BREAKING NEWS

Six Presidents -- The Queen -- A Pope

BREAKING NEWS

Six Presidents -- The Queen -- A Pope

A Life in Journalism

Gene Gibbons

To order additional copies of this book, contact:
Xlibris
844-714-8691
www.Xlibris.com
Orders@Xlibris.com
822371

Contents

FOR BECKY – AND LYNN
And for Sean, Jennie, Chad and Becky
who saw too little of their Dad growing up...

Chapter One
Riding The Whirlwind

HUNTER S. THOMPSON called anyone who covered more than one presidential campaign a "terminal action junkie." He believed these folks suffer from a deadly addiction. Thompson was right except for the terminal part – while seldom life-threatening, careening from one end of the United States to the other covering a presidential campaign is probably as hard a habit to kick as being hooked on drugs. It's almost as much of an adrenaline rush as working at what was once considered the pinnacle of American journalism: being a White House correspondent for a major news organization. I got my first taste of riding the political whirlwind that characterizes how Americans choose their leader as a low-level press aide to Democratic presidential nominee Hubert Humphrey in 1968. He lost and I plunged into journalism. Before I retired, I traveled the country reporting on seven more presidential campaigns, defying a burnout rate that sidelined most of my professional colleagues much sooner. Covering the White House for United Press International and Reuters involved even more cross-country travel and took me all over the world.

I never lost the thrill of the chase in my 40-year career as a reporter. Because of a single-minded dedication to my job that often had serious drawbacks for those dearest to me, I got to rub shoulders with six presidents, the Queen of England, even a pope. I've been to all 50 states, each more than once, and I've visited more than 80 countries.

As a matter of idle curiosity I once listed types of aircraft I've flown on. I counted more than 40, ranging from a Stearman biplane to an Airbus A-380 jumbo jet, the largest airplane in commercial service. I've flown in the backseat of a jet fighter performing aerobatics and experienced a landing and takeoff on an aircraft carrier. I've no idea how many miles I've flown but a conservative estimate is a million or more. (To the surprise of friends and my own chagrin, I accumulated zero frequent flier miles for most of this travel because almost all was on charters or Air Force One.)

My proudest career achievement -- being a presidential debate panelist in 1992. Back then, presidential debates weren't the dime a dozen like they are now: cheap, superficial television programming promoted incessantly by the cable networks. They were few in number, and politically pivotal. The debate that gave me my 15 minutes of fame took place on October 19, 1992 at Michigan State University. It pitted Republican President George H.W. Bush against Democratic challenger Bill Clinton and independent candidate Ross Perot. Like my fellow panelists (PBS newsman Jim Lehrer, CNN anchor Susan Rook and UPI White House correspondent Helen Thomas), I believed Bush won the debate. Clinton won the election. So much for our collective expertise as political handicappers.

In the beginning, with Humphrey, I crisscrossed the United States time and again for more than eight months. He and Richard Nixon made it a matter of personal pride to visit as many states as possible. That election year was a tumultuous one. Dr. Martin Luther King Jr. and Robert Kennedy were assassinated within weeks of each other; race riots exploded throughout the country and protests against the Vietnam War grew in intensity. When Washington DC was convulsed with violent demonstrations after King's slaying, I saw something I never imagined I'd see -- a machine gun nest manned by troops of the 82d Airborne Division on the steps of the U.S. Capitol. I was there when antiwar demonstrators clashed with police at the Democratic National Convention in Chicago. At one point I found myself in the midst of a club-swinging melee outside the Conrad Hilton Hotel, Humphrey's convention headquarters, as a flying squad of Chicago police attacked a group of people who were merely bystanders. There were yells and screams and a lot of broken plate glass. Like the machine gun nest at the Capitol building it was something I never expected to see in America.

Yet I somehow felt insulated. Strange as it seems to write this today, the bloodshed and destruction that swept the country in my youth seemed remote and unthreatening: I was 26 years old, living a dream. There I was, in the midst of politicians and journalists whom I'd read about or seen on television. Not only that, the pace of that life was exhilarating. It wasn't unusual to begin a day in Boston, visit New York, Philadelphia and a town in New Jersey, throw in a stop or two somewhere in the Midwest and wind up late the same day in California.

The grueling pace we kept sometimes brought comic results. In one memorable case, at the end of a very long day exhausted UPI political writer Steve Gerstel stripped to the buff, put his clothes in his suitcase and placed it in the hallway outside his hotel room for pickup. He then took a shower and went to bed. When he awoke the next morning, he realized he'd neglected to unpack any clothes – and his suitcase was gone! Gerstel wrapped himself in a bedspread and made his way to the press bus, reconciled to embarrassment for a while. As the day progressed, colleagues darted from men's store to men's store at various stops, looking for appropriate clothing for their naked friend. I think we travelled halfway across the country before Gerstel was fully dressed.

That all changed over the years – in subsequent elections candidates started confining campaigning to battleground states, foreshadowing the growing polarization of the country. While few people realize it, only a handful of states matter in presidential elections. With the exception of Virginia, the Deep South is reliably Republican, reflecting a conservativism based largely on race and religion. Massachusetts, New York, California and states in the Pacific Northwest are reliably Democratic. The liberalism of these states is generally driven by level of education and income. The nation's once-Democratic industrial midsection and the U.S. Southwest are where presidential elections are decided. Economic issues generally matter most in so-called Rust Belt states like Pennsylvania, Ohio and Michigan because of dwindling manufacturing jobs. Previously rock-ribbed Republican states like New Mexico, Nevada and Arizona are now in play because of their growing percentage of college graduates and Hispanic voters.

Nowadays presidential candidates rely on television and the social media to reach the voters. By the time I retired, it was not unusual for the candidates to stage one campaign rally a day. They'd spend the rest of the time holed up in a hotel room somewhere, taping interviews via satellite hookups with local TV personalities throughout the region. These "interviews" usually feature softball, even fawning questions. An added bonus for the candidates is that the interviews often air as "exclusives" and are repeated again and again, making it a nifty way to get lots of free television airtime.

Studying how running for president evolved during my lifetime would probably be a good way to track U.S. cultural changes and television's metastasis from near-afterthought to the all-powerful information source it is today. When I first trod the campaign trail, there were no TV cameras on the candidates' chartered planes – cameras and crews were relegated to what was known as "the zoo plane." It was called that because of the generally beefy physiques of the individuals who wrestled the television gear from place to place.

At the end of the day, a candidate would frequently venture into the press area in the rear of his charter, drink in hand, and banter with the reporters, most of whom the candidate knew by name. These informal sessions were "off the record," meaning what was said was not for publication. Still, it was a way for journalists to learn about the character and proclivities of the candidate.

It was no secret to anyone who traveled with Hubert Humphrey that he privately believed the Vietnam War was a colossal mistake and would disengage quickly if given the chance. Humphrey used to say "off the record" he couldn't openly break with the policies of President Lyndon B. Johnson because that would trigger a constitutional crisis. Those back-of-the-plane bull sessions allowed reporters to learn what a would-be president was really like. Humphrey, whose public persona was that of a long-winded pol, came across as a thoroughly decent man who still knew what it was like to struggle. He'd often talk about how his wife Muriel sold sandwiches to put him through pharmacy school. He loved his family deeply, especially granddaughter Vicky, a Down's Syndrome child. He was also a baseball and boxing fan and lover of antique cars. You could get a real feel for the personality of a candidate and knowledgeably inform the public of the policies he was likely to pursue as president. There were no TV cameras or tape recorders rolling so the candidates didn't have to worry about falling victim to "gotcha" journalism. When all that fell by the wayside, I believe the public and our system of government suffered.

Part of the fun of covering a presidential campaign was the frat boy atmosphere that often prevailed. FAA safety regulations were widely ignored on the chartered jets we flew on. One tradition was aisle surfing. The surfer, usually a reporter or flight attendant but sometimes a campaign aide, would stand on one of the plastic safety instruction cards next to the cockpit door. As the plane lifted off, usually at a steep angle, he or she would slide down the aisle, swaying from side to side to stay balanced, trying to avoid a wipeout. It was easier said than done.

Another less perilous tradition (which the candidates sometimes joined in) was airborne bowling. Clutching an orange, the designated bowler would sit on the aisle in the rear of the aircraft before takeoff. During the climb-out, the designee would attempt to roll the orange up the aisle and try to hit the cockpit door. This also was easier said than done.

A politically incorrect episode during Democrat George McGovern's 1972 bid for the presidency aptly illustrates the sometimes sophomoric nature of life on the campaign trail. We were flying from Chicago to the West Coast and it was the press plane pilot's birthday. Because of the soft landings he pulled off time after time, the pilot was known as "Perfect Paul." Once we were somewhere over one of the Plains states, the flight attendants lured the birthday boy from the cockpit and pulled off his clothes down to his boxer shorts. Connie Chung, a beautiful young Asian-American television correspondent, then came walking up the aisle wearing a form-fitting wet suit. (Connie had borrowed the wet suit from a German TV crew that was dropping off the campaign to go surfing when we reached the West Coast.) Dangling from her neck was a sign saying "Paul's birthday present."

Amid much hooting and hollering, Connie gave the pilot a kiss. Everyone then sang "Happy Birthday." The festivities concluded, Perfect Paul, still in his underwear, reentered the cockpit and took his seat behind the controls. He then completed his costume by donning a cloth flying helmet and scarf like the ones pioneer aviators wore. In that bizarre garb, he landed the Boeing 727 at LAX, floating the airliner in to touch the runway ever so lightly.

During the 1980 presidential campaign, UPI reporter Ira Allen, temporarily filling in for more senior colleagues, wrote about the flying circus on Ronald Reagan's chartered United Airlines jet. It was a story regulars on the Reagan campaign would never write – there was an unspoken rule that what happened on the campaign plane stayed on the plane. Allen told his readers seat belts were seldom fastened and that the traveling press and female flight attendants frequently exchanged "lustful innuendos." In response, UAL replaced the stewardesses with flamboyant gay men and ordered strict adherence to safety regulations. Many of Allen's news media colleagues were furious. Some TV news people went so far as to harass him physically. Reagan aides gleefully fanned the flames, figuring it was better to have the press fighting among themselves than focusing on the foibles of the candidate. It grew into such a *cause celebre* that Reagan himself finally asked United to restore the original flight attendant crew to the plane. That restored calm but some of those involved in the controversy shunned Allen for years thereafter.

Sometimes the hijinks had a suck-up feel. During the 1988 campaign, George H.W. Bush sought to characterize himself as a good 'ol boy (albeit with an Andover/Yale pedigree) by professing his love for tossing horseshoes, listening to country music and snacking on pork rinds. So on Halloween, at one of the stops several reporters wearing pig masks gathered at the steps of his plane chanting "No more pork rinds! No more pork rinds." Bush, whose ultra-sophisticated sense of humor would have gone over the heads of most of his fellow pork rind lovers, surveyed the crowd and loudly remarked, "Love your mask, Ralph!" His wisecrack was directed at *Washington Times* reporter Ralph Z. Hallow, a dour fellow who wasn't wearing a mask and would never permit himself such silliness.

Bill Clinton was involved in another memorable shenanigan. During his 1996 reelection campaign, the movie "Fargo" was shown repeatedly in the Air Force One press cabin. The Cohn Brothers film is about the comic misadventures of a clutch of hapless hoodlums. We all became so familiar with it we'd turn the sound off and recite the dialogue line by line. A few days before the election Claire Shipman, a TV reporter whose turn it was to fly on the presidential aircraft, mischievously requested another movie before anyone could stop her.

The next morning I was sitting in the motorcade vehicle designated as the wire service car with Ron Fournier of the *Associated Press* when Claire walked by. "See if I'll ever sleep with you again. See if I'll ever let you rub up against me in bed at night," he growled playfully, knowing the woman couldn't hear him.

Fournier's wife at home could. He'd accidently butt-dialed his cellphone and she and their children were listening in to daddy on the campaign trail. It didn't take long for his pager to buzz. It showed his home phone number followed by 9-1-1, indicating an emergency. Ron hastily called back and heard his wife coldly inquire: "WHO are you not sleeping with anymore?" He said it was all a joke and went to great pains to explain the circumstances. That should have been the end of the story. Clinton, however, kept it alive by calling Ron's wife from Air Force One, ostensibly to vouch for him. Instead, he tried to get him in deeper trouble.

"Laurie, this is Bill Clinton. Do you have any idea where Ron is? We haven't seen him since we were in Houston yesterday. He said he was going to get a sandwich and we haven't seen him since," he said. Thinking it was one of her husband's chums, Fournier's wife replied, "Oh, give me a break," and hung up on the president. Fournier called her back and told her what she'd done. "I'm too busy to talk right now. I'm having tea with the Pope," she said.

Sophomoric to be sure, such stunts helped us endure the frenetic, high pressure working conditions and sleep deprivation that campaign coverage entails. The pressure was relentless. Day after day, we had to elbow our way through large crowds at one stop after another, keeping an eye on the candidate, assassination being an ever-present threat. Robert Kennedy was shot and killed on the campaign trail in 1968 and George Wallace grievously wounded in 1972. While there's an understandable tendency to gloss over it, assassinations and assassin attempts figure prominently in American politics: Abraham Lincoln, James Garfield and John F. Kennedy were all murdered and Theodore Roosevelt, Franklin Delano Roosevelt, Harry Truman, Gerald Ford and Ronald Reagan all faced attempted murder. So we were always alert for potential violence.

When the speechmaking started, we also had to be vigilant for an angle with which to frame a report – or an unplanned development, which would likely be front page news. While straining to avoid missing anything, we'd mentally keep composing and re-composing the narrative in order to be ready to write up and file a story as soon as the event ended. It didn't matter who the candidate was – he delivered the same basic speech every time. (It was always a male until Hillary Clinton but that was after my time.) Once a day, the standard stump speech would include a paragraph or two stressing some point or adding a new wrinkle to an issue. Campaign aides would fill in details. That was what then usually became the day's news story.

Except when there was an interesting distraction, that unplanned development I mentioned previously. On the last day of the 1992 presidential campaign, a light plane flew over Bush campaign rally towing a banner that said "Iran-Contra Haunts You Still." This was a reference to Bush's ill-defined role in a Reagan administration scandal involving arms sales to an enemy state – Iran – to win the freedom of a half dozen Americans held hostage by Iranian allies in Lebanon. Bush was outraged – he saw it as a dirty trick played by someone involved with or supporting the Clinton campaign. It was a relatively harmless dirty trick compared with the bordering-on-treason tactics the Trump Campaign engaged in in 2016 – entertaining the idea of, and at one point publicly requesting, help from the Kremlin in digging up dirt on Hillary Clinton. Nevertheless it was one that resulted in stories and news photos unhelpful to Bush on the eve of the election.

Another news-making incident about something as silly as mangled syntax was unhelpful to Democrat George McGovern in his 1972 contest with incumbent Republican President Richard Nixon. It involved the colorful Democratic boss of Brooklyn, a fellow named Meade Esposito. On a dreary Sunday morning late in the election campaign, McGovern and running mate Sargent Shriver, accompanied by a large national and local press contingent, traveled to Esposito's mother's house in Canarsie to meet the political powerbroker and get his long-awaited blessing. Esposito supported someone else for the Democratic presidential nomination because he thought McGovern too liberal and refused to get behind him until a few weeks before the voting. The private reconciliation was brief. Smiling broadly, the participants then came outside and Esposito stepped up to a forest of microphones. "I want youse all to know me and the Brooklyn Democratic organization is behind the McGovern-Shiver ticket to the BITTER end!" he bellowed.

That triggered a wave of stories that Esposito recognized the hard truth of his party's presidential chances: McGovern was lagging badly in the polls and likely to lose. It would be a *bitter* end. Unexpected developments like these would drive the candidates and their campaign aides crazy. But unlike today, unflattering stories were never described as "fake news."

That's not to say normally level-headed presidential contenders maintain their composure when the going gets tough. George H.W. Bush, hands-down the most press-friendly politician I ever knew, adopted "Annoy the Media—Reelect Bush" as his campaign slogan in the waning days of his ultimately futile 1992 bid for a second term. It was said that Hubert H. Humphrey walked in a bathroom at his Minnesota home at the stroke of midnight in 1968 and flushed the toilet, signaling good riddance to a year that saw him lose the presidency to Nixon by less than a percentage point. At a Bush campaign rally in Pennsylvania a few days before the 1992 election, an elderly lady took the suggestion to annoy the media seriously and started poking at a reporter with an umbrella. Seeing what was going on, Bush called out from the podium: "No, no ma'am. Stop. Those people are my friends."

Howard Baker was an exception to the rule of poor loser behavior. Baker, a three-term U.S. senator who died in 2014 at age 88, sought the Republican presidential nomination in 1980, a year when contenders also included Ronald Reagan and George H.W. Bush. As Senate Republican leader, Baker had name recognition and a national following, establishing him as a frontrunner the moment he threw his hat in the ring. I traveled with him on his first campaign swing, a barnstorming tour through New England that was supposed to be crowned by a straw poll victory at a statewide Republican Party caucus in Maine. This would generate positive headlines that would underscore his appeal and give his effort to win the White House a boost. Baker's carefully laid plan collapsed when Bush scored an upset.

I was a UPI Radio correspondent then and accidentally stumbled into what went wrong. I needed a quiet place to do my reports and found a working telephone in an L-shaped cloakroom near the auditorium where the political meeting was taking place. As I prepared to call my news desk an hour or so before the balloting, some of Reagan's supporters came into the cloakroom and began talking strategy. Because of the way the room was configured, they didn't see me lurking nearby. So I kept quiet and eavesdropped. I heard them say while Reagan didn't have enough votes to win the straw poll, some of his votes and Bush's votes combined would carry the day. They thought Bush was a weaker rival than Baker, so they agreed to dump enough votes to Bush to help him win.

The stratagem worked: because Baker lost a test of strength he was expected to win, his campaign essentially blew up on the launch pad.

On the flight back to Washington afterwards, he came back to the press section of his chartered plane and answered questions. That was the last thing most politicians would do. Baker also endured a lot of teasing about his political pratfall.

The most memorable teasing came from Vincent Giato, an ABC News cameraman. An affable man with a puckish sense of humor, Gaito said he'd visited his old Brooklyn neighborhood a few days before starting an assignment to cover Pope John Paul's 1979 visit to the United States. While there, Gaito said he ran into some boyhood friends whom he knew to be Mafia. They were impressed by the fact that he was a network television cameraman often assigned important stories. Gaito said when the group asked what his next job was, he told them he'd be covering the Papal Visit, which was already big news.

His old pals were all over him with congratulations. "THE POPE, VINNIE! THE POPE!!! WHAT A FOOKING HONOR!" one of the wise guys said.

Gaito teased Baker: "You're supposed to win the Maine straw poll. A sure bet! In the bag! You lose to Bush. What a FOOKING honor!" Baker took the teasing in stride. When we finally arrived in D.C., he greeted each of the wives there to meet their newsmen husbands. It was a class act.

Baker continued his campaign for several more weeks but never recovered from his first-inning stumble. He quit the race after disappointing showings in the first set of primaries. Had he become president, I believe he would have been an excellent leader. He was smart, articulate and committed to bipartisanship, which earned him the nickname "The Great Conciliator."

Baker had character and integrity. Although it antagonized many fellow Republicans, he supported Senate ratification of the Panama Canal treaties negotiated by President Carter because he believed the treaties were in the U.S. national interest. Though his wife Joy had alcohol problems, he remained loyal until her death in 1993. Baker subsequently married Nancy Kassebaum, a U.S. Senator from Kansas and the daughter of Alf Landon, the 1936 Republican presidential nominee.

Like me, Baker was a camera buff. Before we were married, my late wife Lynn and I once ran into him and his son taking pictures in the Washington neighborhood where we I lived. Baker asked Lynn to pose, which she did. She was a gorgeous young woman with long red hair, an obvious subject for portraiture. I still have a photo of her I made that day but have no idea what became of Baker's photos.

Like so many prominent Washington figures who fail to live up to their promise, Baker eventually faded from view. I daresay few Americans today know anything about him. That's a shame. Baker was a role model for public service. He served as a U.S. Senator from Tennessee from 1967 to 1985, becoming Republican floor leader in 1977. He retired from the Senate to become Reagan's White House chief of staff, a move many in Washington saw as a step down. "His President needed him. And to be blunt, his country needed him in that position at that particular time. Some things were coming apart, and he was the right person, and perhaps the only person, to pull them back together again," said Trent Lott, a Mississippi senator who succeeded Baker as Senate Republican leader.

Baker was a statesman who deserves more recognition than he has received. While mine was an unusually bookish boyhood, it seems to me the culture then was much more attuned to public figures like him. As a child, I was quite familiar with U.S. history as were most of my playmates. I knew all about Daniel Webster, Henry Clay and other political giants who never reached the presidency but nevertheless contributed to the country's progress. History seems a forgotten subject today despite philosopher George Santayana's warning that "those who don't know history are doomed to repeat it."

All these years later, I often relive what it was like on the campaign trail in my dreams. They're always nightmarish anxiety dreams. I'm trying to file a big story but the typewriter won't work or I can't find any paper or I can't seem to come up with a lede – the all-important first sentence of a news story that is supposed to tell the reader or listener the who, what, where and why of what happened. Always I'm a radio reporter, which adds to the pressure I feel because I not only have to write the story but then record it.

I shudder to think of how many hours I spent doing that. Working bleary-eyed in a hotel room, usually late at night, I did take after take of each of my reports, trying to get the timing and inflection *exactly* right, hoping I wasn't disturbing my neighbors. Because my radio reports couldn't exceed 40 seconds I had to do two or three each night, which usually amounted to two or three hours of work or more. More often than not, I'd fall into bed exhausted at 2:30 or 3 in the morning, facing a 6:30 or 7 AM wakeup. I did this for 16 years. No wonder I still have nightmares!

When I joined Reuters and switched to print, life became easier in some ways, harder in others. While my stories usually ran 500 words or more instead of 80 or 90, I was finished when the writing was done. I also had the support of a much more rigorous editing process. If what I wrote wasn't clear or I made a mistake, editors would clean up my writing and fix my errors. In radio, I was pretty much on my own. On the other hand, once a report was broadcast, it vanished into thin air. If I got it wrong, it was quickly forgotten. Once in print, a story was cast in stone. If the editors missed a mistake or a hint of bias, eagle-eyed readers surely wouldn't -- and then I'd have some explaining to do.

If I erred, Reuters would run a correction. This was embarrassing to a reporter but essential to the news organization for whom he or she worked because its very existence depended on its reputation for honesty and integrity. Most readers used to take these standards for granted. Sadly, the lofty standards of professional journalism maintained in my day are often ignored by the main purveyors of news and information these days, cable television and the social media. What's worse, too many Americans buy into the Big Lie of political propagandists like Fox Television and Briebart "News" that only they provide the truth.

That's not to say legitimate news organizations don't sometimes stretch the facts to make a story more compelling, a practice known as "needling." Reporting the news is after all a business. The idea is to make money to pay for the news gathering, which is expensive, with a little left over as profit. But there's a big difference between sensationalizing a story and putting out "alternative facts." One is hyperbole, the other a lie.

Take my experience covering a 1985 summit between President Reagan and Soviet leader Mikhail Gorbachev in Reykjavík, Iceland. I'd done a lot of legwork to prepare for the summit, talking not only to some of Reagan's foreign policy aides and advisors but also to members of Congress and congressional staff as well as people at Washington think tanks and other scholars. Presidents don't go into major negotiations half-cocked, at least they didn't before Donald Trump. That would be irresponsible. There are widespread consultations. Dozens of folks with various degrees of expertise inside and outside government are − or were -- plugged in. Good reporters know this and have vast networks of "sources." From the bits and pieces of information I gathered "running the traps," I was convinced Reagan planned to go big at the Reykjavik summit, proposing sweeping U.S. and Soviet arms reductions. Before the flight to Iceland, I laid out what I thought was likely to happen to some senior administration officials, conversing with each separately. They didn't challenge my scenario, tacitly confirming I was on the right track. Interpreting winks and nods is an important part of any good journalist's tradecraft.

I wrote a carefully worded story about Reagan's far-reaching aims and after we landed sent it to the local Reuters bureau. Soon it was in the hands of newspaper and broadcast clients around the world. Then all hell broke loose. Other reporters covering the summit jammed the hotel rooms where the White House Press Office had set up shop, clamoring for confirmation or denial.

Amid the clamor, an angry Larry Speakes, the president's spokesman, summoned me into his presence, demanding to know where I'd gotten my information. Speakes suspected a National Security Council staffer named Roman Popadiuk and threatened to fire him. He said my story would wreck the summit – a charge not to be taken lightly since the United States and Russia were then still in the tension-filled standoff known as the Cold War. Popadiuk, who was at the meeting, listened ashen-faced as the tirade went on. Speakes didn't deny my story; he merely said it went too far.

I was confident of my information and declined to identify my sources. But I told Speakes his suspicion was unfounded: Popadiuk wasn't one of them. He accepted my word. Hard as it might seem to believe in this day and age, our confrontation ended with a handshake.

That wasn't the end of the incident. What I wrote was one thing; what went out to subscribers another. An overzealous Reuters editor had taken my copy and stretched it, making the story more sensational. The White House was right – my story *at that moment* did go too far. As the summit unfolded, what Reagan and Gorbachev discussed actually went way beyond what I reported: the complete elimination of nuclear weapons, a deal that ultimately fell apart. But all that happened later.

One advantage of working for a wire service is stories are constantly updated, so after my meeting with Speakes, I went to the offending editor, an Englishman, and told him we needed to put out a new, toned down version of my story. "Tell the White House the British cunt said no," he growled. I was shocked by what he called himself, but the news business ain't for the fainthearted. A heated to-and-fro between me and the editor ensued; I eventually got my way.

Another president, another summit, another instance of how news is gathered and the messiness with which it sometimes gets to the public: George H.W. Bush was in the White House and Gorbachev was in Washington for a series of top-level meetings. The agenda included a day of informal talks at Camp David, a secluded presidential retreat in Maryland's Catoctin Mountains. I was watching from the White House South Lawn as the two leaders departed aboard a big green and white U.S. Marine Corps helicopter. So I saw that Bush was accompanied by a military aide carrying "The Football," a black leather briefcase containing the U.S. nuclear war codes. So instead of writing a straightforward news story, I played up the irony: leaders of the superpowers talking peace literally within an arm's length of nuclear Armageddon. I began my report something like this: *"It was like a scene from a best-selling Cold War spy novel: leaders of the United States and the Soviet Union climbing into a military helicopter and flying off to a secluded location to discuss the fate of the world."*

The next morning I was surprised to see my story on the front page of the *New York Times*, albeit with a different first paragraph, or *lede*, a few different details and a different byline. It was unusual but not unethical; news organizations that subscribe to Reuters or the other news agencies – at the time The Associated Press, United Press International and Agence France Press – pay for their reports and can use them however they wish. But the *Times* front-pager added a new wrinkle to my reporting. Their story said Bush and Gorbachev both were accompanied by aides carrying nuclear war codes. Since I'd been there for their departure and the *Times* was not, I knew this to be untrue. Gorbachev had a single empty-handed bodyguard with him.

The next morning, I got a telephone call. It was Brian "The Digger" Williams, a brash Australian Reuters editor in overall charge of our summit coverage. "Did you see the *Times*, matey?" he asked. "They have two footballs. Can you update your story?"

"Yeah, I saw the Times," I replied. "They weren't there yesterday. They picked my pocket. Did you read their story? It's word-for-word what I filed except for the lede, which claims both Bush and Gorby had their nuclear war codes with them. They back that up with a dodgy quote from Gorbachev's spokesman, who supposedly said 'Of course' when asked if the Soviet leader also brought nuclear war codes to Camp David.

"That's bullshit," I said. "The guy with Gorbachev on the helicopter wasn't carrying anything besides maybe a handgun. And Gorby's spokesman hasn't drawn a sober breath since he arrived in Washington."

The Digger insisted. "The Times has two footballs, matey. It's a better story. We have to match it," he said. I told him to kiss off and hung up. Reuters (and most news organizations) was like that then. You could tell your boss off and get away with it -- as long as you were right.

To my surprise and consternation, Reuters moved a new story a short time later about the informal summit session at Camp David. It carried my byline and was a warmed-over version of what I'd filed the day before, except for this: it reported two footballs. The Digger rewrote my story a bit, lifted the New York Times quote to back up two footballs, and got what he wanted.

There was a comic coda to this. One of the sentences in my original story read, "Seated near Bush in the wool-upholstered cabin of the Sikorsky helicopter was Air Force Major Bruce Kaufman, a military aide whose job this day was to carry "the football," a leather briefcase containing the U.S. nuclear war codes." The *Times* account contained a typo: wool-upholstered became "wood-upholstered." Several years later historian Michael Beschloss and Soviet expert Strobe Talbott wrote <u>At the Highest Levels</u>, a book about the Cold War endgame. In it was a brief reference to the Camp David meeting that obviously relied on information gleaned from the *Times* account. It ridiculously described the cabin of Marine One, the presidential helicopter, as "wood-paneled." As they say, journalism is the first draft of history.

The mission statement driving my professional colleagues and me was "Get it first – but get it right!" That mantra was drilled into me so solidly that shortly after I joined Reuters I couldn't sleep one night after realizing I'd gotten the dates of an upcoming conference wrong. It was a trivial error, easily fixed, and my worries about it turned out to be groundless. But I and most of my colleagues took accuracy so seriously I was afraid I'd be fired for slipshod reporting.

Because we were on the road so often, illicit romance blossomed occasionally, sometimes tragically. A young woman who was a rising star at the New York Times fell in love with the married ace reporter of another big metropolitan newspaper during the 1984 presidential race between Ronald Reagan and Walter Mondale. Reagan won by a landslide, laughing off suggestions that he was too old to be president by declaring in a debate with Mondale he wouldn't make an issue of the fact that his opponent was too young and inexperienced to occupy the Oval Office. When the campaign was over, the young woman's paramour returned to his wife. His shattered lover, whose career nosedived because of the affair, put a gun in her mouth and pulled the trigger, a suicide at age 36.

A less extreme fate befell a handsome unmarried male reporter who engaged in a press plane romance with a White House secretary on a trip to Hawaii during Bill Clinton's presidency. In a bizarre twist, the encounter foreshadowed the Monica Lewinsky scandal. As the chartered Pan Am jetliner flew high over the Pacific, the two lovebirds sat in the rear of the aircraft necking, unmindful of others around them. As their passion intensified, the young woman covered herself with a blanket and lowered her head onto the young man's lap. As the blanket rose and fell, it was obvious to everyone in the vicinity what was going on. Word quickly spread and days later the reporter involved was reassigned to Egypt. Not long after that, the young woman's boss had a new secretary.

Marital breakups were not uncommon. One of the noisier ones followed President Reagan's trip to then-divided Berlin where he delivered his famous "Mr. Gorbachev, tear down this wall!" speech. When Reagan left Europe, two of the reporters traveling with him stayed behind, supposedly to do further reporting but actually for some canoodling in the Azores. The husband of the woman involved became aware of what was going on and phoned the wife of the male to tell her. When the lovebirds arrived back in Washington, their unamused spouses were there at the airport to greet them.

Disrupted personal plans were a way of life. I rushed out of the house without explanation one Saturday evening because George H.W. Bush had been admitted to Bethesda Naval Hospital after suffering an irregular heartbeat at Camp David. There went a date night with Lynn. On another occasion when we'd just begun a nice weekend I had to hustle out to Dulles Airport to cover an airline hijacking. There I ran into Evangelist Billy Graham, who was awaiting a flight. He was eager to offer his two cents worth on how we would avoid such crimes in the future if more Americans brought Christ into their lives.

The most dramatic disruption of family life occurred early on Christmas Day 1991. Even before we'd started to open presents I had to dash to the White House to cover an earthshaking development: the collapse of the Soviet Union. In a brief, totally unexpected speech in Moscow, Soviet President Mikhail Gorbachev announced his resignation and conceded the failure of Communism.

"Destiny so ruled that when I found myself at the helm of this state it already was clear that something was wrong in this country. We had a lot of everything -- land, oil and gas, other natural resources -- and there was intellect and talent in abundance. However, we were living much worse than people in the industrialized countries were living and we were increasingly lagging behind them. The reason was obvious even then. This country was suffocating in the shackles of the bureaucratic command system," Gorbachev said.

This was breaking news on steroids. President Bush, who was spending the holidays with his family at Camp David, returned to the White House to address the American people. I worked through the day churning out copy. We'd planned a big Christmas dinner with several guests, but Lynn postponed it and took the children out for Chinese food. She said it was the best Christmas she ever had.

Looking back, it seems now like a much calmer time. I was in the midst of the hurly burly but wasn't assaulted every waking hour by the ubiquitous nonsense of television and a constant barrage of insults and lies from social media like Facebook and Twitter. Nor were other Americans, or any other nationality for that matter. Life was a lot saner.

While the presidents I covered loom largest in the history books, other newsmakers I encountered made an equal or larger impression on me. Some were presidential contenders: they included legislators like Ed Muskie, Shirley Chisholm, John Lindsey, Lowell Weicker, Scoop Jackson, Bob Dole, and John Anderson. Some were politicians who never became world famous but did their jobs with great integrity, people such as Peter Rodino, Jim Abourezk, Eddie Hebert, Bill Milliken and Bob Ray.

Rodino chaired the House Judiciary Committee, the panel that recommended the impeachment of Richard Nixon. Abourezk was a Lebanese-American who became a U.S. senator from South Dakota but never took himself seriously. Milliken and Ray were Midwestern governors who both seemed qualified for higher office but lacked the ambition – or stomach – to pursue it. I liked them all but covered them without bias. Prominent athletes were another story; I never lost my boyhood sense of awe when I ran into someone who did their news-making on a baseball diamond or football field.

Muskie was Hubert Humphrey's 1968 running mate and the Democratic frontrunner going into the 1972 presidential race. A Maine governor before being elected to the U.S. Senate, he was a man of considerable presence with his lantern jaw, flinty New England appearance, imposing height (he was 6 foot 4) and schoolmaster-stern demeanor. He also had a fiery temper. Early in the campaign, Muskie was the victim of a political dirty trick that dashed his chances of reaching the White House. Campaigning in New Hampshire's important first-in-the-nation presidential primary, he was infuriated by a story in the *Manchester Union-Leader* alleging he privately used the ethnic slur "Canucks" in referring to people of French-Canadian descent. Muskie, a Polish-American who himself was often a target of ethnic stereotyping, was angered even more by the assertion that his wife Jane passed her time on the campaign trail playing cards with friends and telling dirty jokes. All this was based on Nixon reelection campaign fabrications that the arch conservative *Union-Leader* was happy to print.

Muskie held a news conference outside the newspaper's office to denounce the story. He called Union-Leader publisher William Loeb "a gutless coward" for running it and implied Loeb would be sorry if he ever met him. It was snowing heavily as Muskie spoke and at one point he rubbed his eyes. Some of the reporters present thought he was rubbing snow out of his eyes but the *Washington Post's* highly-respected David Broder, one of the fairest, most decent journalists I ever knew, wrote that he was crying. What actually happened is still unclear but Broder's account became how Muskie was defined: emotionally unfit to hold the highest office in the country.

How silly that sounds today given recent history. I got to know Muskie fairly well when I covered Congress and found him to be someone of great character with rock-solid integrity. He returned to the Senate after his failed presidential bid and fathered the modern environmental movement. He later served as Secretary of State under President Carter and helped negotiate the release of the American diplomats held hostage by Iranian militants.

Muskie was typical of giants who strode the halls of Congress when I joined UPI's Capitol Hill staff; political leaders whose towering stature rivaled that of such historic icons as Webster and Clay. Most but not all were New Englanders. Most but not all were Republicans. These were people like George Aiken of Vermont, Margaret Chase Smith of Maine, and Edward Brooke of Massachusetts. Aiken, whose shock of snow white hair, dark horn-rimmed glasses and stooped posture gave him an owlish look, was one of seven GOP senators who denounced fellow Republican Senator Joseph McCarthy of Wisconsin for his unscrupulous anti-communist crusade, hastening McCarthy's downfall. He warned against those who seek victory "through the selfish political exploitation of fear, bigotry, ignorance and intolerance."

Smith, at that time the only woman ever to serve in both houses of Congress, led the opposition to McCarthy. In a Senate floor speech that she called "A Declaration of Conscience" she said his tactics "debased the Senate to the level of a forum of hate and character assassination ... I don't want to see the Republican Party ride to political victory on the four horseman of calumny: fear, ignorance, bigotry and smear," she said.

Brooke, the first African American popularly elected to the Senate, was the first Republican to demand that Richard Nixon resign after the scope of the Watergate Scandal became clear. Sadly, he'll probably be remembered not for political courage but for a romantic entanglement with television diva Barbara Walters. Walters revealed their love affair in Audition, a kiss-and-tell memoir she published in 2008.

There were buffoons as well. Congressman Otto Passman, a Louisiana Democrat, whose constant nervous twitching gave rise to the wisecrack that "he wore out his clothes from the inside" was one. Another was Robert Dornan, a California Republican and Air Force veteran, whose fanatic advocacy of the B-1 Bomber led some colleagues to question his mental health.

Yet another was Republican Nebraska Senator Roman Hruska, who defended one of Richard Nixon's Supreme Court choices against charges that the nominee was mediocre. "So what if he is mediocre? There are a lot of mediocre judges and people and lawyers. They are entitled to a little representation, aren't they? We can't have all Brandeises, Cardozos, and Frankfurters and stuff like that there," Hruska declared.

These were outliers. When Hollywood song and dance man George Murphy was elected to the U.S. Senate from California in 1964, the result was seen as an anomaly. This was before television became the ubiquitous presence in our lives that it is today. Now the George Murphys are the norm – telegenic airheads more interested in celebrity than governance.

Or hanging onto political power, whatever the consequences. I'm convinced that when historians assess the era in which I write, Congressional Republican leaders – former House Speaker Paul Ryan and Senate Majority Leader Mitch McConnell – will not be treated kindly. McConnell showed his disdain for the U.S. Constitution by refusing to even hold hearings on President Barack Obama's effort to elevate a distinguished jurist to the U.S. Supreme Court in 2016, arguing that it was a presidential election year and the voters should decide who would get to fill the vacancy. His abuse of power effectively nullified the votes of the tens of millions of Americans who had elected Obama president. Yet McConnell rammed through the nomination of conservative Amy Coney Barrett to the Supreme Court a few weeks before the 2020 election. Ryan, who retired from Congress after the 2018 elections, rhetorically tried to keep daylight between himself and Donald Trump while sanctioning Trump's egregious actions

I got a hint of McConnell's ruthlessness when he and I sat at the same table at a White House state dinner hosted by President Bush. When I asked him if he knew a friend of mine, *Louisville Courier* reporter Mike Brown, McConnell snarled in reply, "Yes I do. He's the scum of the earth." Brown, an honest, fair journalist and likeable fellow, had apparently written something McConnell didn't like.

Believe it or not there was a time when partisanship wasn't all. Right after the burglary of the Democratic National Committee headquarters that sparked the Watergate scandal, I was speaking to Senator Robert Dole one day and scoffed at speculation that Nixon's campaign committee, known as the Committee to Reelect the President, was behind the break-in. I said it just didn't make sense to do such a thing – it would turn up little of value there. Dole, who chaired the Republican National Committee at the time, had little use for the Nixon political operation. Seizing on the acronym for the organization, he privately called it "CREEP." Dole warned me not to dismiss the speculation out of hand, saying the Nixon team had more than its share of fanatics and screwballs.

Dole was severely wounded while fighting in Italy as a member of the U.S. Army's 10th Mountain Division during World War Two. His injuries left him with a permanently crippled right arm, which might have explained his sardonic sense of humor. Fellow politicians were frequently the target of his acerbic wit. When President Reagan sent former presidents Nixon, Ford and Carter to Cairo to represent the United States at assassinated Egyptian President Anwar Sadat's funeral, Dole studied a front page photo of the trio shown him by a reporter. Pointing at Carter, Ford and Nixon in turn, he then slowly intoned: "See no evil ... Hear no evil ... Evil!"

I admired Dole's legislative leadership skills. During one of the perennial budget battles that nettled Congress when I covered the legislative branch, he displayed his deftness after the Democrats knocked a large hole in a GOP measure supposedly designed to put the nation's financial house in order. In order to undo the move, Dole proposed that business meals no longer be tax deductible. Democrats had long advocated this but didn't really want it to become a reality because it would hurt unionized service industry supporters by reducing their income from tips.

Dole probably would have made a good president. By the time he finally got the Republican nomination in 1996, many Americans considered him too old for the job. In an ironic twist, the good senator from Kansas wound up as a TV pitchman for the male potency pill Viagra. His last appearance on the national stage exposed the mean streak that infected the Republican Party as right-wing extremists became dominant. Defying their former leader, Senate Republicans in 2012 defeated U.S. ratification of a United Nations treaty banning discrimination against disabled people even though Dole favored the pact and came to the Senate floor in a wheelchair to urge its passage.

I was amazed by Dole's warning not to lightly dismiss the possibility of White House involvement in Watergate because it was uncharacteristically politically candid even then. At the time I frankly was a bit shocked. I then still clung to the belief that politics at the national level was almost as pure as the driven snow, that with few exceptions everyone in the upper reaches of the U.S. government was interested only in Truth, Justice and the American Way. But I led a pretty sheltered life before I got to Washington.

Chapter Two

Beginnings

SOONER OR LATER you were going to get dirty: that was a fact of life growing up in Scranton, Pennsylvania. Although the coal mines were mostly gone by the 1950s when I was a child, Scranton still regarded itself as the Anthracite Capitol of the World. Grimy scars of the industry that made it famous -- abandoned breakers, slag heaps and rusting old mining machinery – were scattered throughout the city. We called the slag heaps culm dumps. Some were on fire, giving surrounding neighborhoods a sulphurous rotten egg smell. Culm dumps that weren't burning were enticing off-limits playgrounds for adventurous kids. Parents and policemen considered them attractive nuisances and chased us away whenever we were seen near them. But I still remember what fun it was to climb a mountain of mine waste several blocks from my home. It was a kick to survey the world from atop this four-story manmade mountain. Once we had enough of the view, we'd run headlong back down to ground zero, slipping and sliding all the way. Oh, the joys of childhood. Ragamuffins having the time of our lives. What a bizarre playground it seems now.

I exaggerate. Mary Agnes McNamara Gibbons did NOT have scruffy children. Although money was often tight, as she saw it we were lace curtain Irish, to the manor born. My mother was beautiful, elegant, more than a bit reserved. Like most women those days, she always wore a skirt and blouse at home, often accented with a sweater and apron. For church and social occasions, it was a fine dress, usually complemented with a hat and white gloves. Her children were well-behaved and good-mannered, at least in public. In our circle, playing on a culm dump just wasn't done. When we occasionally broke the rules, we certainly didn't talk about it.

My family was better off economically than most Scrantonians, but still financially a notch below a lot of our friends and neighbors. We lived on the edge of the Green Ridge section of the city, a leafy residential enclave of White Anglo-Saxon Protestant store owners and bankers under siege from up-and-coming Irish Catholics, known to the WASPs as "Paddies" or "Micks." Green Ridge was the place to live in Scranton because it was where the coal barons once lived. Supposedly it was the only part of town that wasn't undermined.

Most of the rest of the city, where there were in fact occasional cave-ins and underground fires from the mining below, was a mishmash of ethnically and religiously segregated neighborhoods. People of Italian, German, Polish and Slavic descent each had their own enclave. Each had its own neighborhood-dominating Roman Catholic Church. Jewish people lived in the Hill Section. We were only vaguely aware of Protestant churches, which were part of different world. There were few African-Americans in Scranton when I was growing up; most of them lived in run-down housing near the central city.

Each ethnic neighborhood had a saloon on nearly every other corner. Think two and three story tenements and single houses whose first floor was often a bar or storefront. These dwellings often had lovingly tended postage stamp-sized yards. Scranton was gritty. It prided itself on being The Friendly City. It was that too.

While I grew up in Scranton, I was born in Baltimore MD, leading my dad to teasingly call me a Balti-moron. My father worked at a Montgomery Ward department store there before the start of World War Two. We left before I was two, however, and some of my earliest, fondest memories are of Pittston PA, another coal town 12 miles south of Scranton. That was where most of my ancestors put down roots when they arrived from Ireland in the mid-to-late 19th Century. It was where my beloved grandmother Nana and the Cotter cousins lived. My family lived there too until I was nearly eight years old.

When I was a toddler, we lived across the street from Nana and the Cotters in what was called a duplex – two houses side-by-side sharing the same foundation. From a bedroom window I'd often see a steam locomotive pulling a train through the countryside north of town. Nearby was Fleming Park, where my dad sometimes took me to watch sandlot baseball. I remember him telling me Charles Lindberg landed there once, and he'd seen the famous aviator in person. I also remember him telling me that during a trip to New York he'd met Babe Ruth, who called him "Sonny" even though he was wearing his first pair of long pants. Although my dad's attire that day signified his entry into the grown-up world, what the Babe called him was perfectly okay.

My favorite relative from my earliest memory till the day she died was Nana. She was my mother's mother, a warm, bespectacled, dumpling-shaped woman who personified the word grandma. She had short, thinning snow-white hair which she wore in a bun, granny eyeglasses, and was loving and kind. Although she never went beyond the eighth grade in school, she was one of the smartest, most well-informed people I've ever known. She was an avid reader and thoroughly open-minded, an unusual trait among most Irish-Americans we knew. She could cook and sew, and had a wonderful sense of humor. Nana was, in short, a delight.

The Cotter cousins were extended family, the children of my mother's sister Trudy, more like siblings than cousins. There were nine of them: Johnny, Tom, Mary, Michael, Susan, Joe, Trudy Ellen, Bob and Kevin. They lived in my grandmother's house. The sprawling two-story white wooden house with a large fenced-in front yard wasn't really her house; the Cotters bought it from her when my uncle returned from the fighting in Europe during World War Two. But she still lived there and was the family matriarch, regally ruling over her clan. On summer evenings, my Aunt Trudy's physician husband, a rabid baseball fan with curly dark red hair, would gather a bunch of kids in his big front yard and tap out popups and grounders. Catch a ball in the air and earn a nickel, enough for a Popsicle at the neighborhood grocery store. Fielding a ground ball was worth a penny. Even poor athletes like me could scramble after enough grounders to earn a Popsicle before it got dark.

My mother's brothers John, Tom and Joe, a Jesuit priest, often visited. After the baseball was over, we kids would try to put off bedtime by joining the adults on Nana's front porch for conversation and word games. If only all of life were as much fun as the summer evenings of my early youth.

While we had a close relationship with my mother's side of the family, we saw my dad's family less often. My father, a 4-F civilian who helped build B-29 bombers during World War Two, seemed closer to his two sisters than he was with his father and his three brothers. I didn't much care for my paternal grandfather, a gruff, great bear of a man with snow white hair. He scared me, perhaps because I didn't know him well. My dad's family had owned a small brewery and Gibbons Beer was still a well-known local brand, albeit with different, unrelated owners. Its simple, catchy radio ad jingle helped me learn how to spell my name. "G-I-B-B-O-N-S, Pure refreshing Gibbons. If it's Gibbons, it's good. So next time you should say 'Gimme, gimme Gibbons!" was how the jingle went.

There were also other amusements during my formative years. John C. Kehoe, a local coal baron and politician, owned a Sunday newspaper that my father worked on briefly. He wrote a column immodestly called "As Kehoe Knows it" that took aim each week at political enemies, whom he usually attacked with cruel nicknames. Kehoe called one of his favorite targets "Baggy Pants" McGuire. This individual came to our home for some reason once and my cousin John and I fell all over ourselves trying to check out his clothes.

Half-way through my second year of grade school, we moved to Scranton, where my dad managed a general insurance agency owned by two of my mother's brothers. He found it hard to get along with his in-laws. That often provoked parental arguments. Work-related tensions weren't the only cause of domestic tension: my father suffered "the curse of the Irish" and spent a lot of his non-working time in local saloons.

While he was seldom drunk, he was probably a functioning alcoholic, which caused me no end of anxiety and embarrassment as a kid. It was also a cause of familial distress since my mom and dad seemed to argue a lot and often went for days without speaking. That they loved each other was never in doubt. They were always close when my dad wasn't drinking and as they grew older, they became inseparable. My dad had been on the wagon for several years when he died at age 68. My mother followed him two years later. A diary she left behind made it clear the cause was a broken heart.

My boyhood world had four reference points: the white frame two story house where we I lived; St. Paul's Roman Catholic Church and School two blocks away; Circle Field, a small cinder-field two blocks near the railroad tracks where my brothers Charlie and Joe and I often played baseball; and my father's insurance agency on the sixth floor of a downtown office building.

Our four bedroom, one bathroom house wasn't fancy but had its charms. My favorite place was the kitchen. I used to love to back up against the radiator and stick my nose in a book while toasting my rear end. Reading was then and still is my main form of entertainment -- television was then in its infancy and unlike most of our neighbors and friends, we didn't own a TV set.

One of the best things my brothers and I had going in those days was Landmark Books, an inexpensive, well-written series of histories and biographies published by Random House. The series was the brainchild of famed book editor Bennett Cerf, who launched it in 1948 after failing to find a book about the Pilgrims for his children while vacationing on Cape Cod. "Not a single author was an academic. Cerf clearly preferred skilled wordsmiths, the more famous the better, who could engage a general audience," historian David Spear said in The Story of Landmark Books, an article published in the journal of the American Historical Association.

"The early years of the series relied on such literati as war correspondent Quentin Reynolds, Pulitzer Prize winner MacKinlay Kantor, double Pulitzer Prize recipient Robert Penn Warren and Nobel Prize winner Pearl Buck," Spear wrote. It was enlightening, and better yet, fun to read about American statesmen, soldiers and Indian chiefs and foreign notables like Sun Yet Sen. (Pearl Buck authored the biography of the Chinese philosopher-politician who became the first president of the Republic of China.)

The United States entered World War Two nine months before I was born and the conflict affected my childhood deeply. As a toddler I must have been aware of my parents' anxieties because by the time I was in grade school I'd developed full-fledged neuroses. The threat of a World War Three was never far from my mind. I was convinced it was inevitable; it was just a matter of time.

In retrospect, I think the fact that my mother and dad were devout Catholics had a lot to do with it. The Catholic Church was forever warning about the march of "godless Communism," exemplified by the persecution of the faithful in Eastern Europe, most notably Cardinal Josef Mindszenty, who was imprisoned in Hungary. There was also the Virgin Mary's supposed revelations to three shepherd children in Fatima, Portugal. The Catholic Church taught that the mother of Christ appeared to the children six separate times between May and October of 1917 and imparted to them three "secrets" about the fate of the world. During a visit to Portugal in 2019, I learned that the so-called "Miracle of Fatima" coincided with political upheaval in the country that culminated in the dictatorship of Antonio Salazar, who allied himself with the Catholic Church for more than 40 years.

Another likely reason for my abiding fear was that I was an avid reader and constantly tackled books far beyond my age and grade level. I liked history and biography but was almost obsessed by one of the World War Two books my parents owned, Up Front by cartoonist Bill Mauldin, which I leafed through again and again. When Mauldin's book of sketches of GI dogfaces Willy and Joe was reissued in 2000, I bought a copy and added it to my library.

As I reflect on the menacing climate in which I grew up, it's useful to add that government actions also contributed to my fear that a world war with Russia could erupt anytime. On the first Wednesday of every month, the sound of air raid sirens shattered the morning stillness. Radio programs were frequently interrupted by CONELRAD tests. (The acronym stood for the tongue-twisting bureaucratic title of the emergency public broadcasting system that would come into play in the event of attack during the Cold War: *Control of Emergency Radiation*. If that weren't enough, tense military face-offs over divided Berlin or brushfire wars like the one in Korea were constantly in the headlines. So it was little wonder I was often gripped with anxiety.

For Catholic families in my formative years, a neighborhood was defined by its parish. Ours was Saint Paul's, whose pastor was Monsignor John Vaughn, a florid-faced, overstuffed man who seemed to chiefly worship the Sunday collection. Every year, he published a booklet that listed his parishioners, the amounts each gave to the church over the previous annum and how the church spent the money. It was a Catholic Social Register of sorts that separated the affluent sheep from the poor or parsimonious goats.

Monsignor Vaughn was not my friend. I had a morning paper route, which kept me busy from 5:30 AM until just before school each day. The monsignor wanted his newspaper before he said 6 o'clock Mass every morning and complained if it was late. Since the parish rectory was at the end of my route, I had to race there first, then race back to where I picked up my papers and set out on my rounds at a normal pace. If the monsignor tipped me like most of my customers, I might not have minded. But he never gave me a nickel. I've had a jaundiced opinion of clerics since, viewing them generally as a pompous, privileged bunch.

Not that my opinion meant much then: much of what we did in those days revolved around religion in even though my parents were more liberal than those of most of my friends. No meat on Fridays. No movies not sanctioned by the church. Nine o'clock mass on Sundays. Lent was especially difficult. Every Friday afternoon after school during the penitential season we had to attend the Stations of the Cross, a ponderous retelling of Christ's passion frequently punctuated by the sprinkling of holy water and the generation of clouds of incense. It generally took 90 minutes, meaning it was getting dark by the time the service ended. This was torturous because it was springtime and I wanted to be outside playing baseball.

My favorite sport was cause for another grudge I had with Monsignor Vaughn. Across the street from his church was a large sandlot in one corner of which was a baseball backstop. It attracted every kid in the neighborhood and was perfect for playing baseball, which we did from sunup to sundown whenever we could.

But our field of dreams lasted only a season or two before it was paved over and turned into a parking lot. After that we did most of our baseball playing at Circle Field, a postage stamp-size vacant lot with more cinders than dirt. It was bordered by a drainage ditch on one end and heavily used railroad tracks on the other. You had to be desperate to want to play baseball there.

Several times in my professional life I got to set foot on the real thing – a Major League Baseball diamond. Twice I was with President George H.W. Bush, who threw out the first pitch at Opening Day ceremonies of the Baltimore Orioles and Texas Rangers. On another occasion, I was with President Clinton at a game between the New York Mets and Los Angeles Dodgers marking the 50th anniversary of Hall of Famer Jackie Robinson's becoming the first black player in modern major league baseball. During the game, Robinson's jersey number "42" was permanently retired. That started a baseball tradition – every year on April 15, every big league ballplayer now wears number 42 to honor the man who broke the color barrier in America's national pastime.

My biggest thrill, however, was being a member of the grounds-keeping crew at a Seattle Mariners-Minnesota Twins game on August 29, 2010. The experience was one of the prizes offered at a Seattle charity auction and my daughter Jennie and her husband Eric got it for me as a 68th birthday present by making the winning bid. Not only did I get to dash around Safeco Field between innings and mingle with the players – my name was flashed on the scoreboard at one point. It was a boyhood dream come true. Not one I ever anticipated growing up in Scranton.

We moved there in 1950. I entered second grade at St. Paul's parish school, where one of my classmates was Joe Biden. I don't remember what he was like then – in fact, I don't remember him as a classmate at all; he and his family moved to Delaware when he was 10. But the future politician returned to Scranton to visit his grandmother every summer and I sometimes played baseball with him. He was quiet and a pretty good ballplayer as I recall.

Years later, I had a reunion with Sister Eunice, the nun who'd taught second grade, a warm, gentle woman who was among my favorite teachers. She claimed she'd followed my career, and of course she'd followed Biden. "You children would go home for lunch each day and Joe Biden apparently ate a big lunch because he'd fall asleep in the afternoon," she told me. "I used to call him Bye Bye Biden." A few weeks later, I saw a former Biden aide who worked at the White House and told her of my visit with Sister Eunice. I asked her to tell Biden about it the next time she saw him. When she reported back, she said emphatically, "Biden really dislikes that nun!"

I was staggered. I couldn't imagine anyone disliking Sister Eunice. The young woman explained that when Biden was young he stuttered, and he remembered my favorite nun mocked him because of his affliction. I thought he simply misunderstood But I've since learned Biden was probably right: several of our other second grade classmates weren't fond of our teacher either.

"She called me 'Reegy Deegy' instead of my name and was a nun whose attention I didn't seek. I don't remember any kindness from her," Evelyn Regan Kuhn told me as I prepared a news story about the matter after Biden's election as president.

Biden let bygones be bygones. When he learned that his childhood tormentor was observing her 100th birthday – he was at this point Vice

President – he got her telephone number and called her to extend his best wishes.

I was timid as a kid. Worse, I was scared of my own shadow. I was afraid of dogs, afraid of the water and, as noted previously, had lots of other phobias. Anxieties have plagued me all my life but as an adult I've constantly forced myself to confront my fears. For a long time after we moved to Scranton, I was often the target of schoolyard bullies. I didn't fight back, inviting further attacks. Like all my classmates, I walked to and from school. There were two routes home, one almost twice as long as the other. When school ended each day, I'd try to figure out which direction my tormentors were taking and then take the other.

Becoming a bully myself finally ended my ordeal. A new boy entered our parochial school, fresh meat for facing the gauntlet. His first name was Earl, a name strange to our ears, and he was Protestant to boot. In an act completely out of character, I knocked him to the floor of our fourth grade classroom before the start of class one day. The nun who taught us didn't see what happened. Earl didn't cry or tattle. I was hailed as a Defender of the Faith by my chums and finally accepted into the tribe.

My closest friend was first cousin Johnny Cotter, known as Cotz. We spent a lot of time in each other's company and went to high school together at Scranton Prep. It was Cotz who hung a nickname on me it took a long time to outlive – Choo Choo, or Chooch for short. It derived from my adolescent love of model railroading.

I was the godfather of Cotz's first child but in adulthood we grew apart. He preceded me into the news business and eventually became a well-known New York tabloid newspaper editor – a form of journalism I detest. Cotz was a brash, facile writer skilled in stretching the facts with a bad-boy streak that endeared him to men and women alike. He was immortalized as one of the characters in a short-lived Broadway show called "Lucky Guy" starring actor Tom Hanks. Cotz wasn't lucky himself. He died of a sudden heart attack before he was 50.

For a time I expected to sell insurance like my Dad when I grew up. He'd opened his own business after splitting with his in-laws. In the summertime I sometimes worked in his one room office in one of Scranton's largest buildings, helping to file papers and answer the telephone. Once or twice a week my dad would drive out to Montrose or Susquehanna, rural communities where he had satellite offices. I often went with him. That was my favorite part of my job.

An encounter with Harry Truman when I was 10 years old might help explain how I wound up in the news business. The year was 1952 and the 33d president, beset by corruption in Washington and an unpopular war in Korea, was traveling the country trying to help Adlai Stevenson succeed him. Truman was on a fool's errand and probably knew it. The anti-intellectualism often prevalent in American politics was running strong, and Stevenson, the Democratic governor of Illinois, was widely thought too brainy. "Egghead" was the term used to demean him. (When a woman once told him every intelligent American was in his corner, Stevenson replied: "Ah, but I need a majority.)

Like my father, I supported the Republican in the presidential race, General Dwight Eisenhower, who was immensely popular because of his leadership of the war in Europe during World War Two. You probably find this hard to believe -- interested in presidential politics *at age ten?*

Yes, I was a nerdy kid. I'd learned to read before I entered kindergarten and quickly became interested in current affairs. When most of my contemporaries were still plodding through the elementary school primer *Dick & Jane*, I was reading such weighty tomes as John Gunther's The Riddle of MacArthur. I was so curious about the world I lived in that my grandmother nicknamed me "Dr. Why?" My curiosity has been a lifelong gift – and curse.

Though I liked Ike, my dad took me out of school to hear Truman speak at a campaign rally in Scranton. It was a cold, misty October morning and I remember my dad calling out, "Hello, Mr. President," as the dapper Man from Missouri, surrounded by Secret Service agents and local politicians, strode briskly through Courthouse Square on his way to the podium. I believe Truman's response was a jaunty "Good Morning!" In his speech, Truman knocked the press. "You have a good newspaper with the courage to give you the facts, the Scranton Times. I want to say to you that sort of newspaper is in the minority these days. I have been all over the United States, from one end of the country to the other, and about 90 percent of the press is against the Democrats," he said.

Truman then turned his ire on the Republicans, showing off his "Give 'em hell, Harry" style. "For 20 years, the Democratic Party has been working to promote the interests and the welfare of the plain people of this country. That was the meaning and the purpose of Franklin Roosevelt's New Deal – and of Harry Truman's Fair Deal," he said. "At every session of Congress -- as (local Democratic congressman) Harry

Mitchell can tell you – we have had to struggle with the Republican obstructionists. They have put things in the way of every progressive measure we have offered.

"This goes on all the time – day in and day out – until the last few weeks of the campaign for President," Truman continued. "And then they come around and tell you that they have been for everything. Then suddenly, as you will find, the Republican candidates begin to take an interest in the people, begin to sing a strange new song to the people of the country. It is called the 'me too' song. It's a marvelous thing to hear."

I vividly recall getting to school late and telling my classmates all about my experience. So I can truthfully state that at age 10 I got my first taste of political reporting. Thus began my lifelong fascination with national politics. Maybe also my lifelong frustration that my chosen profession of political journalism so often falls short of my high standards for it.

I saw Truman again in 1968 when Hubert H. Humphrey was running for president. I was a campaign aide and in the entourage when the then-Vice President and Maine Sen. Edmund Muskie, his Democratic running mate, visited the former president at his modest Independence MO home. The two story white frame house at 219 Delaware Street is still there and open to visitors. Truman, a feisty 84-year old by then, greeted Humphrey and Muskie on his narrow front porch and predicted they'd win. According to news accounts of the meeting, Truman said the key to victory was to "See as many people as you can and tell them the truth, even if it hurts."

Had Truman known who I was he might have whacked me with his cane, because I was an eight-year old know-it-all when he fired General Douglas MacArthur in 1951. MacArthur was one of my heroes. I loved his insouciance: his corncob pipe, aviator sunglasses and the scrambled eggs on the visor of his crushed Army cap. Outraged by his dismissal – a move I later realized was long overdue because of MacArthur's arrogance and insubordination – I sat down and wrote an angry letter to the president:

> Dear Mr. Truman,
>   I think you are very wrong about firing MacArthur. He was the brains of the Army. He and "Ike" and "Blood & Guts" and a couple more are responsible for this country's victory.

He was a very gallant leader and he would have to give his wholehearted support to keep freedom. You said "He did not give his wholehearted support. This is wrong. All this country needs is a few more MacArthurs. England wanted him fired because he would ruin their plans. They are dealing with Red China. To save this country, I would drop the "A" bomb.

Did you get the book, "Why Doesn't Somebody Kill Stalin?" There is a wall 12 feet thick, not even his top army leaders may see him. I learned this because I read – I read the war story too. I always wait for the paper, as soon as it comes I read about the war. But when I saw the headlines yesterday, I didn't even read the funnies. I read the story of MacArthur. I am a good reader. I even read the story about the time those men tried to take your life. I heard your broadcast. My father saw it on TV. This country will be ruined if it doesn't have good Army leaders.

Why don't you people in Washington wise up?

Yours truly.
Eugene Gibbons

P.S. I am in the third grade. Please answer.
E.G.

My dad showed the letter to a neighbor who worked for the local newspaper, and it wound up in print. The letter was my first brush with celebrity though few people believed I wrote it. For the record, I did. I never got a response. Years later, the Scranton Times resurrected the letter in a hometown-boy-makes-good story on my involvement in the 1992 presidential campaign debate.

More than 130,000 people lived in Scranton in the 1950's, making it the third largest city in Pennsylvania. There was always lots to do. My friends and I were deep into sports, played baseball, built model airplanes, collected bubble gum trading cards and flirted with girls. My first date was Judy Gilroy. When we were both in fourth grade, she accepted my invitation to have after-school sodas at Huber's Drug Store. When the big day came, I headed off to our meeting with the exact change in my pocket. When Judy showed up with her younger brother, I had to run home for another dime.

My childhood crush went on to become a flight attendant. There's a sad coda to the story. Though we hadn't been in touch in years, I was saddened to learn that as a young adult Judy committed suicide. When I think of her now and then, it always brings to mind my parents' amusement at our innocent pre-adolescent romance.

Like most cities its size, Scranton had a major league farm team – the Scranton Miners of the Class A Eastern League, one of the lower rungs of professional baseball. Every Saturday and Sunday the team was in town during the spring and summer, my brother Charlie and I haunted its premises, an aging old ballpark with a wooden grandstand. We were members of the Knothole Gang, a promotional gimmick which let us get into games for a quarter.

In 1952 the parent big league club – the American League's Saint Louis Browns – played an exhibition with the Miners, winning it 4-2. Charlie and I were in heaven. One of the Browns' players was Leroy "Satchel" Paige, an old Negro League player who was perhaps the best pitcher in baseball history. He was either close to or in his 50s then and thought by many to be too old to play baseball, a prejudice he mocked by sitting in a rocking chair in the pitchers' bullpen. He promised Charlie and me an autograph "after the game," but forgetful of or ignoring his promise started toward the clubhouse when the last out was made. My younger brother would have none of that. He vaulted over the fence separating the ballfield from the stands and grabbed Satchel Paige by the sleeve of his uniform. Charlie wouldn't let go until our quarry, who's now enshrined in the Baseball Hall of Fame, signed our scorecards for us.

Bespectacled and bookish, I longed to be popular and a good athlete like my brother Charlie, who excelled at everything he touched, baseball and girls in particular. Instead, I was something of a loner, often with my nose stuck in a book or off in an imaginary world playing with my Lionel trains. As I got older, a lot of my free time was taken up working at part-time jobs – delivering newspapers in the morning and groceries after school. I was a summer camp counselor in high school and worked various low-paying, unattractive summer jobs in college.

One year I delivered samples of a new detergent called "Mr. Clean" house to house. I walked from one end of Scranton to the other but never got the sexual thank you from a grateful or lonely housewife that some workmates boasted about. For several weeks the next year, I worked for a neighbor whose small business built scales to weigh railroad coal cars. The job involved some heavy labor and I once nearly lost my right hand when a steel I-beam slipped off a jack as it was being hoisted into position. I still have a scar from that.

Because I wasn't skilled enough to make my high school baseball team, I learned to play tennis and together with a pal named Frank Connolly once won the local YMCA junior doubles championship. Throughout my youth, I longed to be part of Scranton's moneyed elite. But my father, a child of wealth whose family was among those victimized by Great Depression, was too unfocused to ever really succeed. It seemed to me he constantly chased impossible dreams and went off on benders to escape his frustrations. I was determined to be the man my dad sought to be: financially comfortable, someone others admired. If my goal in life was to be summed up in a nutshell, it would probably be becoming a person of consequence.

Although my dad never went to college and my mother completed only two years, they instilled in my brothers and me a thirst for learning and an undying belief that anything was possible. Perhaps the greatest gift they gave us was the love of reading I mentioned previously. One of my earliest memories is of my father reading to Charlie and me. (Our brother Joe, the youngest in the family, was born a few years later. I teased him unmercifully when he was a child and he squawked about it every time, getting me in trouble with our parents.)

Each evening, we heard a chapter or more of a classic: Treasure Island, Robinson Crusoe, The Adventures of Pinocchio, Swiss Family Robinson. What a cast of characters! Long John Silver was one of my favorites, but Jim Hawkins had a special place in my heart too. Years later, when I did a fair amount of long distance blue water sailing, I learned that "shiver me timbers" was not just a pirate saying: boats actually shake and shiver in the turbulence of a storm at sea. Pinocchio? An excellent primer on politics. And the castaway hero of Daniel Defoe's masterpiece? A lesson on the reliance of self-importance. Once, during a sad passage in "Little Women," I burst out crying. My dad took me in his arms and told me it was okay to cry, that it was manly to have compassion for the suffering of others.

My parents were unusual for their day and religious convictions. Although we were raised in a church not known for openness to intellectual inquiry, we were encouraged to question authority, to seek truth wherever we found it. Still the church had a profound influence on me. It wasn't until I was in the army that I rejected the ecclesiastical strictures of no meat on Friday, no missing Mass on Sunday and all the rubrics drilled into me in parochial school.

Living through the nerve-wracking Cuban Missile Crisis in October 1962 was probably the worst emotional ordeal I've ever been through short of the death of Lynn. I was a sophomore in college, working weekends at Radio Station WSCR in Scranton. For 13 days we hovered on the brink of nuclear war. President John F. Kennedy ordered a naval blockade of Cuba and put other U.S. armed forces on high alert. The crisis escalated when an American spy plane on a reconnaissance mission over Cuba was shot down, its pilot killed.

How well I remember when the war fever broke: NBC News Correspondent Sandor Vanocur breathlessly breaking into a Sunday night radio broadcast to announce that Soviet Premier Nikita Khrushchev had agreed to withdraw Soviet nuclear missiles from Cuba. It was almost like being reborn. The world would get to go on. Sanity would prevail over madness.

It was taken for granted I would go to college, becoming the first in my immediate family to get a degree. There was only one choice: the University of Scranton, a Jesuit institution with about 3,000 students, most of them locals. My beloved Uncle Joe was a member of the Jesuit order. I attended an all-male Jesuit high school, Scranton Prep. Moreover, almost every one of my high school classmates was headed to the same place.

Scranton U at the time was also all-male. Unlike Prep, there was no after-school detention or mandatory Latin or ban on smoking. Otherwise there was little distinction. The education it offered was considered the *sine qua non* of academia by nearly everyone who went there. Critics said the Jesuits were great at turning out accountants and cops. I think they were probably right. The sanitized curriculum included a heavy dose of Catholic theology and the philosophy of St. Thomas Aquinas, neither of which helps develop proficiency in critical thinking.

I was an English major which played to my strength, given my love of literature. The instruction was weak with one exception – Professor Matthew O'Rourke, who inspired me to become a writer. In the spring semester of my freshman year, I played on the college tennis team, never winning a match. I was also active on the campus newspaper, wrote for the literary magazine and was heavily involved in the campus radio station. I hosted a jazz program that aired on weekends and eventually became station manager, a position I screwed up by neglecting to apply to the Federal Communications Commission for renewal of the station's broadcasting license in a timely manner.

This was undoubtedly partly due to the fact that I'd lined up a part-time job with a commercial radio station, to which I devoted a good deal of time and attention. My preoccupation with broadcasting meant I had a lackluster social life which I now regret, although it was okay with me at the time.

As things turned out, broadcasting was my life's work until I was more than 40. But I always thought of myself as a writer. Though I was a UPI Audio reporter, I wrote newspaper stories every chance I got. When I joined Reuters, I was initially intimidated by the pressure of churning out much longer, detailed copy "under the gun" of deadline pressure. Until the day I retired I worried about being fired because I doubted my ability to compete with better connected, more facile wordsmiths. So I worked longer and harder than most. Adopting Woody Allen's philosophy that 80 percent of life is just showing up, I worked long hours, often neglecting to claim overtime, and grabbed every trip I could get. Some were almost beyond belief. On a trip with Bill Clinton, we left Knoxville, Tennessee on a Friday afternoon at 4 PM, flew to Italy, Hungary, Bosnia and Croatia – and were back in Washington DC before midnight Saturday.

My high profile work enabled me to sign up with a speaker's bureau and earn extra money by telling my stories to civic groups. It was a lucrative sideline. Sometimes I made as much as $3,000 for a 45-minute talk, helping defray the cost of my children's tuition bills. As glamorous as this might seem, it was often lonely and physically demanding – hop on a plane after work, fly halfway across the country and get back in time to put in a few hours of work the next day

Here I was fortunate. Just as my parents were unusually open-minded when it came to education for their day and time, nothing I did in my working life would have been possible without my wife Lynn. We met at the headquarters of the Democratic National Committee in the Watergate office building, the place where Richard Nixon's downfall began. I was a newly-hired United Press International reporter and needed to fill out some job application forms. I'd previously worked at the DNC, which was just down the street from my apartment. On the afternoon I went there to borrow a typewriter, my wife of 41 years was a working as a volunteer.

Lynn wanted to be a doctor. But she abandoned her dreams when we married and devoted her life to our children and me. A few days after she turned 65, she died in her sleep. Just when she was enjoying her greatest pleasure – her grandchildren, whom she loved dearly – she quietly slipped away. Her death was characteristic of the way she lived, never wanting anyone to make a fuss about her. I tried to capture Lynn's essence in an essay I wrote for her funeral program:

"A beautiful soul."

That's how Jon Potfay describes Lynn, who unexpectedly died in her sleep early on the morning of July 13. She had not been ill.

Jon, our beloved son-in-law and a cardiologist, said a heart attack is almost always the cause of sudden death. He said what happened to Lynn could not have been anticipated, or prevented. Something broke in her circulatory system, her heart fluttered for a second or two, she flew to God. Lynn died peacefully, a serene look on her face. It was almost as if she had earned the reward of a good death for her magnificent life, which touched the lives of so many, many, many others, always for the better.

Lynn was forever on the lookout for a chance to help. Perhaps because her mother was blind, she believed to her very core we are all dependent on the kindness of others – most of all those of us on the margin. She was especially drawn to newly-arrived immigrants struggling to make a home in America. She taught them to speak English, giving them the most essential tool for finding their way in a new world.

Lynn didn't stop there. She helped her students fill out employment forms and badgered folks with jobs to hire them. She accompanied them to the bank to get a car loan, found them medical and dental care they could afford, got them books for their children. When necessary, she slipped them a dollar, or ten. She asked for nothing in return. Selflessness was part of Lynn's DNA. I called her my Mother Teresa and it wasn't a compliment. I often worried her generosity would put us in the poorhouse.

Lynn's love was boundless, but it began with her family. She was a model mother and wife, a devoted sister, a revered sister-and-mother-in-law, the adored grandmother of Charlie, Eli, Zoe and Hobbes. (How she would have delighted in Lily, Libbie and Nell, all of whom were born after she died.)

I think the last months of Lynn's life were especially happy. She was surrounded by family and friends at Becky and Jon's wedding. She saw Sean and Dayna and Zoe often. Chad, as always, was her special child, her blue-eyed boy, as attentive to her as she was to him. Jennie and Eric and their three sons made Seattle a love-filled suburb of Washington for her. And just last week, we celebrated her 65th birthday.

Lynn's life was not without difficulties. Her congenital back trouble gave her constant, sometimes excruciating pain. Because of this, her mobility was increasingly limited. Yet she shared with me my love of motion, uncomplainingly for the most part. We were in Seattle and Florida in January, in France in April, in Seattle and Hawaii for most of June.

I will always remember and cherish the last night of my beloved Lynn's life. We had been babysitting five-month-old Hobbes for two days to give his parents a brief break from the rigors of parenthood. We'd survived that delightful ordeal with flying colors. A trivial health concern of mine had been lifted. We talked and laughed over dinner, and made plans for a bright future. Lynn's mother was born in Montana and she'd always wanted to go there. I wanted to go to the Swiss Alps as well, but for once in my life put her wishes first. We were going to go to Montana in August.

As hard as the hours have been since I found my beautiful wife resting peacefully, asleep forever, it's been a wonderful consolation to see the great outpouring of love for her. It has become abundantly clear she will be missed by so many beyond her immediate family.

It's the only monument Lynn would have wished. Oh, how she will be missed.

There's so much more to say about Lynn. You'll find it elsewhere in this book. If God is love, she was godly though she didn't believe in God.

I'm glad to see she didn't live to see greed and hate become American political mainstream. Four years after Lynn died, I remarried. My wife Becky is in many ways a mirror image; loving, selfless and kind. We met when she traveled from her home in South Carolina to visit her daughter, who lived next door to me in Virginia. We married three years later in Charleston SC. My oldest grandson Charlie, then nine years old, was my best man. The bride's 15-year old granddaughter Anna Banks was her maid of honor. Becky shares my love of motion. Seldom are we at home.

II

Growing up, I had no intention of becoming a newsman even though journalists and journalism were part of my life. As I've noted, our neighbor was an editor for the local newspaper. Dorothy Kilgallen, a celebrated New York gossip columnist, was a distant relative. My father worked in newspaper advertising for awhile. And as I also noted previously, I was interested in current events from childhood, writing the president when I thought he made a mistake.

Jim Bishop, whose syndicated columns often recreated historic events, was one of my newspaper favorites. I also enjoyed Walter Winchell's daily tidbits about the entertainment world and Westbrook Pegler's political tirades. I read the editorial page faithfully, seldom fully comprehending the issues raised. I was what later came to be called a news junkie.

My addiction to printer's ink notwithstanding, my hero and role model was Dr. John Cotter, a physician uncle by marriage who landed on Omaha Beach in the first hour of the D-Day invasion of Europe. On that fateful day, his second wedding anniversary, he earned the Distinguished Service Cross, a decoration for bravery second only to the Medal of Honor. That, in itself, was remarkable. What was even more remarkable was that he was a medical officer, a doctor. Seldom do non-combatants get that exalted a decoration.

"Captain Cotter landed early in the assault on the coast of France as part of the (116th) Regimental Medical Detachment. At this time the beach was subjected to intense enemy rifle, machine gun and artillery fire and numerous casualties had been inflicted," his DSC citation said. "With complete disregard for his own safety, Captain Cotter administered medical attention to the wounded under this heavy fire.

His fortitude and devotion to duty in rendering aid to the wounded under such hazardous and difficult conditions inspired those who saw him to a more determined effort in meeting the enemy."

After-action reports said German soldiers deliberately shot at U.S. medical personnel, whose Red Cross helmets and armbands made them easy targets. Many doctors and medical corpsmen were killed on Omaha Beach that day, including my uncle's best friend, Captain Robert Ware. My uncle, who suffered only superficial shrapnel wounds during nearly a year of combat in World War Two, seldom spoke of his ordeal. He died of a heart attack at age 50, possibly a delayed action casualty of the war.

Despite his brusque, often intimidating manner, I deeply admired "Uncle John" and, like him, wanted to be a doctor. Once when I was in high school, he let me go with him to a hospital emergency room where I watched him treat a boy who'd nearly severed his thumb. I nearly fainted as he sutured and dressed the wound. I pretty much decided then medicine probably wasn't for me.

On June 6, 1984, I followed my uncle to Omaha Beach. It was the most memorable presidential trip I ever made. Ronald Reagan was president and the occasion was the 40th anniversary of D-Day. The celebration, on a sparkling summer day far different from the stormy weather of the invasion, started at Pointe du Hoc, a promontory overlooking the Normandy invasion beaches. It was there U.S. Army Rangers, in one of the greatest exploits in the history of warfare, used ropes and ladders to scale a 100-foot cliff under withering enemy fire to knock out a German gun emplacement. The guns had been moved to a nearby pasture. The Rangers found and destroyed them there. Even today, the wind-swept promontory bears the scars of battle: the landscape is pockmarked with shell craters and littered with the rubble of Nazi bunkers.

Reagan commemorated the feat of arms that took place there with soaring Shakespearean rhetoric. (Indeed, the Bard deserved a credit line. Columnist Peggy Noonan, then a White House speechwriter, was inspired by the St. Crispin's Day speech in Shakespeare's Henry V, "...we few, we happy few, we band of brothers," in penning the lines). Standing in front of a granite monument shaped in the form of a bayonet and flanked by 62 Ranger veterans – by now gray-haired old men, Reagan declared: *"These are the boys of Pointe du Hoc. These are the men who took* the cliffs. These are the champions who helped free a continent. These are the heroes who helped end a war."

Gentlemen, I look at you and I think of the words of Stephen Spender's poem. You are men who in your 'lives fought for life...and left the vivid air signed with your honor.'" It was the Great Communicator at his finest; I still get a lump in my throat writing the words of that speech.

There was another emotional Reagan speech at the U.S. Military Cemetery overlooking Omaha Beach. More than 9,000 American war dead are buried there in a 172-acre grove considered U.S. territory, their graves point west toward the United States. The dead include 41 sets of brothers, including two of President Teddy Roosevelt's four sons, Theodore and Quentin Roosevelt.

TR Jr., an Army brigadier general and Medal of Honor winner, was the only allied general to land on D-Day with the first wave of troops. He died of a heart attack one month later at age 56. Quentin Roosevelt was an Army aviator killed in World War One. Originally buried at Chamery, France, his body was exhumed and transferred to Normandy.

Reagan's speech borrowed from a posthumous letter a California woman wrote to her D-Day veteran father. In it, she regretted that he'd died before he could realize his postwar dream to return to the battlefield and pay homage to his fallen comrades.

"I'm going there someday, Dad, and I'll see the beaches and the barricades and the monuments. I'll see the graves and I'll put flowers there just as you wanted to do. I'll never forget what you went through, Dad, nor will I let anyone else forget – and Dad, I'll always be proud," Reagan said, quoting Lisa Zanetta Hann.

In the afternoon there was a parade on Utah Beach as Reagan, Britain's Queen Elizabeth, French President Francois Mitterrand and Canadian Prime Minister Pierre Trudeau, leaders of the allied nations, looked on from a reviewing stand. Also present were King Olav V of Norway, Queen Beatrix of the Netherlands, King Baudouin of Belgium and Grand Duke Jean of Luxembourg. Bagpipes skirled, flags swirled, soldiers and sailors in colorful dress uniform marched in close formation, allied warships lay at anchor offshore; the pageantry was breathtaking.

We flew out of the port of Cherbourg after the ceremonies, and the ride to the airport was electrifying. As our motorcade rumbled through one tiny French village after another, crowds lined the sides of the narrow road waving French and American flags. There was an especially enthusiastic welcome in the ancient village of St. Mare-Eglise, where paratroops of the 82d Airborne Division landed. Red, white and blue bunting was everywhere and dangling from the steeple of the village church was a mannequin clutching a parachute. It depicted the ordeal of Pvt. John Steele, whose canopy caught on the church steeple during his descent into battle.

I came away that day with a priceless souvenir – a small engraved brass paperweight in a leather case adorned with the presidential seal. Reagan had the mementos made for each of the other heads of state and members of his senior staff. I got mine by mistake – I was in the press pool that accompanied the president from London to Normandy by helicopter. On departure from Winfield House, the U.S. ambassador's residence in London, we were steered to the wrong chopper – the one meant for Reagan's top aides. Somewhere over the English Channel, a Marine crewman passed around the gift-wrapped keepsakes, unwittingly giving them to the wrong people. I gave mine to my aunt to commemorate the heroism of her late husband.

Ten years later, I returned to Normandy with President Bill Clinton for the 50th anniversary of D-Day. It was a different kind of visit. We sailed from Portsmouth England on June 5 aboard the aircraft carrier USS George Washington, and anchored off the French coast at nightfall. Watching the lights twinkle on in the villages was mystical; fifty years earlier the greatest armada in history had assembled off this coast, prepared for a clash of arms to determine the future of the world. It was foggy by dawn and the seas were rough. Adding to the verisimilitude with D-Day itself, a nearby destroyer fired a 21-gun salute during a watery wreath-laying ceremony.

As the ceremony unfolded, I could imagine what it must have been like to be aboard a landing craft churning through rough seas toward shore, carrying seasick troops packed shoulder to shoulder toward an uncertain fate as naval gunfire pounded the beaches and warplanes roared overhead. It must have been hell on earth. Clinton's main speech at the U.S. military cemetery that day included passages that resembled Reagan's words. He noted that many D-Day veterans were in the audience.

"Oh they may walk with a little less spring in their step, and their ranks are growing thinner. But let us never forget, when they were younger, these men saved the world," Clinton said.

One of the veterans there was Florida Congressman Sam Gibbons, who parachuted in behind enemy lines with the 101st Airborne Division. He wasn't related but we were friends. He once told me that as he led a group of paratroopers toward their initial objective, they came across a badly wounded German soldier begging to be out of his misery. Gibbons said they gave the man some water and moved on. That bothered him for the rest of his life. He said maybe they should have administered a coup de grace.

There was some political theatre after the speeches that upset me. Clinton walked Omaha Beach with two elderly veterans of the 116th Regiment, my uncle's unit. At one point, he knelt down and arranged some small stones in the form of a cross as Eddie Adams, a famous news photographer, snapped away. Clinton's action seemed politically calculated, a desecration of sacred ground. After a stop in Paris following the D-Day commemoration, he went on to Oxford where as a Rhodes Scholar he'd done post-graduate work, to receive an honorary degree. I thought that too insensitive and inappropriate. While Clinton and most others who eventually became America's leaders were hiding out in study halls, thousands of their fellow countrymen were fighting and dying in Vietnam.

In 2010, my uncle's son Bob and his wife Alisa and Lynn and I visited Normandy, today a gentle, pastoral region far removed from the blood and thunder that etched it into history. Traces of D-Day and the hedgerow fighting that followed are easy to find. On grassy bluffs overlooking Omaha Beach, concrete German gun emplacements with walls three or four feet thick, some still bristling with artillery pieces, convey a sense of menace. In the sleepy farming village of Saint Mare-Eglise, that mannequin representing the unlucky American paratrooper who caught on the church steeple on D-Day still swings in the wind. If you look closely as you drive past the ancient stone buildings and sheds that flank the winding country roads, you'll often see tell-tale pitting left by bullets and shrapnel.

We hired a guide for our visit and followed the footsteps of Captain Cotter from the Dog Green sector of Omaha Beach, the deadly beachhead he stormed on D-Day, to the town of Saint-Lo. Now largely forgotten, it was a major World War Two battleground. It was here American troops broke through German defenses, paving the way for the allied race to the Elbe. Saint-Lo was where the tide of the war turned, making the defeat of Nazi Germany all but inevitable.

Our journey of remembrance took just a few hours – Saint-Lo is only about 30 miles from the Normandy beaches. In 1944 it took U.S. troops nearly seven weeks and thousands of casualties in savage hedgerow fighting to cover that ground. The German Wehrmacht resisted fiercely, so a push allied planners expected to take nine days wasn't completed until July 18. According to British historian Antony Beevor, author of D-Day and the Battle for Normandy, allied and German casualty rates in the initial phase of the allied invasion of Europe were equivalent to those suffered in horrific clashes between Russian and German armies on the Eastern Front. "The general advance from 7 to 20 July had cost the Americans some 40,000 casualties," Beevor said.

Saint-Lo is the locale of a memorial chapel honoring the city's American liberators. Jean Mignon, who was instrumental in creating the monument, told us a U.S. Army doctor had saved his brother's life. He said his brother was born in the summer of 1944 with a potentially fatal birth defect. He recalled that the doctor who treated the baby told the boy's parents he knew what he was doing because "I'm a children's doctor in civilian life." That doctor might well have been my uncle. He was a pediatrician.

I suspect that it was on the trip to honor my uncle that Lynn started to die. She was often unwell; twice she spent much of the day in bed. She begged off a walking tour of the section of Paris around Notre Dame. Later that day, she sat on a park bench and waited as I scurried around Luxembourg Gardens taking pictures. Still later, she passed up dinner, choosing to rest while Bob, Alicia and I went off to a restaurant. She felt too ill to accompany us on one of the three days we were in Normandy. I chalked it all up to her bad back. Like her father and brother, Lynn suffered from spinal stenosis, an acutely painful degeneration of the spinal column. Yet she pushed on, usually without complaint.

Some elements of our trip to France had aspects of a late-blooming romance. How she loved seeing Claude Monet's home at Giverny! The Impressionist master was probably her favorite artist. What I remember most was how excited she was seeing remnants of ancient Rome at a museum in Evereux. We had a pleasant dinner at a small French restaurant afterward and drove back to Paris on Easter Sunday morning.

Though Lynn never spoke of it, our visit to Normandy must have been stressful emotionally. There we were, tracing the footsteps of a World War Two hero. Lynn's father, also a doctor and World War Two veteran, was something of a monster because of his wartime service. He was badly injured in Sicily when a surgical tent he was in collapsed under enemy shelling. That and other life-threatening experiences took a toll on him mentally: he probably suffered from PTSD. His demons apparently drove him to mistreat his children. As I discovered too late, throughout their childhood, he often subjected Lynn and her brother Norden to emotional abuse.

The day after Lynn's funeral, I gave my son Chad a few of her favorite things: an IPod filled with classical music and a set of noise-cancelling headphones. Chad asked me if he could also take something else and showed me a set of his mother's handwritten notes. I'd never seen them before. "The seeds of my life sprouted from Hitler's grave," she wrote.

In a cramped script obviously edited and re-edited many times over, Lynn told how her father and mother, a Red Cross psychiatric social worker also close to the European frontlines during World War Two, took out their psychoses on her and her brother, subjecting them to emotional torment. What frightened Lynn most, though, was when her dad threatened to banish her brother, her only sibling. He would send the boy to an orphanage or to prison, Bill Weingarten vowed. Once or two, he threatened to kill his son. Lynn wrote that she was so desperate to escape the madness she sometimes considered suicide. "But the knife was dull," she said.

Lynn's mother died soon after we married. I didn't really know her. Her dad, who was semi-retired when Lynn and I met, was very demanding but didn't seem a tortured soul. Perhaps his demons were stilled by then. Neither parent was at our wedding; they were angry with Lynn for marrying me without their permission. Lynn's father became ill before Becky, the youngest of our four children, was born. She shuttled constantly between our home in Alexandria VA and his home in Chevy Chase MD, a distance of 13 miles, to take care of her father, frantically trying to play dutiful daughter as well as wife and mother. Her heavy burden took its toll on our marriage. When Bill Weingarten died in 1979 it was something of a relief.

At times during our life together, Lynn tried to share her pain. I'm of Irish stock. Stoicism is a character trait: emotion is frowned on in the tribe I come from. Need a shoulder to cry on? Not my job. Go see the chaplain. I've since realized Lynn's childhood shaped her life. If someone hurt or was in need, she HAD to help. It was her way of keeping her painful memories at bay. Her way of trying to gentle the world. Her way of staying alive. She did all sorts of good works with no hope of salvation.

It grieves me to see the history, standards and sacrifice of my family and so many others – history, standards and sacrifice that made for an America always striving to do better – under assault from the deceit and demagoguery and cruelty and hatred that roils our country in the second decade of the 21st Century. World War Two was a powerful unifier; it arguably led to a post-war period where our country flourished. Racial segregation slowly, often painfully ended, women slowly gained greater equality. We even launched a war on poverty. When I arrived in Washington, the only lapel pins worn by politicians signified that the person wearing it had earned a medal for bravery in the war or had been wounded and held a Purple Heart. Now almost every politician sports an American flag lapel pin. Those who don't are criticized as being unpatriotic.

Political theorist Hannah Arendt wrote of the "banality of evil" in a book about Adolf Eichmann's trial in Israel for his role in the Holocaust. I've always been terrified by the aspect of human nature that allows normal people to rationalize horrific behavior. Germany was the birthplace of Brahms and Beethoven. It was deeply religious and blessed with great natural beauty. Yet during twelve years of Nazi rule, the darkest depravity became the norm.

In 2014, I visited the Eagle's Nest, Adolf Hitler's retreat in the Bavarian Alps. A stout, sprawling stone building, it sits atop a mountain overlooking the village of Berchtesgaden, with sweeping views in every direction. It was built as a 50th birthday gift for Hitler and reeks of the kind of excess you'd expect: grand meeting halls with marble everywhere, gigantic fireplaces and a gold-plated elevator big enough to accommodate limousines rising from an exterior entranceway. Der Fuhrer visited the place only 14 times and never slept there: he was fearful of heights!

You'd think we Americans would learn from history. But less than three quarters of a century after we took down Hitler, a case can be made we're repeating it. What I worry about in my old age is a return to the uncertain times of my youth. Air raid sirens wailing once a month, just a drill to test the system. Or is it? Public appeals for civil defense volunteers. Visions of U.S. towns and cities shattered and pestilence-ridden like those of Europe after World War Two. These were nightmares that haunted me as a child.

Before the benighted presidency of Donald J. Trump, it was unthinkable for any American leader, Republican or Democrat, to go anywhere near the political accelerants that have ignited historical bonfires. Yet Trump's four years were a frightening flirtation with totalitarianism. It can't happen here? It damn near did – and the threat it will happen is still very real.

I blame television and the social media for much of what's gone wrong with our country. A thriving democracy depends on a well-informed citizenry and, until recently, Americans were reasonably well informed. We read books, magazines and newspapers, and discussed current events at the dinner table or around the water cooler. American history was taught in school. So were civics and geography. Baseball, a sport that encourages wisdom and reflection because of its focus on history and statistics, was the national pastime. Politicians at the national level put the country first: when Republican Richard Nixon resigned the presidency, it was Republican congressional leaders Hugh Scott, John Rhodes and Barry Goldwater who told him he had to go. (State and local politics was another story, particularly in parts of the South. But scoundrels seldom went much higher.)

Television in its early years was a force for the good in American life. When my parents finally bought a TV set, it opened up a whole new world. Every week brought excellent drama on such shows as *Playhouse 90*, *Alfred Hitchcock Presents* and *GE Theater* (hosted by then-actor Ronald Reagan). There were excellent documentaries, such as CBS Reports *Harvest of Shame*, which spotlighted the mistreatment of migrant farm workers. TV news, then as now, was generally superficial. But the news presenters, Chet Huntley, David Brinkley, Douglas Edwards and Walter Cronkite among them, usually had a print news background and understood and adhered to journalistic standards and practices.

I was a freshman in college when the first big red flag was raised. The alarmist was a public official, Federal Communications Commission (FCC) chairman Newton Minow. In a 1961 speech to the National Association of Broadcasters that sparked much discussion at that time, Minow deplored what was happening.

"When television is good, nothing – not the theater, not the magazines or newspapers – nothing is better. But when television is bad, nothing is worse," he said. The most quoted part of Minow's speech was his description of television as "a vast wasteland." His was a voice crying in the wilderness given what the airwaves have since become.

Our country's leadership remained above this – for a time. I spent much of my career documenting the changes. One of the change agents was Newt Gingrich, to my mind an individual keen only on stroking his ego and amassing political power. Bill Clinton, a brilliant but undisciplined man also hungry for power, was another.

There were others too and, yes, early symptoms of the malignancy that I fear might yet devour our country had already appeared before the Georgia Republican and Arkansas Democrat – and Trump -- arrived on the scene. The Vietnam War and the Civil Rights Movement both engendered great bitterness; so did the decline of the U.S. manufacturing sector, exemplified by the deteriorating standards of Detroit automakers, which prompted a flood of foreign imports.

But these national growing pains were rationally discussed and addressed until cable news came on the scene. Soon after the U.S. House of Representatives reluctantly allowed live TV broadcasts of its proceedings. Gingrich recognized the presence of the cameras as a golden opportunity for self-promotion. Early in each day's House session is a time devoted to one-minute speeches. Congressmen traditionally used it to deliver brief remarks about a constituent or activity in their district they thought deserving of recognition (and could get political credit for providing.) The house chamber was almost always empty during this exercise. It was harmless political pandering to the folks back home.

Gingrich, at the time a powerless back-bencher, saw an opening to break out of the crowd. Three or four times a week, there he'd deliver one-minute speeches short on substance but long on fiery rhetoric. No matter that there was no-one else in the chamber to listen. People throughout the country with nothing better to do than watch TV saw and heard him, and he quickly made a name for himself. The audience Gingrich tapped into was almost by definition under or unemployed, bored, angry and ill-informed. It was like touching a match to a bucket of gasoline.

Clinton broke with political tradition when he ran for president in 1992 by making the rounds of TV gabfests like the Phil Donahue Show, Larry King Live and Oprah. These were usually show- biz light, where aspiring actors and comedians engaged in inane chit-chat with the hosts. Until the then-Arkansas governor defied the taboo, they were considered beneath the dignity of presidents or presidential candidates. On a telecast hosted by Arsenio Hall, an African-American comedian and talk show host, Clinton donned dark glasses and tooted a saxophone, identifying himself as a cool cat while subliminally suggesting his opponent was old and out of touch.

Behind in the polls, Bush succumbed to the pressure to follow suit and reluctantly agreed to a Larry King interview on CNN. He had little regard for the medium, privately referring to TV news reporters as "breathless wonders." The King show format included call-in questions from viewers and one of the callers was George Stephanopoulos, a Clinton campaign aide who went on to a top job at the White House. CNN insisted Stephanopoulos was chosen at random to be one of the questioners. I found that hard to believe.

When he left the White House, Stephanopoulos became a television "journalist," following a well-worn path between politics and the TV anchor booth. When I broke into the news business, any link with the political world was usually a disqualifier. I was unusual – I'd worked for Humphrey, albeit in a lowly, press-related job. But for television, no problem: its ranks are littered with former pols and political aides, including Diane Sawyer, who worked for Nixon; the late Tim Russert, an aide to New York Democratic Senator Daniel Patrick Moynihan; Chris Matthews, a Jimmy Carter speechwriter; Brian Williams, who also worked in the Carter White House; and the aforementioned Stephanopoulos. During the 2016 campaign, CNN hired Corey Lewandoski, Donald Trump's onetime campaign manager, as a political analyst even though *he was still on Trump's campaign payroll!*

I learned firsthand how television creates its own reality as a panelist at that presidential campaign debate I mentioned previously. Nothing said that night made history. There were no ringing declarations or statements of principle, no political ten strikes or gaffes to affect the outcome.

Nothing said that night made history. There were no ringing declarations or statements of principal, no political ten strikes or gaffes to affect the outcome of the 1992 presidential race. What struck me was how nervous Bush and Clinton were. Both were uneasy: you could tell by their body language. Not Perot. The know-it-all interloper wasn't nervous at all. He seemed to be enjoying the limelight. I asked Bush a question about his repudiation of a pledge not to raise taxes and Clinton about a financial crisis then gripping the U.S. savings and loan industry. I forget what I asked Perot.

When I saw Perot in Bermuda at the finish of a sailboat race 14 years later and reminded him I'd been one of the questioners at the East Lansing debate, he snorted dismissively, "Good for you!" For a few weeks after the debate, I was famous. People recognized me at the supermarket, old girl friends got in touch, a few strangers even wrote asking for autographed photos. My kids were embarrassed by this. My celebrity lasted less than a month. I was glad to see it go.

We panelists privately agreed Bush won the debate. Sitting 10 feet away from him and the others, it was our judgment that he turned in the most commanding performance. When the post-debate polls came out however, they showed the public considered Clinton the winner. I didn't understand it until about six weeks later, when my son Sean returned from a college semester abroad and we watched a videotape of the debate. On the TV screen, Clinton seemed more appealing. He was more telegenic and appeared much more affable. What's more, the medium worked against Bush technically. The tie he wore looked funny on television and distracted attention whenever he spoke. Clinton, of course, went on to win the election.

The 1992 election might have marked the beginning of a death spiral for the kind of society I'd always imagined our country to be – too loud and cocky and way too unequal to be sure, but always seeking to improve. Ronald Reagan once inadvertently sounded the death knell. He was trying to repeat a line from Mark Twain – "Facts are stubborn things!" but misread the quote and said instead, "Facts are *stupid* things!"

Television, in my opinion, has done much to make it so. It has become the main vehicle for delivering public information. Yet it's forever blurring the difference between fact and fiction. Opinion is offered up as fact. There's very little original reporting: what was once disdained as "rip and read" journalism – merely re-reporting news gathered by the wire services and major newspapers – is now established practice. I'm also not enamored of the 24/7 news cycle: it's destructive of serious journalism. More often than not, initial reports are wrong. Military strategists call this the "fog of war." The newsroom mantra used to be, "If your mother tells you she loves you – check it out." A companion rule was, "If it seems too good to be true it usually is." Yet the tendency in newsrooms nowadays is to "go with it" with little if any double-checking.

The public is drenched by a firehose of information which might or might not be true.

Another of my problems with new journalism is the practitioners' lack of experience. There used to be an apprenticeship and winnowing process in the news business: reporters and editors usually started at the local level, covering the police beat and city hall. More talented individuals moved on to the state capitol and covered the governor or state legislature. The best wound up in New York, the editorial center of the major news organizations, or Washington, the seat of national decision-making, or going abroad as foreign correspondents. By the time a journalist arrived at the top, he or she was generally well-grounded on public policy and the issues of the day. The chief requirement for success in TV "news": good looks. A woman who became a well-known television news figure (with few journalistic credentials for the post) once told me: "It's not what you know. It's who you blow." Is it any wonder that in 2016 we elected an individual who revels in his ignorance President of the United States?

Lyndon Johnson is the first president I actually met. I'd seen Truman of course, and John F. Kennedy when he visited Milford PA on September 24, 1973, a few weeks before he was assassinated. To help pay my way through college, I worked part time as an announcer/news reporter for WSCR, the NBC Radio affiliate in Scranton, and went to Milford to cover a Kennedy speech on conservation. The speech was unmemorable, but in my mind's eye I still see Kennedy in the midst of an entourage, walking down a trail on his way to the podium, his hands jammed into the pockets of his suitcoat, one of his trademarks. Kennedy's assassination affected me deeply. Despite all the seamy details of his personal life that have been exposed since, I think it's fair to say JFK was the most inspirational figure of my generation. He was young, handsome, cool, chic and sophisticated; above all, a leader. He had guided America through what to this day remains the most dangerous two weeks of the nuclear age – the 1962 Cuban Missile Crisis – only to be snatched away little more than a year later.

Like many my age, I still know where I was when the news came: in the first semester of my junior year at the University of Scranton, at a philosophy class taught by Rev. Joseph Devlin, S.J., a kindly bear of a man who was one of my favorite teachers. During his lecture, Father Devlin was called to the door of the class and came back to announce

Kennedy had been shot in Dallas. Soon thereafter came word the President was dead. Class was dismissed and a miasma descended on our little corner of the world. Together with my family, I sleepwalked through the days that followed, watching JFK's wake and funeral on television. It was as sorrowful as a death in the family. During the 1968 presidential campaign, the late David Broder of the Washington Post, a writer regarded as the nation's preeminent political journalist, remarked that it would take another 20 years for the nation to recover from the Kennedy assassination. As I write this a half century later, I doubt we'll ever recover.

My encounter with Kennedy's successor was physically painful. My first job after the army was working in the press office of the Democratic National Committee and I was invited to a White House reception after a DNC meeting. Awestruck doesn't begin to describe it. The reception was in the East Room and I was thrilled to be there. I was talking to three other guests when LBJ walked up and joined us. He knew the three others, so I introduced myself.

When someone in the group asked a question about Vietnam, Johnson responded not to his questioner but to me, perhaps because I was youngest and still had a military haircut. He jabbed his index finger into my breastbone as he made his points. There I was, a few months past nervousness at the sight of a captain or major standing at attention before the commander-in-chief. Johnson's forefinger thrusts hurt like hell but I didn't flinch. That experience told me I had the right stuff to succeed in Washington: a high tolerance for indignities from politicians. When LBJ headed back to his ranch on January 20, 1968 at the conclusion of his presidency, Texas Republican Congressman George H.W. Bush was among those at Andrews Air Force Base to see him off. The bipartisan goodwill gesture was so characteristic of Bush and so rare in American politics nowadays.

I deplore the incivility that afflicts modern political discourse. Our society is complex, our issues full of varying shades of gray. There are no blacks and whites, and seldom is anything ever resolved as cleanly as TV reality shows pretend. That's just one of the problems. TV "journalists" are seldom well-versed enough in the facts to challenger liars; they're often more interested in their celebrity than their preparedness. The brief "sound bites" that litter TV news put a premium on being provocative rather than profound, and an insult will get you wall-to-wall airtime.

Social media like Facebook and Twitter have worsened the problem, allowing lies to be spread far and wide without any effective rebuttal. Nazi propaganda minister Joseph Goebbels would have been ecstatic to work in today's environment. The media barons – people like Rupert Murdock, the late Roger Ailes and Les Moonves to call a few names -- should be ashamed of the damage they've done. Indeed Moonves gave the game away in during the 2016 presidential race when he said Trump's candidacy "may not be good for America, but it's damn good for CBS.

"Man, who would have expected the ride we're all having right now … The money's rolling in and this is fun," he said.

Moonves was eventually ousted as CEO of CBS, not because of his glee at the torching of the U.S. presidential election process but because of a long history of sexual harassment of women. It figures – in the anything goes age in which we now live, there are few truth tellers. The only thing sacred is money and power.

Chapter Three

The Gipper

RONALD REAGAN WAS our first television president. A master of optics of leadership, he was often oblivious to everyday happenings. Andrew Card, who went on to become White House Chief of State under George W. Bush, once told me: "Reagan knew my name and he knew my face. But in the six years I worked for him, he never once put the two together." Clark Clifford, an advisor to several Democratic presidents, called Reagan "an amiable dunce." That was unfair.

While not an intellectual, Reagan was bright. His writing was clear and succinct, his instincts good. But he often seemed to live in a separate world. At White House news conferences, which were rare during his presidency, he worked from a seating chart to call on reporters whom he saw every day. More than once, he called on people who weren't there, making it obvious his encounters with the news media were carefully choreographed.

Indeed, Larry Speakes, the White House spokesman for six of Reagan's eight years in office, had a sign on his desk boasting of the image-making that became fine art on his watch. "You don't tell us how to stage the news. We don't tell you how to cover it," the sign said. I once accidentally tested Reagan's acuity by becoming tongue-tied going through the receiving line at a White House Christmas party. "Merry President, Mr. Christmas!" I said. Reagan smiled and nodded. "And the same to you," he replied.

We denizens of the White House press room called the 40th president "The Gipper" – a reference to his starring role as George Gipp, a college football player who died young, in the motion picture "Knute Rockne of Notre Dame." He had a captivating kind of everyman *Aw Shucks* manner that made him immensely likeable even to those who disliked his politics. White House aides used to say he was forever writing a personal check to someone whose hard luck story he'd read about in a newspaper. Many checks never got cashed: the recipients held onto them as souvenirs. Because of this, Reagan's checking account balance was often incorrect. One of Reagan's favorite people in the White House press corps was freelancer Trude Feldman, a furtive food-hoarding woman thought by most of her colleagues to be mentally ill. He gave her one of his last interviews before leaving office in 1981. It ran in the *Wall Street Journal*. Though he opened his 1980 run for the presidency with what was widely regarded as dog whistle to diehard segregationists in the Deep South, holding a campaign rally in Neshoba County, Mississippi near where three civil rights workers were murdered in 1964, he interrupted his White House schedule two years later to visit a black family victimized by a Ku Klux Klan cross burning in a Maryland suburb of Washington. "I came out to let you know that this [cross burning] isn't something that should happen in America," The Washington Post quoted him as saying.

Reagan also had a puckish side. His wife Nancy was often the victim. A bust of Lincoln sat on a pedestal near the door to the Oval Office. Sometimes when he knew the First Lady was about to visit, he'd slip out the door and turn the bust to the wall. Mrs. Reagan, who was probably in on the joke, would turn the bust so it was facing forward again and then complain about the standards of West Wing housekeeping.

Reagan's grip on reality wasn't always firm. In his early days in office, whenever he spoke to a veteran's group, he'd would tell a story about a crippled American bomber struggling to stay aloft while returning from a World War Two raid on Germany. He'd vividly describe how the pilot kept the plane flying until it reached the English Channel, where the crew could bail out and be picked up by allied search and rescue boats.

After giving the order to begin parachuting, Reagan said, the pilot heard a groan on the intercom, leading him to discover a wounded tail gunner stuck in a jammed turret. His voice swelling with emotion, Reagan would then roll into the climax of his story. "The pilot took that young man's hand and said: "It's okay, son. We'll ride her down together."

After a dramatic pause, he'd conclude matter-of-factly: "Medal of Honor. Posthumously awarded!" By then there usually wasn't a dry eye in the house.

The only problem was the story wasn't true – not that I or any of my colleagues in the White House press corps was smart or observant enough to figure that out. It took an outsider filling in on a Reagan trip – Lars-Erik Nelson, a brilliant Newsday reporter who died suddenly at the height of his career – to wonder how anyone could have known about the heroism Reagan recounted since the only witnesses – the pilot and the wounded crewman – supposedly perished together. Lars could find nothing in World War Two Medal of Honor citations that even came close to the incident Reagan described. Then, acting on a hunch, he started checking old movie scripts and, *voila*, discovered that Reagan's account of extraordinary valor was straight out of Hollywood. It was the storyline of a movie starring matinee idol Dana Andrews. Lar's expose got nationwide play and strengthened the impression of Reagan's critics that he sometimes failed to distinguish between fact and fiction.

A few weeks after Reagan's story went up in smoke, I was aboard a Pan Am jet chartered to ferry the White House press corps on a presidential trip to Alabama and Georgia. One of the stranger conventions of White House travel was that the press plane departed after Air Force one but landed first, permitting TV camera crews to record the president's plane departing and arriving. On this trip, the legs between stops were short and the skies were clotted with thunderstorms. Lacking much room for maneuver as he hurried to get into the landing pattern ahead of Air Force One, the press plane pilot flew through one of the smaller storm cells, causing the jet to pitch and plunge like it was about to go out of control. Most of us had all we could do to get our seat belts buckled, but Sam Donaldson of ABC News, a leather-lunged television correspondent always intent on being the center of attention, somehow managed to push himself up from his seat and stand in the aisle. "IT'S OKAY, SONS. WE'LL RIDE HER DOWN TOGETHER!" Donaldson bellowed as the rest of us cowered in terror.

I discovered years later Reagan's story actually had a factual basis. In 2018, Britain's Royal Air Force celebrated its centennial with a series of static aircraft displays, one of which took place at Washington Dulles International Airport. It included a Lancaster bomber, one of the largest warplanes in World War Two. Thinking the show might make for some interesting photos, I persuaded Becky to go to the event with me. While there, I got into a discussion with a young RAF pilot who'd flown the Lancaster. It was named after Canadian Pilot-Officer Andrew Mynarski, who'd been awarded Britain's highest decoration for bravery posthumously for his actions during the war. The pilot told me Mynarski had nursed his badly damaged, flaming Lancaster back to England after a raid on Germany and ordered the crew to bail out. But he then discovered the tail gunner was trapped in his turret. Ignoring the crewman's insistence that he save himself, the pilot struggled desperately to free him. Finally, with his parachute on fire, Mynarski leaped from the plane and fell to his death. The plane crashed, cartwheeling as it hit the ground, causing the tailgunner's turret to separate from the fuselage. He walked away unscathed, living to tell of his captain's heroics. It seems pretty clear the incident inspired the movie to which Reagan referred.

Another trip memorable for a Reagan gaffe and some white knuckle flying took him, and us, to Brazil, Columbia, Costa Rica and Honduras. The trip began on an unfortunate note when Reagan, at a dinner in his honor in Brasilia, Brazil's futuristic capital, toasted "the people of Bolivia." The next day, on a flight to Sao Paulo, our chartered press plane held over the airport for nearly an hour, bouncing up and down through dirty gray clouds as a line of storms swept over the city. There supposedly was also a radar problem. Amid fearful shouts from the traveling press, a White House official ordered the pilots to return to Brasilia. It couldn't be done. They were low on fuel, they said. After what seemed an eternity, the plane finally landed uneventfully.

As we left Brazil a day or so later, yet another flying adventure occurred. The U.S. television networks overloaded a cargo plane chartered to transport their equipment from country to country, causing it to clip some runway lights as it struggled to take off. The mishap sheered the plane's landing gear. It made a belly landing; no-one was hurt. But an all-news radio station back in Washington erroneously reported the White House press plane had crashed. When we arrived in Columbia, everyone frantically called home to assure our loved ones we were okay. I later learned that one of my neighbors intercepted another who was on her way to our house to console my family. She'd heard the radio report but was persuaded to await more information before acting.

Not for nothing was Reagan known as "the Teflon president." The bomber story, his errant toast in Brazil and a host of other gaffes would have made any other politician a laughingstock at the time. With Reagan, the missteps were treated like the harmless confabulations of a much loved, if slightly daft old uncle. There were many differences between perception and reality. Reagan rarely went to church, but the pious considered him one of them. His military record was hardly illustrious: unlike many of his Hollywood contemporaries who saw combat in World War Two, Reagan made training films on a Los Angeles sound stage. But much of the public considered him some sort of war hero. He was seen as the embodiment of "Family Values." Yet he was the first divorced president, and for a time he and his wife Nancy were estranged from his adopted son Michael. Despite his Irish charm, there was a hard edge to Reagan. His display of anger toward the moderator of a New Hampshire debate during the 1980 presidential campaign was a turning point in the primary race, cementing his image as someone who couldn't be pushed around. Visiting Neshoba County on the opening day of the general campaign, was also at odds with Reagan's avuncular image. Critics saw it as dog-whistling racists.

The variance between perception and reality extended to policy. Reagan was, and is, regarded as a ruthless tax cutter. But when a massive tax cut he pushed through Congress early in his presidency proved to be unwise, he embraced a corrective tax reform package that brought about the biggest tax increase in U.S. history. He also pushed for immigration reform and other bipartisan policies that would make him unwelcome in today's Republican Party. Whenever Reagan disappointed his staunchest allies, the cry would go up from the Republican right: "Let Reagan be Reagan!" it was aides and advisors who got the blame.

Reagan's relationship with the Russians was the greatest case study of his political evolution. He entered the White House a hard-liner, branding the Soviet Union an "Evil Empire." When he left office, friendly relations were in full flower. Reagan seemed to doubt the Russians were even communist anymore.

Two episodes in Reagan's diplomatic shape-shifting stand out in my mind: the 1985 summit between him and Soviet leader Mikhail Gorbachev in Reykjavik Iceland and their 1988 summit in Moscow. As noted previously, I'd been tipped that Reagan would propose sweeping arms reductions in Reykjavik and filed a story to that effect when we arrived in Iceland. Little did I think the two leaders would seriously discuss eliminating their respective nuclear arsenals altogether. To my surprise, they did exactly that. Their talks broke down when Reagan refused to abandon a U.S. program to shoot down incoming enemy missiles called the Strategic Defense Initiative. As we headed toward the Keflavic airport after the summit collapsed, the press busses passed a cemetery. Looking out the window despondently, I happened to spot a man and woman standing next to an open grave clutching each other, a portrait of grief. Were they mourning the loss of a parent? Or a child, I wondered. To me, the tableau epitomized the dashed hopes of Mankind. The image of that Icelandic couple has stuck with me.

I was convinced Reykjavik would spell the end of the thaw in the Cold War and U.S. and Russian hostility would become more dangerous than ever. To my surprise, the talks continued. Three years later, Reagan and Gorbachev met in Moscow, partners for peace. It was almost surreal. Gorbachev at one point led the onetime outspoken adversary of Soviet Communism on a tour of Red Square, introducing him to Russian schoolkids as "Grandpa Reagan." It was a remarkable scene: the two leaders walking along together, waving to an excited crowd, for all intent allies and friends. The Moscow visit ushered in a new era in relations between the superpowers unimaginable a year or two earlier. Besides the photogenic stroll through Red Square, Reagan gave a speech to students at Moscow University followed by a no-holds-barred question and answer session that was televised throughout the Soviet Union; met with Russian dissidents at Spaso House, the U.S. ambassador's residence; and went window-shopping with Nancy through the fashionable Moscow shopping area known as the Arbat. During their stroll, UPI's redoubtable Helen Thomas got manhandled by an overzealous Russian cop. Mrs. Reagan went to her rescue. That's the way it was in those days: members of the White House press corps weren't seen as enemies by the people they covered, unlike the hostile environment that prevailed under Donald Trump.

Years after the Reagan visit, an aide told me of a presidential aside following his Moscow University appearance. During his speech, Reagan stood in the shadow of a massive statue of Vladimir Ilyich Lenin, the father of Soviet communism. "Wasn't that wonderful," he remarked as he stepped away from the podium. "Lenin had to look at my backside for the last hour and a half!"

Reagan's pursuit of harmonious relations with Russia grew out John Hinckley Jr's attempt to assassinate him outside the Washington Hilton hotel in March 1981. Reagan believed God had spared his life to make the world safer. Soon after he left the hospital, he sent a handwritten letter to then-Soviet leader Leonid Brezhnev saying the two superpowers had to work together to reduce tensions.

"The peoples of the world, despite differences in racial and ethnic origin, have very much in common. They want the dignity of having some control over their individual destiny. They want to work at the craft or trade of their own choosing and to be fairly rewarded. They want to raise their families in peace without harming anyone or suffering harm themselves," Reagan wrote. "Mr. President, should we not be concerned with eliminating the obstacles which prevent our people—those we represent—from achieving their most cherished goals?"

Insiders said Brezhnev was receptive to the olive branch Reagan offered. But he died of a heart attack before he could follow up.

The 1988 Moscow summit was one of the brightest moment in my career as a journalist. It was a great story, played out on a stage that included such world-famous backdrops as the Kremlin, St. Basil's Cathedral and Lenin's Tomb, and Reuters assembled an international all-star team of writers and editors to cover it. As White House correspondent with all the sources needed to make our reportage sparkle, I was the star of the show. At an unprecedented news conference in the Kremlin broadcast live in both the U.S. and Russia, Reagan replied "no" when a reporter asked if he still believed the Soviet Union was an evil empire. That description belonged to "another time, another era," he said.

I've always been fascinated with aviation, to the point of taking a private flying lesson when I was in the army. (I couldn't afford to continue and dropped the idea of getting a pilot's license.) I liked to ride in the press plane cockpit and did so whenever I could wangle an invitation. So I was in the jump seat as we took off from Moscow's Sheremetyevo Airport after the summit and saw firsthand graphic evidence of the technology gap that contributed to the Cold War's peaceful conclusion. A German Lufthansa jetliner took off before us and as it climbed through triple deck cloud cover, its radio transmissions to Russian air controllers were clear and crisp. The Russian transmissions, on the other hand, crackled with static and were often difficult to understand. "That's incredible," I remarked to the pilots. "Their radio technology sounds far behind. No wonder they're so scared of Star Wars." I referred to the futuristic Reagan administration program to develop a shield against intercontinental ballistic missiles.

"Let me show you something," the co-pilot said, pulling out an aviation chart. He pointed to a symbol on the map designating a navigation beacon and said there were hundreds of them between Stockholm, our first western waypoint, and our destination of London. "We don't need them. We rely on inertial navigation," he said. "But there are hundreds of them in Western Europe and thousands of them in the United States. And the Russians have very few." It made me wonder why U.S. policymakers considered Russia to be such a menace for so many years. It seemed pretty primitive to me. Indeed, many referred to the country as "Upper Volta with missiles."

Reagan's trip to Russia was the first of several I made to that country. I was also there with Presidents George H.W. Bush and Bill Clinton. Lynn accompanied me on yet another trip after I retired in 2010. On that trip, part of a vacation cruise that included a half dozen ports of call in Northern Europe, we toured majestic St. Petersburg, seeing such landmarks as the Hermitage art museum and Tsar Peter the Great's Winter Palace. The city, known in the Stalinist era as Leningrad, suffered horrendously when besieged by the Nazis during World War Two. The two-and-a-half year siege resulted in mass starvation and the deaths of an estimated 1.5 million Russian soldiers and civilians. More than a half century later signs on some buildings still designated safe areas during bombardments and some of the trenches were still visible.

Before a Bush trip to Russia in 1990, I was a member of the advance team; at the time and perhaps still, the White House assigned a regular in the White House press corps to the group of aides and advisors who laid the groundwork for presidential visits to other countries. This individual would advise on news coverage requirements and gather information on people and places on the itinerary, so the press corps would have this background material during the actual visit. Though Bush had been Reagan's vice president, we started from scratch. The U.S. Embassy had few if any files concerning the 1988 summit. Furthermore, the quickest way to raise the hackles of Bush's team was to talk about how something had been done during Reagan's visit. It just wouldn't do to follow in Reagan's footsteps.

Included in the mission was a side trip to Kiev in the Ukraine, then an integral part of the Soviet Union. Located there is a massive statute of a woman, her hands bound behind her with barbed wire, trying to shield an infant. It was a monument to the victims of a World War Two Nazi massacre at Babi Yar where more than 100,000 mostly Jewish men, women and children were slaughtered, the largest mass killing during the Holocaust. Bush was to lay a wreath there. Traveling with us were top Kremlin officials involved in arranging the presidential visit. As our Boeing 707 U.S. military transport climbed out of Moscow, Mike Gould, an air force officer assigned to the White House, sat at a window making notes on the surface-to-air missile sites deployed around the capital. Seated across the aisle from him was the head of the KGB, seemingly unruffled by the American spying. Gould later became a three star general and superintendent of the U.S. Air Force Academy.

I often enjoyed dinner and after-hours companionship with Dr. Larry Mohr, an army physician on the president's medical team, during the pre-advance trip. An American friend of his who was doing some high level medical consulting in Moscow arranged for us to visit a Kremlin museum where the possessions of the tsars were on display. It was the kind of Alice in Wonderland experience White House connections often produced: the museum was open to few Western visitors. I was amazed at the carriages, jewelry, art, furniture and other artifacts preserved there. Seeing the riches and splendor of Russian aristocrats who led a very poor nation, I could understand why there had been a Revolution.

After retiring from the army, Mohr went on to teach at the Medical University of South Carolina. In 2016 he suffered an accident that left him paralyzed from the waist down. He was standing on the deck of his house one evening and leaned against a railing. When it gave way he fell 15 feet, severing his spine. It was the kind of tragedy that's hard to understand. Before becoming a doctor, Mohr was a paratrooper in the 82d Airborne Division and earned the Silver Star in combat in Vietnam. Fortunately, he's still able to lead a productive life, consulting on medical issues and teaching at MUSC. I've never forgotten Mohr's kindnesses to me when he was a White House doctor. I try to stay in touch with him.

Covering the Reagan White House was intensely competitive, even more so I think than other presidencies. Perhaps this was because several of the president's California cronies occupied key positions, people like Mike Deaver, Ed Meese and Bill Casey were presidential aides and

William French Smith as Attorney General. (Meese later replaced Smith at the Justice Department and Casey became CIA director.) Others like Justin Dart were members of Reagan's kitchen cabinet, an unofficial group of advisors. Each had their favorite reporters and as so often happens in Washington advanced their ideas with selective leaks to the press. James Baker was Reagan's chief of staff during the first four years of his presidency. He and his inner circle were especially adept at press relations.

I barely held my own, breaking enough stories to keep my editors satisfied but not enough to guarantee job security. I was among the first to report Donald Regan's adversarial relationship with Nancy Reagan, which quickly led to Regan's unceremonious ouster as White House chief of staff. Regan, a former Wall Street banker who used to boast he had "Fuck You" money (he was too rich to be pushed around), got his revenge with a juicy tidbit in a tell-all memoir called <u>For the Record: From Wall Street to Washington.</u> His disclosure that Nancy Reagan used a Hollywood astrologer to organize her husband's presidential schedule caused a brief sensation.

I got another less sensational scoop that left me shaking my head. In 1983 I learned that close relatives of several top administration officials held plum U.S. Information Agency jobs in some of the world's major cities. Former Secretary of State Alexander Haig's daughter worked at the agency's office in London; Defense Secretary Caspar Weinberger's son was in New York. National Security Advisor Bill Clark's daughter was stationed in Bonn. There were other examples as well. If it wasn't nepotism it was close. I broke the news while U.S.I.A. Director Charles Wick was on a goodwill tour of several Asian nations. My story generated unwelcome attention that dogged him everywhere he went.

Wick, one of Reagan's old show biz pals, was furious. "We do not think it serves the national interest to discriminate against a few highly qualified people who happen to be related to outstanding national leaders who are serving their country with commitment and personal sacrifice," he said at a Bangkok news conference.

When he returned to Washington, Wick invited me and UPI editor Ron Cohen to join him for lunch, where he insisted my story was unfair. He reiterated that the U.S.I.A. employees in question were highly qualified. I said that wasn't the point; the issue was whether they were hired and given attractive assignments because of their connections. We argued a bit and finally agreed to disagree about the fairness of what I'd reported. I then told Wick that my daughter Becky, then five, was at the White House with me while I was putting the finishing touches on the story and was invited to help herself to the president's jellybeans. (Reagan's favorite candy. He devoured them by the handful.) In many countries, if I'd embarrassed the leaders, I would have been ducking down allies, dodging bullets, I said.

"What you're telling me is you accept people' hospitality – and then kick 'em in the head," Wick growled. I thought it a rather strange reaction from the man in charge of U.S. image-making.

Lynn and my family paid a price for all the hours I put in and all the globetrotting I did. I was often away, and when I was home I frequently was so caught up in my work it left little time for wife and children. I was also often stressed out from the pressures of the job. Many times I'd tell myself as I drove home in the evening I had to set aside my frustrations about missing a story or ruminations about what was likely to happen next at the White House and just relax and play with the kids. But my good intentions usually evaporated when I walked in the door and encountered the maddening clamor of everyday life. Instead of interacting with family members, I'd often retreat to my man cave in the basement and read a book or watch a movie.

Even when I was home, work a constant presence. Editors would call at all hours asking me to get a White House comment on a remote development in some far-flung corner of the world. Occasionally a White House press aide would call with an announcement. Carter White House Press Secretary Jody Powell himself phoned one morning at 2 AM to read me a statement about how the U.S. government viewed some international development. Lynn, whose dad was a doctor, said the number of after-hours calls I got far exceeded what her father ever received. Adding insult to injury, I became obsessed with sailing. I bought a boat, the first of three I owned. Soon I was gone for long stretches practicing for or competing in long-distance ocean races. My family didn't share my enthusiasm for sailing so I pursued the sport alone. It's one of my great regrets that family relationships often came last in my life.

There were some consolations for those near and dear. Our family vacations were usually tied to presidential vacations. Families could fly on the White House press charter for a nominal cost. So Lynn and the kids got to go to Sea Isle GA with Jimmy Carter; to Santa Barbara with Reagan; and to Kennebunkport ME with George H.W. Bush. This was good and bad, of course. What Lynn and the kids saw as a timeout from everyday life was anything but a timeout for me – I was working. If anything, presidential vacations were even more stressful than the normal routine because stories were harder to come by.

Reagan went to Santa Barbara often – at least a half dozen times a year, often for a week but for a whole month in August. He and his wife Nancy would go off to their mountain hideaway, *Rancho del Cielo*, while the rest of the presidential entourage stayed in beautiful Santa Barbara 27 miles south. Reagan made little news. He liked to clear brush and chop wood, and he and Nancy went horseback riding. That was about it. The networks mounted a television camera with a powerful telephoto lens on a mountaintop overlooking Reagan's ranch, to my mind a gross invasion of privacy, and frequently showed blurred, grainy footage of the Reagans on horseback on the evening news. Reagan joked that he was often tempted to clutch his chest and pretend to fall off his horse, a prank that instantly would have caused worldwide alarm. He never did that, but his sense of humor once got him in trouble. Doing a microphone check before his weekly radio speech on August 14 1984, he declared: "I have decided to outlaw Russia forever. We begin the bombing in five minutes." That was the only real news from the Western White House that I can recall in eight years of covering California vacations. NBC newsman Marvin Kalb later reported that the Russians responded with a joke of their own a few days later: a fake message to Soviet forces ordering them into offensive positions. Kalb said the message briefly led Japan to put its forces on heightened alert.

I never got to the ranch during Reagan's presidency. The White House press corps was allowed to visit only once: for a bill-signing ceremony in the driveway. I wasn't on that particular trip. But in 2015, I arranged a personal tour for my wife Becky and me through the Young America Foundation, a conservative political organization that now owns the property. We were astonished at how modest the property was. There were only a few rooms in the ranch-house itself, and the furnishings were like those you'd find in any American home: the living room fixtures included a naugahyde armchair. Over the fireplace was the only indication of the residents' prominence – a handcrafted presidential seal made by an admirer who'd hammered thousands of thumbtacks into a plank to form the familiar emblem.

The Reagans' bedroom was even more frugal than the rest of the dwelling. Two old single beds had been wired together to form a king-size bed. But the mattresses were too short to accommodate someone of Reagan's stature. So there was a small table at the end of Reagan's side of the bed that served as a footrest. A McGyver solution if ever there was one! Hanging outside near the front door of the house was a wrought-iron sign of the kind you'd see in a suburban subdivision. "The Reagans. 1600 Pennsylvania Avenue," it said. There was a pond nearby with a canoe alongside it. Painted on the prow was the word "LOVE," bespeaking the Reagans' romance.

On a Reagan trip to California in 1983, I had a close encounter with the Queen of England, Elizabeth II. The British monarch was on her first (and only) trip to the West Coast of the United States, a trip that included stops in San Diego, Los Angeles, Santa Barbara, San Francisco, Sacramento, Yosemite National Park and Seattle. Accompanied by Prince Philip, the queen visited President and Mrs. Reagan at their ranch, where she and her husband were served Mexican food for lunch. (It wasn't the first time the British Royals were served such commoner fare by American hosts. When King George VI and his wife visited Franklin and Eleanor Roosevelt at their private home in Hyde Park NY in 1939, the repast at one meal was hot dogs.) After lunch at the ranch, the royal party went on to San Francisco. The Reagans followed 24 hours later for several days of socializing.

Both parties were staying at the St. Francis Hotel. When I went to my room I found it was already occupied. It was the only time in more than thirty years of White House travel that I experienced such a problem. I was swamped with work – a main story to write, a news analysis about the U.S.-British relationship to go with it and a weekend feature to complete – so I didn't have time to get it fixed just then. Fearing my suitcase would wind up in the wrong place, I found a member of the White House travel office staff and asked him to help me get it off the baggage truck. That way it would be safe with me until the room arrangement was straightened out.

He agreed and took me to a hotel sub-basement where the baggage truck was located. I quickly found my bag and headed off to the press workspace in a hotel ballroom. On the elevator, I punched in the floor where I thought it was – and stepped off on the floor where the Queen was living. Her floor should have been inaccessible to folks like me. But I'd come from a secure area and the elevator wasn't locked out on that level.

There I was, in shirtsleeves, lugging a suitcase. The Queen and Prince Philip, along with a bodyguard, were coming down the hallway, on their way to some event. The Queen was wearing a floor length gown and a tiara. Her husband was in formal clothes, his chest bedecked with medals and ribbons. "How are you, your Majesty?" I said. That violated the first rule of royal protocol: one must never speak to a queen or king until first spoken to. The Queen gave me a haughty look and swept into a waiting elevator while I got back in the elevator I'd arrived in. It was all I could do to avoid reflecting my ancestors' antipathy toward the English and shout, "Up the Irish, blaggard!"

The next day Queen Elizabeth had a dinner party for the Reagans aboard the royal yacht Brittania and I was in the "pool," covering the get-together as a representatives of the larger press corps. It was quite an experience. As we boarded the "yacht" – a vessel as large as an ocean liner – we were greeted by a British naval officer with a spyglass under his arm. Just like a Horatio Hornblower movie! We then moved through a passageway stacked with boxes of Cheerios. The quantity of the cereal seemed extraordinary. When I asked about it, I was told it was a farewell gift to the Queen, who would sail in the morning. It was San Francisco's way of saying "cheerio!" There was also another whimsical touch: the British Union Jack hung flew from street lampposts throughout San Francisco but it had been hung upside down. I didn't know it until then, but there's a right way and a wrong way to hang the Union Jack – the flag is not symmetrical. In a classically tongue-in-cheek British riposte, the presidential ensign flew from the topmast of the Brittania – upside down.

Proximity to the British royals always seemed to get me in hot water. When Queen Elizabeth made a state visit to Washington during President George H.W. Bush's tenure, he greeted her at a White House South Lawn arrival ceremony but someone failed to lower the podium for her response. When the Queen began talking the only thing the audience could see was her broad-brimmed blue hat, so I said in my Reuters dispatch she resembled "a talking toadstool."

Shortly thereafter, there was a Royal reception for the White House press corps to which I was invited. I shook hands with the Queen in the receiving line, but forgot my manners when she approached NBC Correspondent Jim Miklaszewski and me later on in the gathering. She spoke to Miklaszewski and they exchanged pleasantries. Mindful that the president taking her to a major league baseball game that night, I asked if she'd been briefed on the intricacies of the game. Speaking before being spoken to again! She pleasantly but curtly replied that she had not.

My third breach of etiquette occurred at Buckingham Palace. Bush senior was in London for an international conference and Queen Elizabeth entertained him at lunch. Once again I was in the press pool. There was some military pageantry in an inner courtyard of the palace before the lunch. The pool was then escorted back to the presidential motorcade to await the conclusion of the socializing.

As we waited, I took a picture of a palace sentry in his scarlet tunic and bearskin hat. When I snapped the shutter, a red-faced sergeant major with a walrus mustache marched up and sternly shouted: "SIR, ONE MUST NEVER TAKE PICTURES IN THE FORECOURT OF THE PALACE – EVER!" He then spun on his heel and walked away. Undeterred, I took another. "Gibbons! Didn't you hear what he just said?" one of my colleagues remonstrated. "Fuck 'em," I said. "If it wasn't for us, they'd all be speaking German." I think I was channeling one of my Irish ancestors. I'm ordinarily much too polite to act as boorishly as I did.

Reagan travelled to 24 countries during his presidency. I was on more than half the trips, including the most memorable ones: his visit to Normandy for the 40th anniversary of D-Day, his "Mr. Gorbachev, tear down this wall!" speech in Berlin and his visit to China.

We flew into now-defunct Tempelhof Airport on the trip to Berlin. It was once one of the most famous airports in Europe because of the 1948 Berlin Airlift, a Cold War delivery operation of food and supplies that stymied a Soviet blockade of Western sectors of the divided city. Apartment buildings lined both sides of the runway, making for hair-raising landings.

Reagan's June 12 1987 speech at the Brandenburg Gate was something of an afterthought. According to Peter Robinson, one of his speechwriters, the West German government asked that he stop in Berlin on his way home from an Economic Summit in Venice to help the city celebrate its 750th anniversary and his schedule was adjusted accordingly. What followed was one of the electrifying events of Reagan's presidency. Standing in front of a massive crowd, Reagan delivered an impassioned address broadcast throughout Eastern Europe.

"Behind me stands a wall that encircles the free sectors of this city, part of a vast system of barriers that divides the entire continent of Europe," Reagan said. "General Secretary Gorbachev, if you seek peace, if you seek prosperity for the Soviet Union and Eastern Europe, if you seek liberalization, come here to this gate. Mr. Gorbachev, open this gate! Mr. Gorbachev, tear down this wall!"

To my undying regret, I was not actually at the speech. I was in the press filing center back at Tempelhof, watching what unfolded on television. My dispatch was written and ready to go. As soon as Reagan uttered his immortal words, I hit the send button and out it went to Reuters subscribers all over the world. Such was sometimes the lot of wire service reporters in those days. Even though we had laptop computers then, they had to be hooked up to a telephone line in order to send copy. It wasn't much later that mobile telephones came along, letting folks like me file a story right from the scene. How I now wish I skipped being first with the story and witnessed what happened up close and personal.

Reagan's China trip included a trip to Xian to see the terracotta soldiers, clay sculptures representing the armies of Qin Shi Huang, the first emperor of China. There one of the funniest moments of my career occurred. Over the years, the White House press corps has had its share of colorful characters. Perhaps the most legendary was Naomi Nover, whose husband Barney was a longtime Washington correspondent for the *Denver Post*. After Barney died, Naomi herself became a journalist – at least in her own mind. She established the Nover News Service, which had no known clients, became accredited because of the sympathy of some of her late husband's colleagues in the news business and started traveling the world with presidents. Lord only knows where she got the money. Imagine how costly it is to lease a jumbo jet and its crew for a week or more. Yet that's what news organizations who sent reporters on presidential trips did. The expense of chartering a press plane was divided among them. Then there was the cost of first class hotels, meals and incidental expenses. The cost of an average White House trip to a foreign country ran into thousands of dollars per journalist. Naomi wore her snow white hair in a bun and always wore identical tailored navy blue dresses that made her look like the schoolteacher she once was. Everyone agreed she closely resembled the famous Gilbert Stuart portrait of George Washington.

The terracotta soldiers – archers, horsemen and other military figures, together with horse-drawn chariots and weapons – were buried with Emperor Qin sometime after 221 B.C. They were discovered by Chinese farmers in 1974. When we were in Xian, the archeological excavation that unearthed the army was enclosed in a huge airplane hanger-style building. A wooden staircase descended into the excavation pit. It was clear this was reserved for the Reagans: a living Chinese soldier armed with a sub-machine gun barred to anyone not in the official party. Naomi approached the staircase, determined to go down among the terracotta figures herself in order to get a good photo. When the sentry blocked her way, she tried to slip around him. She was persistent and he was becoming exasperated. Seeing what was going on, Gary Schuster of the *Detroit News,* a man with a keen sense of humor, walked over to the soldier, flipped open his wallet and produced a $1 bill. He pointed to George Washington's portrait on the currency and then to Naomi. "Very…important…person…in…our…country," he intoned. The soldier snapped to attention and stepped aside, letting Naomi scoot into the pit to get the snapshot she wanted.

China in the mid-1980s reminded me of the South Korea I knew when I was stationed there in the army in the mid-1960s. I was convinced my grandchildren would speak Chinese if it developed as rapidly as South Korea had. We saw the Great Wall. Even better, Reagan's entire entourage was invited to a state dinner in the Great Hall of the People on Tiananmen Square. Hundreds were killed there a few years later during a student uprising brutally quashed by Chinese authorities. That set the country's march toward global preeminence back for years but I was correct about one thing -- my oldest grandchild Charlie had a Chinese nanny as an infant and some of the first words he spoke were Chinese.

I returned to China with Bush senior in 1989, a few months before the Tiananmen Massacre. His was a trip down Memory Lane. Bush had been U.S. Ambassador to China under President Gerald Ford and, among other things, revisited the tiny Methodist church in a run-down Beijing neighborhood where he'd once worshipped. After the service he reminisced about riding a Chinese-made Pigeon bicycle throughout Beijing when he was an envoy. But the trip was blighted by an incident that reflected the political turmoil roiling the country when the secret police kept Chinese dissident Fang Lizhi from attending a dinner hosted by Bush. Fang came to the hotel where the White House Press Corps was staying to protest his treatment and a scene straight out of a cops-and-robbers Hollywood comedy ensued. The dissident and we reporters ran up and down stairs and hopped on and off elevators, engaging in a running news conference while playing hide and seek with secret police pursuers. Fang was subsequently arrested and jailed for several months. U.S. pressure eventually brought about his release and he migrated to the United States, where he died in 2012.

People have wondered if Reagan suffered from the Alzheimer's Disease that afflicted him in later life while he was in office. In the final years of his presidency, media colleagues and I sometimes suspected he was becoming senile. But one of my encounters with him left me scratching my head about that speculation. I'd just jumped from financially ailing United Press International to flourishing Reuters, moving from one cubicle in the White House press room to another, when my new boss made a request: the board chairman of Reuters, Lord MacGregor of Durris, was coming to Washington, he said, and could I arrange for him to sit in on White House press secretary Marlin Fitzwater's daily news briefing? I thought I might be able do even better. I knew Reagan reserved time on his Thursday afternoon schedule every week to meet prominent visitors from around the country and the world. I thought the head of Reuters, and a British aristocrat to boot, might qualify. So I asked Fitzwater deputy Rusty Brashear if a meeting could be arranged. He agreed to set one up.

During the weeks between his promise and the Reuters executive's arrival, Brashear left the White House for a job in private industry. What I believed was in the works wasn't happening. I learned this just a week before the prospective meeting. Fortunately, the White House press office scrambled to my rescue. I then learned Lord MacGregor was NOT Reuters board chairman, but chairman of an advisory board with no executive power. In for a dime, in for a dollar, I thought, and let events go forward.

On the appointed day, the British peer came to the White House and Reagan aides took us to the Cabinet Room to await the meeting. It was red carpet treatment since people with appointments to see the president usually waited in a West Wing reception room. Lord MacGregor, a dapper, affable man with an impressive bow tie who looked like he'd stepped out of a theatrical performance on London's West End, was beside himself with excitement and pulled out a sheaf of notes. It was a speech he planned to make to Reagan about a journalism conference he'd just been to in Singapore.

I advised him an oration would be inappropriate; the meeting would be brief, just handshakes and a photo. But if an opening arose, I said, he could mention the conference in passing.

Soon Reagan appeared at the Cabinet Room door. "Well, Gene, who've you brought to see me today?" he said. It was as though I saw him every Thursday, bringing interesting people with me. He then ushered us into the Oval Office. As we posed for a photo, Lord MacGregor brought up the subject he wished to discuss. Reagan was all ears. He knew about the conference and asked questions about it. I was astonished. I'd not known about the conference until that day and Marlin Fitzwater told me the president hadn't been briefed about it. We finally surmised that he'd read about it in the newspaper -- somebody said there'd been a story about it in *The Washington Post* a few days earlier.

Several years later, after Reagan died, Army Brigadier General John Hutton, who'd been his military physician, told me he believed people started to slip into dementia around age 75. Hutton said he himself had just turned 75 and was starting to slip. He died of Alzheimer's 10 years later. Reagan was nearly 78 when he left office.

Reagan's presidency was as transformational as Franklin Delano Roosevelt's. He led a peaceful revolution that reshaped the country dramatically. But unlike FDR, who in my opinion put America on a course toward greatness that made us the envy of the world with progressive policies like fair labor standards and Social Security retirement benefits, Reagan's tenure arguably started a steady decline. He governed pragmatically but his rhetoric became reality. Like television, he blurred the difference between fact and fantasy. His famous statement, "government is not the solution to our problem – government is the problem," became the mantra of the Republican Right. Forgotten is the qualifier he placed on the statement, which he made in his first inaugural address: "In this present crisis … "

America was suffering a crisis of confidence when Reagan took office, a crisis exacerbated by government policies that led to over-regulation, spiraling inflation and long lines at gas stations. No doubt reforms were needed. But Reagan's acolytes seized on his blaming government to throw the baby out with the bathwater.

Indeed, radical activist Grover Norquist, a self-appointed keeper of the Reagan flame, said his goal was "to cut government in half in twenty five years, to get it down to the size where we can drown it in the bathtub." A darling of cable television talk shows because of his knack for inflammatory comments, Norquist came to wield so much political power that many Republican members of Congress put allegiance to him and his anti-tax dogmas ahead of their sworn oath to preserve and defend the Constitution and signed onto his pledge to never raise taxes.

The basic mission of government is to provide for the common defense and promote the general welfare. A democracy cannot function without compromise. Reagan and Democratic House Speaker Thomas "Tip" O'Neill famously fought tooth-and-nail over policy by day, gave a little to get a little and enjoyed a whiskey and friendly banter together at night. They had their political differences but at the end of the day they were both Americans. The same spirit prevailed under President George H.W. Bush.

This political bonhomie was never countenanced by Reagan's conservative disciples, and a lot of them liked it even less when Bush engaged in it. Political differences became non-negotiable. Taxes were not just unpopular, taxes were evil. Deficits were evil too, but America's leaders must never, ever raise taxes to help soak up the red ink. That could only happen through spending cuts, no matter how draconian or laughable.

One money-saving proposal advanced during Reagan's presidency was to consider catsup a vegetable to meet nourishment requirements under the school lunch program. A civil defense official advised the citizenry to protect themselves in the event of nuclear war by taking a door to one of their rooms off its hinges and using it to provide overhead cover on a hole they'd dig in their backyard.

The Constitution's fundamental principle that our country is governed by the rule of law, not of men was disregarded by Reagan's underlings (his role has never been clearly established). The United States sold arms to enemy Iran to try to win the release of American hostages held by Iranian-backed terrorists in Lebanon. They then used the money to try to overthrow a leftist government in Nicaragua, even though U.S. spending to accomplish the latter had been expressly forbidden by

Congress. Reagan broke an air traffic controllers' strike, which ultimately broke the back of the U.S. labor movement, leading to wage stagnation and the income inequality that gave rise to the anger that helped elect Donald Trump. And he promoted the myth of U.S. exceptionalism, a notion that overlooked the fact that Americans historically were as capable of wrongdoing as any other people, as shown by slavery, the brutal mistreatment of blacks and Native Americans, colonial wars in Latin America and the Philippines and other evils.

When the news media brought such national embarrassments to public attention, it made people uncomfortable, prompting right wing howls of "liberal press." President John F. Kennedy was widely criticized for cancelling 22 White House subscriptions to the New York Herald Tribune in 1962 because of what he felt was its unfair coverage. There was no similar pushback against anti-press sentiment that arose and intensified on the Republican right during Reagan's presidency.

The howling about press-bias became a cacophony in the late 1990s and early 21st century, with Fox "News" powerfully amplifying the outcry. Fox was created and led not by a journalist but by right-wing political operative Roger Ailes. Ailes, who was forced into retirement in 2017 amid allegations that he traded TV stardom for sexual favors from a number of Fox's female employees. He first gained prominence as a media advisor to Richard M. Nixon during Nixon's 1968 campaign for the presidency and subsequently served Reagan and George H.W. Bush in a similar capacity. Disparaging other, more legitimate news organizations by insisting that it was the only purveyor of "Fair and Balanced" information, Fox quickly became the most powerful propaganda organ the world has ever seen.

To be sure, many of those in journalism tilt toward the left, including me, although I've consistently tried to vote for whomever I thought would do the best job for the country, including Presidents George H.W. and George W. Bush. Folks like me tend to favor a more expansive government role in the life of the country than those on the right. Unlike most of our countrymen, we tend to be skeptical and irreligious. But on the print side of the news business -- I can't say the same for television – professional standards strongly discourage showing any favoritism to one side or the other in the ongoing national debate over public policy.

I think we journalists have done a poor job of educating the public about the difference between hard news on the one hand and columns and editorials on the other. Hard news sticks to just the facts of a news-making development while editorials and columns are opinionated about what happens. The editorial pages of the New York Times and the Washington Post generally take a liberal stance although conservative opinion is found there too, witness Washington Post columnists Kathleen Parker and George Will and columnists Bret Stephens and Ross Douthat for the New York Times. The Wall Street Journal has always taken a conservative tack editorially but its editorial pages also reflect liberal thought. The front pages and news sections of all three newspapers should be and generally are free of any slant.

In an effort to be truly fair and balanced, journalists lean over backwards to report both sides of a story, which too often leads to false equivalence. Sometimes the facts of a situation are entirely one-sided. It's an empirical fact that the sun *always* rises in the east. If some insist it sometimes rises in the west they're simply incorrect: there's no two ways around it. Since time immemorial politicians have tried to cast inconvenient facts in the most favorable light – a practice known as "spinning"-- but until Donald Trump, outright lying was political suicide.

Reagan's brush with death in 1981 and near miraculous recovery from the assassination attempt made him a mythic figure in the public mind. He displayed extraordinary good humor during the ordeal, reportedly telling wife Nancy at one point, "Honey, I forgot to duck." I was on Capitol Hill the day Reagan was shot. What happened I know only from television and the firsthand accounts of some of my colleagues.

One of the most memorable moments of the crisis was Secretary of State Alexander Haig's panicky, much-ridiculed "As of now, I am in control here" statement in the White House press room in the first hours after the shooting as top officials scrambled to manage the crisis. It was a performance from which Haig never recovered. Nor were presidential security arrangements ever the same again. Because Reagan's would-be assassin fired from a press pen outside the Washington Hilton Hotel as the president departed a speechmaking event, the U.S. Secret Service constantly subjected the White House Press Corps to bag checks and electronic frisks with a magnetic metal detector (commonly called "mag") thereafter. "I've been magged so much on this trip, from now on I'll have to turn north to get a hard on," Reuters photographer Larry Rubenstein quipped during a presidential visit to Europe.

I was traveling with Reagan little over two years later when another, less well known security incident occurred. It happened at the Augusta

National Country Club where the annual Masters golf tournament, the most prestigious event in professional golf, takes place. Reagan was playing golf on October 22 1983 with a foursome that also included Secretary of State George Schultz when an unemployed Georgia man whose marriage was on the rocks stormed into the pro shop waving a handgun and demanding to speak to the president. Five people in the shop, one of them a White House aide, were taken hostage. Reagan did try to talk to the gunman by telephone in an effort to resolve the situation. In fact he made five attempts. But the connection was bad, which only intensified the man's agitation. The siege finally ended peacefully after a two hour standoff and everyone heaved enormous sighs of relief.

Sometime that night, however, we were all awakened and ordered to prepare to leave for Washington immediately. A terrorist truck bombing of military barracks in Beirut had killed 220 U.S. Marines, 18 sailors and three soldiers on peacekeeping duty in Lebanon. Another 115 Americans were wounded. There were crisis meetings on Reagan's return and for a nerve-wracking time it looked like we might be on the threshold of major conflict in the Middle East or even World War III.

There were political recriminations arising from the massacre to be sure -- under U.S. rules of engagement, barracks sentries carried loaded weapons but without any rounds in the chambers, delaying their reaction time. Those "Rules of Engagement" definitely raised questions. But partisan criticism of Reagan and other administration officials endured paled by comparison with the intense, prolonged barrage of second guessing that congressional Republicans leveled at Secretary of State Hillary Clinton after four U.S. diplomats were killed in Bengazi, Libya. That deadly incident was a major issue in the 2016 presidential race, as was Mrs. Clinton's use of a private email server even though her predecessor, Republican Secretary of State Colin Powell, did the same thing. What's sauce for the goose often isn't sauce for the gander in American politics. I've never understood why not.

Reagan's presidential library atop a hill in Simi, CA is a soaring monument to his memory. It houses the Boeing 707 that served as his primary Air Force One (AF1 is the call sign of any aircraft carrying the president), a Sikorsky helicopter that was his Marine One (the U.S. Marine Corps provides helicopter support to the president) and a presidential limousine. It also houses a section of the Berlin Wall that evokes Reagan's "Mr. Gorbachev, tear down this wall!" speech, several of his saddles and the Jeep he used at his ranch. Reagan and his wife Nancy (Rawhide and Rainbow were their Secret Service codenames) are buried next to the library.

Lynn and our children were with me when Reagan broke ground for his library in November 1988, a few weeks after George H.W. Bush was elected to succeed him. The afternoon was sunny and warm, the start of a Thanksgiving trip to California, and the atmosphere was festive. "As my time in Washington draws to its close, I've had occasion to reflect on the astonishing journey I've been privileged to make from the banks of the Rock River (at his Illinois birthplace) to this glorious site overlooking the mighty Pacific," Reagan said. "The journey has not just been my own. It seems I've been guided by a force much larger than myself, a force made up of ideas and beliefs about what this country is and what it could be."

It was strange to visit the library 17 years later with my wife Becky, to board an airplane I'd flown on many times and see the artifacts of a presidency I'd known firsthand. I'll always regret a missed opportunity to get Reagan to reflect further on the highs and lows of his remarkable life. A few days before he left office, he agreed to a 30-minute wire service interview with Helen Thomas of UPI, Terence Hunt of the Associated Press and me.

I argued beforehand for a "soft" question-and-answer. Instead of pursuing a headline story, we'd go after a feature: Reagan's thoughts about his greatest achievement, his biggest failure, the funniest thing that happened to him as president. That sort of thing. My colleagues agreed. But as soon as we entered the Oval Office, Thomas became a relentless prosecutor, pressing Reagan to admit wrongdoing in the Iran-Contra scandal. Reagan's defenses came up. Our half hour with him became an eternity, for us as well as him. We wound up with several notebook pages full of meaningless verbiage, but nothing to hang a story on. I was embarrassed, and angry at Helen – but she was oblivious to having squandered a chance to collect some quotes for the history books.

Less than six years after he left the White House, Reagan announced to the nation that he 'd been diagnosed with Alzheimer's Disease. He did so in a handwritten letter:

Nov. 5, 1994

My Fellow Americans,

I have recently been told that I am one of the millions of Americans who will be afflicted with Alzheimer's Disease. Upon learning this news, Nancy and I had to decide whether as private citizens we would keep this a private matter or whether we would make this news known in a public way.

In the past Nancy suffered from breast cancer and I had my cancer surgeries. We found through our open disclosures we were able to raise public awareness. We were happy that as a result many more people underwent testing. They were treated in early stages and able to return to normal, healthy lives.

So now, we feel it is important to share it with you. In opening our hearts, we hope this might promote greater awareness of this condition. Perhaps it will encourage a clearer understanding of the individuals and families who are affected by it.

At the moment I feel just fine. I intend to live the remainder of the years God gives me on this earth doing the things I have always done. I will continue to share life's journey with my beloved Nancy and my family. I plan to enjoy the great outdoors and stay in touch with my friends and supporters.

Unfortunately, as Alzheimer's Disease progresses, the family often bears a heavy burden. I only wish there was some way I could spare Nancy from this painful experience. When the time comes I am confident that with your help she will face it with faith and courage.

In closing let me thank you, the American people for giving me the great honor of allowing me to serve as your President. When the Lord calls me home, whenever that may be, I will leave with the greatest love for this country of ours and eternal optimism for its future.

I now begin the journey that will lead me into the sunset of my life. I know that for America there will always be a bright dawn ahead.

Thank you, my friends. May God always bless you.

Sincerely,

Ronald Reagan

In a book entitled "Riding with Reagan," John Barletta, who served on the 41st president's Secret Service detail, paints a charming picture of Reagan as he slipped into senility He says the man he and his fellow agents called "Rawhide" became a child again, looking forward to his daily visit to a park near his Los Angeles home where he'd shyly ask the children at play if he could join in their game of soccer. He would often ask Barletta, who retired from the U.S.S.S. to become his companion, to get him a cookie.

My take on the Gipper: he was a pleasant, albeit distant man personally. He served with great integrity, humility and distinction, the Iran-Contra matter notwithstanding. He was able to articulate a vision of America that inspired confidence in the country, making the citizenry proud. On balance, however, I believe his presidency was bad for America because of the anti-government ideology – pathology might be a better word -- it advanced. Too many Americans became convinced that government is pernicious, robbing from hard-working citizens to support the shiftless. Too few understand that while there are inevitable headline-making screw-ups, the day-in, day-out work of government benefits every American immensely. Regulation of the nation's food and drugs helps keep people healthier than they would be otherwise; air traffic control makes flying safer; roads, bridges, highways and other elements of the infrastructure enables smoother travel and transportation; and the nation's armed forces protect us from would-be evildoers throughout the world. To the extent the Gipper's rhetoric contributed to the wholly negative view of government leaders and institutions that's much too prevalent in the United States, I'd give the Reagan presidency a fair to middling rating at best. History's verdict may be different.

Chapter Four

Poppy

A FEW DAYS AFTER my wife Lynn died, Former President George H.W. Bush called me to express his sympathy. It was so like the man – kind, decent, a friend. He was then 88 years old, and time was the most valuable thing he had. Yet he spent some of it to console someone who needed comfort. He could have easily had his staff prepare a letter of sympathy and have a robo-pen sign it. But as the comedians would have had him say, that "wouldn't be prudent."

I first met Bush when he became chairman of the Republican National Committee in 1973 and named Pete Teeley his press secretary. I knew Pete from when he worked for New York Sen. Jacob Javits. So he invited me to a small gathering with the new boss of the Republican Party at RNC headquarters near the U.S. Capitol. I liked Bush instantly. He was down-to-earth, smart and funny, the kind of guy it's fun to kick back with over a beer. In the more than 40 years since, that first impression has never changed.

A memory. We're on a trip, or perhaps conversing in a White House hallway, when George H.W. Bush, 41st President of the United States, tells me and whomever I'm with, that Arthur Adler, a men's fine clothier in Washington, is having a sale. "If you need any suits," he says, "Arthur Adler has a two-for-one sale right now." Patrician, but unassuming. A regular guy. A day or two later, I went into Arthur Adler and bought two suits, two of the nicest I ever owned. They weren't especially expensive. Every time I wore one of them, I glowed with pride because of how I'd happened to buy them. Haberdashery advice from the most powerful man in the world.

Two years before his condolence call, I'd seen Bush and his wife Barbara at their oceanfront home in Kennebunkport. Lynn and I were in Maine after a Harvard fellowship I'd had, and the Bushes invited us over for drinks. We found them frail and showing other signs of aging, but they were also lively and charming. Bush had difficulty walking and leaned on a cane. He said he suffered from "Parkinsonian syndrome." The once-buxom Mrs. Bush had lost a lot of weight and seemed tiny, but said she felt good.

It was a charming evening, a high point of my life. I told Bush about a course Lynn and I had audited – a course on the presidency taught by Prof. Richard Parker, one of the best lecturers I've ever listened to and also a consummate showman. His course was worth every moment not only for the content, but also for the performance art. "Parker compared you and Harry Truman," I told the former president. "He said you both followed charismatic presidents whose policies didn't work out the way they hoped, so you each had to clean up the messes they left and create your own legacy. "You got a B-plus. Maybe even an A-minus," I teased.

"How did George W. do?" Mrs. Bush asked. I had no response.

There was a poignant moment toward the end of our visit. I had to help the former president rise from his chair when he tried to get up to bid us farewell. "Hold onto me for a few moments till I get my balance, Gene," he said. This once-athletic man told me he fell often, and was constantly on the lookout for a way to cushion his fall. A golf cart parked next to the Bushes' door had this sign taped to its windshield: "Hands Off -- 41 Only!"

"There has to be a story behind that," I said. Bush didn't hear me, but Mrs. Bush replied, "We have to do that. Otherwise the grandkids would run off with it." It was the last time I saw Bush ambulatory: he was confined to a wheelchair at every subsequent visit

Over dinner later than night, Jean Becker, Bush's chief of staff, told Lynn and me one of her boss's favorite pastimes was planning his funeral. My wife Becky and I attended it eight years later. It was a singular honor. Washington's majestic National Cathedral seats 3,200 people. Since a presidential funeral is a State Ceremony, most of those seats were reserved for U.S. and foreign leaders and other dignitaries including, in Bush's case, Britain's Prince Charles, German Chancellor Angela

Merkel, Jordan's King Hassan and former Polish president Lech Walesa. To be among the chosen few to also be included will always be among my most cherished memories.

It also prompted a precious exchange with my granddaughter Libbie, then four years old. A few weeks after the funeral we were visiting, and Libbie began toying with a photograph of President Bush and her mom taken during a Kennebunkport vacation one summer when her mom was about 10 years old. When I told Libbie about the photo, she asked: "Did President Bush die? I told her he had, at the end of a long and good life, and that wife Becky and I had been at his funeral.

"Was Gorbachev there?" Libbie asked.

I was so startled I nearly fell over. Why on earth would a four year-old ask such a question, I wondered. I soon knew the answer. During a trip to Moscow with Bush, I'd picked up nesting dolls of him and the Soviet leader that I'd given to my daughter. Libbie liked to play with them and was especially fascinated with the Gorbachev doll because of the birthmark on his forehead. To her, Bush and Gorbachev were as inseparable as Mutt and Jeff. Thus her question. It made very good sense.

Bush to my mind was the best president I covered, followed by Gerald Ford. While we'll never know, his skillful, compassionate response to the decline and fall of the Soviet Union just might have prevented World War Three. Never before in history had a great empire collapsed without bloodshed; most politicians in Bush's position would have been tempted to gloat. "I hope you noticed that the United States has not engaged in condescending statements aimed at damaging the Soviet Union," he told Soviet President Mikhail Gorbachev at their first summit, which took place in Malta, specifically mentioning that he'd taken flak domestically for avoiding a more aggressive approach. "I am a cautious man, but I am not a coward; and my administration will seek to avoid doing anything that would damage your position in the world," Bush said.

The Bush-Gorbachev meeting in Malta was called the "Seasick Summit" because a fierce winter storm raked the Mediterranean island during their talks. A day before the summit began Bush flew out to the U.S. aircraft carrier Forrestal to see flight operations. He was watching from a catwalk just off the bridge when an F-14 "Tomcat" jet fighter with afterburners blazing roared past the carrier, creating a thunderous sonic boom. The ship's captain was ready to hang the pilot but the former Navy pilot would have none of that. Bush was among the first greeters when the show-off landed, sparing him what at the very least would have been a thorough tongue-lashing.

Bush enlisted in Navy on his 18th birthday during World War Two and became the sea service's second-youngest pilot. He flew a TBM-1C "Avenger" off the carrier San Jacinto in the Pacific and was shot down during a raid on the Japanese-held island of Chichi Jima on September 2 1944. In an extraordinary twist of fate, he was rescued by a U.S. submarine lurking off the island; his two crewmembers were killed. "For a while there I thought I was done," Bush told biographer Jon Meachum. Once during his son George's first term as president, I visited him at his office in Houston where he proudly showed me the nameplate of a new Navy carrier then under construction: CVN 77, the U.S.S. George H.W. Bush. I was proud to be at the warship's christening in 2006. Lynn wasn't with me because she was in Seattle helping daughter Jennie with her firstborn, my grandson Charlie. At a party the night before Bush's daughter Doro broke a bottle of champagne over the carrier's keel and named the mighty carrier after her dad, I showed him a photo of baby Charlie. "This is what's important in life! This is what life's all about," he said, nodding at the image as he gave me a thumbs up. Lynn and I both attended the commissioning ceremony of the carrier three years later.

Bush's handling of the first Gulf War was a textbook example of leadership but a U.S. miscalculation might have started it. A week or two before Iraq invaded Kuwait, Jim Gerstenzang of the Los Angeles Times, CNN's Frank Sesno and I had dinner with National Security Adviser Brent Scowcroft. We asked about the threatening noises Iraq was making toward its neighbor. Scowcroft told us the United States suspected Kuwait was stealing Iraqi oil and that Saddam Hussein would punish them by taking over two small Kuwaiti-owned islands. The U.S. would do nothing in such an event, he said.

What clearly was not expected was a full-blown Iraqi invasion of Kuwait, an action that threatened the West's oil lifeline by putting Saudi Arabia at risk. The crisis erupted as Bush was on his way to Aspen CO for a day-long meeting with British Prime Minister Margaret Thatcher. Characteristically self-effacing, Bush later reported that Thatcher told him, "Remember George, this is no time to go wobbly!" It was yet another example of the self-denigration rarely seen in a politician. Once the situation clarified, Bush was resolute. "This will not stand," he said at an impromptu news conference. When ABC's Ann Compton asked him to elaborate, Bush brusquely brushed her off. Characteristically, he later sent her a note of apology.

Calmly and methodically, Bush set about rolling back the Iraqi invasion. Together with Secretary of State James Baker, his longtime friend and confidant, he knitted together a global coalition that even included the Soviet Union even though Iraq was a Soviet client state. The United States and the allies poured hundreds of thousands of troops into the Persian Gulf region amid a torrent of threats from an Iraqi spokesman nicknamed "Baghdad Bob" and Saddam Hussein's promise of "the mother of all battles."

As preparations for war moved along feverishly, Bush worked to win the support of a leery Congress. The lawmakers narrowly agreed to back him. After heated debate, a resolution authorizing use of force was approved by the Senate on a 52-47 vote and by the House on a 250-187 vote. Rank-and-file Democrats defied their leaders, who opposed the move. It was the strongest congressional action since the 1964 Gulf of Tonkin resolution, which authorized use of force in Vietnam.

The run-up to war was a time of great tension and much foreign travel. So it was that over Thanksgiving in 1990 I was on a trip that started in what was then Czechoslovakia, went on to Germany, then to France, from there to Saudi Arabia and on to Egypt before a final stop in Switzerland. To my amazement, Simon Peller, a Reuters employee, was Bush's translator when he and Czech President Vaclav Havel addressed a massive crowd in Prague's Wenceslas Square.

It was emotional moment for Peller. He told me over dinner that night he'd been beaten up in the square a year earlier during the Czech "Velvet Revolution" that wrested the country from communism. Peller said he wept with joy to stand there with Bush and his country's leader. He was especially moved that Bush quoted the words of Thomas Jefferson and Woodrow Wilson on freedom and liberty. These words inspired him and his countrymen during the dark days of communist oppression, he said. Bush had left a page of his speech behind on the podium and Peller had kept it as a souvenir. I suggested he give it to me to get autographed.

I was on Air Force One for a flight to Germany the next day. It has changed since; but in my day, writers and photographers for Reuters, AP and UPI had permanently assigned seats in the rear of the aircraft. Representatives of the major newspapers, radio and television networks and the news magazines occupied the other press cabin seats on a rotating basis. When Bush came back to chat, I got him to sign the memento and told him of Peller's comments about Jefferson and Wilson. I thought he'd be impressed to hear of a concrete example of the power of American ideas. Bush was not into deep thinking that day. "When that guy told me we'd be doing consecutive translation, I thought, 'Christ, we'll be here all day!'" he said.

The stop in Germany was to visit Chancellor Helmut Kohl's hometown of Oggersheim to sample a local delicacy. It was a good example of Bush's leadership style: he put great store in personal relationships to advance his diplomacy. Then it was on to France where the headline story was Soviet President Mikhail Gorbachev's acquiescence to the use of force, if necessary, to expel Iraq from Kuwait. Word also came while we were in Paris that several thousand Westerners in Iraq were free to leave. That showed the strength of Bush's leadership. It was feared that Saddam Hussein would use the Westerners as human shields, but Bush essentially wrote them off. His unstated reason, I think, was that in wartime, some unfortunately become expendable. Once he did that, their value as hostages evaporated.

After France, it was Saudi Arabia, first stop Jeddah, where Bush met the Emir of Kuwait. Their meeting lasted long into the night and we had a departure at dawn. It was customary at such times to buddy up, to exchange wakeup calls with a colleague in case the hotel failed to call. Part of the deal was to eyeball the buddy in the lobby to make sure he or she was up and ready to go.

My buddy in this instance was Terry Hunt of the AP. When we found each other in the lobby, he was carrying a gift-wrapped package and said it contained a tea kettle. "It's a gift from the hotel. Didn't you get one?" he asked.

Hunt said he knew what it was because UPI's Helen Thomas had opened her package. He said he planned to re-gift his to someone as a Christmas present. I thought nothing of it, nor did I think of the Secret Service warning we heard again and again since leaving Washington: that there was credible intelligence that enemy agents were tracking our movements, so we should watch our personal belongings closely and take nothing from anyone we didn't know. Hunt later told me he recalled the warning after we boarded Air Force One and worried throughout the flight to the Saudi city of Dhahran that the package would explode.

The Jeddah-Dhahran flight was brief, but we were escorted by fighter planes, issued gas masks and briefed on their use. Saddam had used chemical weapons in Iraq's war with Iran and war planners worried he'd use them again. (The thought of soldiers having to wear heavy protective suits in the desert heat was a great concern, and U.S. officials suggested that if Iraq used chemical weapons it would provoke a nuclear response.) From my stint in the Army I knew the gas mask briefing included an exposure to tear gas. You remove the mask, get a whiff of the agent and put it on again. It's enough to make you gag and cough and drives home a powerful message: a gas mask is highly effective and should always be used. As the sergeant briefing us aboard Air Force One concluded his spiel, I jokingly asked, "Aren't you supposed to pop a can of CS (tear gas) now, Sarge"? With a look of horror on his face, the sergeant replied, "Not on this airplane, sir!"

Seeing our troops in the desert poised for war was gut-wrenching. Bush visited three outfits: a U.S. infantry group, where I met a soldier from Scranton; a British outfit renowned for its World War Two performance in North Africa, which earned its members the nickname "Desert Rats"; and a Marine battalion near the Kuwaiti border. Illustrating how faraway events constantly impinge on what the president is doing, news came from London that Margaret Thatcher was out as British prime minister, forcing White House officials to stop and grind out a statement expressing Bush's views on the development. "On a personal basis, I'll miss her. I think everyone in America will agree Margaret Thatcher has been an outstanding ally for the United States," Bush said.

We left the Marines after nightfall. During our visit, the press helicopter sank into the sand up to the passenger compartment. The crew had to climb aboard, start the engines and put the chopper into a low hover before we could get on the aircraft. As we lifted off through a cloud of dust, it was hard to shake the feeling that we were leaving fellow Americans behind to face a cataclysm. Less than ninety days later they were in combat. Fortunately, the war was short and there were relatively few U.S. casualties. 219 Americans died, 35 of them from friendly fire.

From Saudi Arabia we flew to Cairo, where I saw the Pyramids for the first time. (I returned five years later with Hillary Clinton.) Not only did I see them and the Sphinx, I actually got into the burial chamber in the center of the Great Pyramid, a foray not for the claustrophobic. It involved duck-walking down an entryway that was perhaps four feet wide, four feet tall and about 80 yards long. Once into the entryway, there was no turning back – it was one-way traffic in and out. By the time I reached the empty burial vault, a room maybe 30 feet wide and 12 feet high, my knees and thighs were screaming with pain. Was it worth it? Probably not. There was nothing to see.

I did the whole tourist routine during the Giza visit, riding a camel for a photo in front of the Sphinx. My other memory of the Egyptian capital was a military museum whose grounds were crowded with tanks and artillery. I thought it was strange to display armaments that were no match for Israel in three successive wars.

After Cairo, it was on to Switzerland and the most bizarre episode in all of my thousands of miles of travels with presidents: The Battle of Geneva Airport. The final stop was a hastily-arranged addition to the schedule to accommodate a meeting between Bush and President Hafez Assad of Syria. With little time to lay the groundwork, Swiss officials were understandably anxious to prevent any glitches. Their nervousness collided with one of the quirks of White House news coverage – in those days, whenever Air Force One landed, the press "pool" expanded to include additional television crews, so each of the networks would have its own motorcade footage. The TV people had cause for this – the assassination of President John F. Kennedy and the assassination attempts on Presidents Gerald Ford and Ronald Reagan were all motorcade-related. But the White House advance team had neglected to brief Swiss police. So when Bush's jet rolled to a stop, the gendarmes got jumpy seeing a bunch of people moving toward the plane.

One policeman pulled a gun when commands to halt were ignored, a move that enraged impetuous White House chief of staff John Sununu. While Bush was in talks with Assad, Sununu summoned and scolded the Swiss interior minister. Suddenly word spread that the Swiss police had surrounded Air Force One and would only let the president get aboard. Aides said no-one need worry because the plane wouldn't take off until everyone on the manifest was present and accounted for. It was preposterous – no government would embarrass the head of state of another in such a manner, let alone the President of the United States. But Bush's bone-tired, jet lagged entourage wasn't thinking clearly.

When we finally headed back to the airport, everyone had a chip on their shoulder. One of the photographers hit a policeman, starting a melee. Two senior White House aides, protocol officer Joseph Reed and communications adviser Sig Rogich, got roughed up in the fracas. Shortly after takeoff, White House spokesman Marlin Fitzwater stormed into the press cabin and denounced the Swiss "barbaric" behavior. He said the United States would lodge a diplomatic protest. I filed a report from the plane about the tumultuous end to Bush's trip. After n a few weeks, however, the incident was forgotten. U.S.-Swiss relations survived.

Bush made 26 foreign trips as president and I was on most of them. He went to Europe 11 times, to Asia twice and to South America once. He and other presidents I covered liked to travel because a high-level meeting in a far-off foreign capital or even a stump speech in the American heartland usually generated more favorable publicity than the daily grind in Washington. But the pace is hectic and 18-hour days are the norm, so perhaps it isn't surprising that presidential travel sometimes becomes detached from reality.

There were two occasions when Bush probably wished he'd stayed home; when he threw up on Prime Minister Kiichi Miyazaawa during a state visit to Japan in 1991, and when he spoke at a grocer's convention in Florida in 1992. His embarrassing moment in Tokyo came toward the end of a trip that also included visits to Australia, Singapore and South Korea. The stop in Tokyo was politically charged. Bush was accompanied by top U.S. auto industry executives and his aim was to staunch the flow of Japanese auto imports flooding the American market. Little did I and my colleagues know that he was suffering from stomach flu.

Since Bush's presence at a state dinner hosted by the prime minister was unlikely to make any news, my Reuters colleague Steve Holland and I planned to take the night off. I asked our local office to assign a reporter to cover the event. My first inkling that maybe that wasn't a good idea came when I went to my room to freshen up before Holland and I went to dinner. I was just about to leave when I got a call from Reuters' Tokyo bureau chief saying something unusual had happened. He said before the dinner Bush briefly left the receiving line and had gone into a bathroom. When he emerged, photographers noticed he seemed a bit pale and was wearing a different tie. The Reuters guy wondered if he was sick.

I said I'd check it out: Reuters was heavily into news that moves financial markets and there was a saying at the time that when a president sneezes, Wall Street gets pneumonia. I made some calls to members of Bush's staff. Everyone I spoke to said he was fine. But as I entered the press workplace in a hotel ballroom, television screens in the front of the room cut from a Japanese quiz show to live pictures of the prime minister's residence with a U.S. military ambulance in front. "Oh, shit!" I muttered. I thought my career had crashed and burned. Being out of position for an event like that is not good for job security. Fortunately Holland and I recovered quickly and got the news out that Bush's illness was nothing serious. It was a sobering reminder that when covering the president, news people can never relax.

Bush's supermarket fiasco couldn't have happened at a worse time: at the start of his 1992 reelection campaign, when he was fighting a public perception that he was out of touch with the nation he led. It was a good example of how the news media sometimes gets things wrong because of unprofessional internal crosscurrents. It also showed how Bush's tendency to be overpolite sometimes got him in trouble. This combustible mix came together at a grocer's trade fair in Orlando, where he was shown the latest in supermarket scanner technology. I was with him as a member of the press "pool" and saw nothing newsworthy. Andrew Rosenthal of the New York Times was back in the press room and, based on a snarky pool report, wrote a front page news story that Bush was astonished by commonplace checkout equipment, suggesting he had no idea how average Americans lived.

An explanation of press "pools" and pool reports is appropriate here. When I was a member, the White House press corps usually consisted of 40 or 50 writers and broadcasters, half as many photographers and about two dozen TV camera crew members. On foreign trips it was larger. News organizations in Europe and Asia would send representatives, sometimes swelling the press corps to 300 people or more.

It was physically impossible to have a group this size at most presidential events, so a representative of each sub-category – newspapers, radio, television and news magazines – would cover the event and share the information with everyone else. Every news organization took a turn at being in the press pool: the representatives rotated. Reuters, the AP and UPI were always pool members because our stories went out to other news organizations. We "pooled" our information by definition. For internal consumption only, pool reports were often playfully written, meant to amuse as well as inform. One sophomoric example, recounting President Jimmy Carter's church attendance one Sunday, reported that Carter was wearing a necktie "handcrafted by the CIA" that warned the country of Senegal in code "they'd better watch their ass for the next six months." When James Deaken, a short-tempered reporter for the St. Louis Post-Dispatch, angrily objected that he couldn't tell which parts of the report were true and which were false, the writer whimsically replied: "Everything that's not patently absurd is true."

Most presidents chafed at the idea of having to take a press pool along whenever they left the White House, feeling it impinged on the little privacy they had while serving in the nation's highest office. A week or so before his inaugural, Bush asked AP White House Correspondent Terence Hunt and me to come to his office for an off-the-record conversation. What he wanted was more freedom of movement to enjoy unofficial after-hours functions. "If Bar and I want to go out to dinner to the home of some friends, why is it necessary to take a pool along? It's a waste of your time and your employers' money. It'd all be private. We wouldn't be making any news," he said.

Trying to be as diplomatic as possible, Hunt explained that the pool was a death watch – that if the president was hurt or killed in an accident or attack while going to or from a private event, independent observers would be on to tell the public what happened.

Bush was unimpressed. "What if I got hungry in the middle of the night and went to the refrigerator in the White House kitchen and grabbed a piece of chicken – and the bone got stuck in my throat and choked me to death. You wouldn't be around for that," he said. The discussion went nowhere: Bush put up with the pool coverage he tried to get rid of throughout his presidency.

New York Times editor Tom Wicker observed that journalists are often like children playing with pieces of colored glass. I agree. I was often at odds with my professional colleagues because of their fascination with happenings that to me seemed trivial. I also believe even top public officials are entitled a zone of privacy. Some of my colleagues undoubtedly saw me as "in the tank," too soft on the people I covered. I believed they were unreasonably difficult and that informing the public suffered as a result.

We journalists generally see ourselves as champions of truth, justice and the American way. But making mischief is sometimes the norm. It can be deadly. Admiral Jeremy Boorda is a case in point. Boorda rose to the rank of four-star admiral after entering the Navy as an enlisted man and became Chief of Naval Operations in the mid-1990s. I met him when we sailed to Normandy aboard the USS George Washington for the 50th anniversary of D-Day. After learning that *Newsweek* was about to publish a story that he'd worn two Vietnam combat decorations he didn't merit, something he called "an honest mistake," Borda committed suicide, leaving a family behind.

Another example was the torrent of Wikileaks stories that helped doom Hillary Clinton's presidential bid in 2016. The stories provided entertaining glimpses of the foibles of Clinton insiders, especially campaign manager John Podesta, but disclosed little useful information for voters. News organizations knew, or should have known, of the dubious provenance of the material, that it was likely part of a Russian disinformation campaign designed to damage the former first lady. Yet they went with it anyway, helping put Donald Trump in the White House.

I got into a serious dustup with colleagues over professional standards during a trip to South Asia with Mrs. Clinton in 1995. It involved a pool assignment. The then-first lady was accompanied by daughter Chelsea, whom I and the other reporters agreed was off-limits. She was not a newsmaker; we did not write about or otherwise cover her.

We visited the Taj Mahal while we were in India, and I was with Mrs. Clinton and Chelsea on a tour of the breathtaking mausoleum conducted by an Indian official. Besides Mrs. Clinton's Secret Service bodyguards, the only other person present was Lisa Caputo, the first lady's press secretary. Our tour guide had a thick accent. After he showed us through the white marble monument built in the 17th century by Mughal emperor Shah Jahan to honor a beloved wife who died in childbirth, we briefly stood at the entrance talking. I asked a few follow-up questions, then turned to Chelsea and asked her what she thought of what we'd just seen. I wasn't seeking a quote but merely being polite, including her in the conversation. Chelsea's reply was graceful, something to the effect that when she was a little girl, she always thought of the Taj Mahal as a fairytale palace but it was even more beautiful than she imagined.

As we walked to the motorcade, Lisa Caputo asked me if I'd gotten the quote. I told her I hadn't. I didn't tell her I hadn't written it down because I considered it off the record. Perhaps I should have. Lisa whipped out a pocket recorder and played Chelsea's comment back for me. Thinking she wanted it published, I passed it on to the others covering the trip. At that next stop, Ann Compton of ABC News tried to get Chelsea to repeat what she'd said on camera. Mrs. Clinton was furious.

I interceded. I explained to the others the circumstances that led me to give them the quote, said it was all a misunderstanding and that we therefore shouldn't consider it part of the story. *Washington Post* writer Molly Moore said she planned to use the quote. I told her if she did, I'd file a story about us.

We'd been in Pakistan before arriving in India and after the last event there, a dinner at the historic Red Fort in Lahore, gift-wrapped small rugs awaited us in the press van. They were gifts from the governor of Punjab Province. We climbed aboard Mrs. Clinton's plane with them without telling the Secret Service. They quickly found out and refused to let the plane take off until the rugs were inspected. I told Molly that if others in the first lady's entourage had committed such a security breach, we'd report it. So I was prepared to embarrass us – I'd write a story about OUR security breach. That ended the matter.

Returning to Bush senior, I helped trigger a flurry of stories about his hatred of broccoli that subsequently became part of his image. I was sitting in my White House press room cubicle one day when a photographer came by and told me the president was looking for me. He said Bush had walked into the press briefing room waving a Reuters story. I hadn't written it, nor had anyone else on the Reuters White House team. A general assignment reporter had, telling the public California broccoli growers planned to send a truckload of broccoli to the White House as a publicity stunt. They were reacting to an item in *U.S. News & World Report* that Bush had banned the vegetable from meals on Air Force One. The photographer said Bush declared in mock anger he didn't want the shipment and wouldn't accept it.

There was a state dinner for visiting Polish Prime Minister Thaddeus Mazowiecki that evening and I covered the exchange of toasts. Afterwards Bush, who was in an ebullient mood, introduced me to Mazowiecki and asked me what I wanted to ask them about. "Well sir, as the representative of Reuters, I guess I'd better ask you about broccoli," I said, teasing him about his outburst earlier in the day. Bush played along, saying he hated broccoli but had been made to eat it when he was a child. Now that he was president, he would no longer eat it, he said.

He then jokingly asked Mazowiecki if Poland wanted the broccoli shipment headed to Washington. Mazowiecki, who was probably unfamiliar with the vegetable, seemed bewildered by the president's remarks. I wrote a three or four paragraph story about the exchange, light humor known in the news business as a "bright." The next day, Bush held a televised news conference and someone asked him about it. He responded with a tirade about the evils of broccoli, etching the character trait into the public mind.

I've never understood the disconnect between Bush's public persona and what he was really like. In reality the 41st president was a lot of things Ronald Reagan was not: war hero, excellent athlete, devoted family man, a regular churchgoer. But he was perceived by much of the public as aristocratic, aloof and weak. *Newsweek* ran a cover story during the 1988 presidential campaign that did a lot to define him, unfairly. The cover picture showed Bush aboard "Fidelity," his beloved high speed power boat, with a banner splashed across it suggesting his biggest political problem was "The Wimp Factor." Cartoonist Gary Trudeau, a fellow Yale alumnus, depicted Bush as a lightweight in the comic strip *Doonesbury*, declaring he had "put his manhood in a blind trust."

No doubt about it, Bush WAS preppie. He wore colored watch wristbands, played tennis and golf and had an estate in Maine where he liked to go boating. Not exactly a match with your average citizen. He sometimes spouted strange syntax. On the golf course, he factiously called himself "Mr. Smooth." When he served in a tennis match, he "unleashed Chiang" – a reference to Chinese strongman Chiang Kai Shek, a hero of the Republican right. That wasn't a match with your average citizen, either.

But unlike Reagan, who was affable but detached, the man friends called "Poppy" (his nickname in college) was genuinely interested in others. During one Maine vacation, he engaged in a day-long "pentathlon": golf, tennis, jogging, horseshoes and softball. My daughter Becky, a good athlete then about nine, played in the softball game and got a hit. AP photographer Scott Crabtree got a shot of Bush leaping to catch an errant throw as she scooted toward first base. I've always regretted failing to get a copy of the photos.

Bush was a big baseball fan. He captained his Yale baseball team and kept his old first baseman's mitt in a drawer of his desk in the Oval Office. Ted Williams was a friend. Once, when I playfully suggested he attend the Baltimore Orioles' Opening Day ceremonies, saying it would help him in the polls, Bush sent me a tongue-in-cheek response in one of his famous handwritten notes:

Dear Gene –

I don't believe in polls. I do believe a President must make the tough calls.

Thus I'm prepared to sacrifice and make the decision that benefits our national pastime. – stay tuned –

George Bush

In 1991, Bush set the stage for the annual Baseball All-Star Game with a White House Rose Garden ceremony celebrating two of the sport's greatest feats: Williams' .406 batting average in 1941, the last time anyone has hit over .400; and Joe DiMaggio's 56 game hitting streak. That record has never been broken. Bush presented each with the Presidential Medal of Freedom.

It was unabashed hero worship. "Who, even now, does not marvel at the Splendid Splinter and the Yankee Clipper. These genuine heroes thrilled Americans with real deeds," he said, using nicknames the sportswriters bestowed on Williams and DiMaggio. Afterwards, he and the honorees flew to Toronto for the all-star game.

In one of those "pinch me, I'm dreaming" moments I was with them, occupying in the Reuters seat on Air Force One. Williams was my childhood baseball hero. I used the same model baseball bat, wore my baseball cap like him, often pretended to be him. My brother Charlie, retaliating for something I'd done to make him angry, sent off a harshly worded letter to Williams demanding an signed picture and put my name on it. He was trying to wreck my fondest dream: securing a Ted Williams autograph. Two weeks later, a signed picture arrived. I was thrilled. (I learned much later in life Boston Red Sox clubhouse attendant Johnny Orlando replied to most of William's mail. But no matter.)

The trip to Toronto was like being on a field trip to the biggest baseball game in history with the biggest stars of the game on the school bus with us. There he was, bigger than life, Ted Williams himself! And Joe DiMaggio to boot! Williams, a scourge of journalists during his playing career, was more friendly toward the knights of the White House, visiting the press cabin for 10 minutes or so. The aloof DiMaggio stayed up front. Barbara Bush also came back to the press cabin, collected our cardboard trip credentials and got Williams and DiMaggio to sign them. I wanted to give mine to the Baseball Hall of Fame in Cooperstown NY – they were interested in the momento. But my late wife Lynn vetoed the idea, saying we could use the money the souvenir is probably worth in our retirement. I still have it. It's in my safe deposit box.

When we landed in Canada, the magic was gone. Now it was the President of the United States, arriving on an official visit, with all the pomp and panoply involved. A red carpet, a phalanx of Canadian Mounties in their distinctive scarlet and blue uniforms and a bevy of official greeters were there to provide a formal welcome. Looking around during the ruffles and flourishes, I witnessed a scene that would have made a great photograph: Williams and DiMaggio, standing near the motorcade. Obviously confused about which one of the cars they should get in, they huddled together trying to make sense of a world they did not understand, yesterday's giants become bewildered old men.

I saw my first big league baseball game when I was 10 years old. The New York Yankees played the Chicago White Sox at Yankee Stadium and my favorite uncle, the hero of D-Day, took Cotz and me to the game. It had to be on a Wednesday; that was Dr. Cotter's day off. Bob Turley, known as "Bullet Bob" because of his blazing fastball, hit Chicago shortstop Minnie Minoso in the head with a pitch and fractured his skull. Baseball players didn't wear helmets then. Minoso survived. He was still playing professional baseball when he was more than 50 years old.

Another memory of the game was getting a souvenir baseball supposedly autographed by the Yankees but actually signed by a machine. I knew it wasn't real but cherished it anyway. I also remember my Uncle John being irked because he felt his son and I spent more time looking at men and boys with ducktails, a style of haircut then in vogue, then we did following the action on the field. My uncle was an avid baseball fan. He listened to games on the radio, tracking hits, runs and errors on a homemade scorecard while picking slivers of World War Two shrapnel out of his hands and arms. He'd drop the bits of steel into an ashtray, where they landed with a clink. I was broken-hearted when my family hero died. I was in the army myself, serving in South Korea. There was no instant international communication in the mid-1960s. My cousin sent me a letter saying his father had died of a heart attack. I sat in a field in far-off Korea sobbing.

Like my Uncle John, I loved baseball. My childhood dream was to play in the big leagues. But I wasn't good at the sport and only the talented kids got to play on Little League teams those days. I played a lot of sandlot baseball. Once in a while, other players included Joe Biden, the former U.S. senator and vice president whose political comeback in 2020 catapulted him into the presidency. We were in second grade together at St. Paul's School in the Green Ridge section of Scranton, but then his family moved to Delaware. Biden often returned to his birthplace to visit his grandmother and there'd often be pickup games near her home.

Our second grade teacher was Sister Eunice, whom I remembered as one of the kindest, best teachers I ever had. When I was invited to give the University of Scranton commencement address in 1996, I visited her in retirement. She said she remembered me but of course she remembered my famous classmate.

"You children would go home for lunch and Joe Biden must have had a big meal every day, because he'd fall asleep in class in the afternoon," she said. "I used to call him 'Bye, Bye Biden!"

When I got back to Washington, I told a member of Biden's staff about my meeting with Sister Eunice and asked that she give him the nun's regards. I saw the staffer again a few weeks later and she reported: "Senator Biden hates that nun!" She explained that Biden stuttered as a child and said the nun mocked him. I couldn't believe she'd do any such thing: it conflicted with everything I remembered about her. But the more I've learned about Sister Eunice from some of her other former students, the more I've become convinced Biden was right.

The future president moved to Wilmington Delaware after second grade. But he often came back to Scranton to visit his grandmother and on several occasions we played sandlot baseball together. Biden was a good ballplayer and as was usually involved in choosing sides. The process could be painful for klutzes like me. "Awwww, Gibbons!!! Do I have to take him?" was a familiar refrain. Biden didn't do that as I recall. He treated everyone playing with respect.

When I wasn't throwing a ball around, I was pouring over my baseball cards. Fleers and Topps were the big sellers, one card and a large stick of bubblegum for a penny, six cards and gum for a nickel. Besides Ted Williams, New York Yankee up-and-comer Mickey Mantle – real name Charles Eugene Mantle – was one of my favorites. The New York Giants' Monte Irvin, one of the first African Americans to reach the pinnacle of professional baseball, was another. But just a notch behind my idol Ted Williams was Bill Howerton, a professional ballplayer who lived a just a few blocks away. Over a four year career in the National League, Howerton played for the St. Louis Cardinals, Pittsburgh Pirates and New York Giants. He appeared in 247 games and compiled a .281 lifetime batting average. An average-sized, sandy haired man with an infectious grin, he operated a soda fountain and convenience store about a block from my school in the off-season. I would stop in, order a Coke or some penny candy and shyly engage him in conversation. Howerton was unassuming and infinitely patient. In 1952, he was waived out of baseball, returned to his native state of California and spent the rest of his working life as a long haul truck driver.

More than 40 years later, he came back to Scranton to be with his son, the University of Scranton baseball coach. Several years before he died at age 80, I reunited with him at a nursing home. It was a Saturday afternoon noon in late autumn and when I saw his big grin, I instantly remembered his kindly manner. I wanted to make him the centerpiece of a baseball old timer magazine article but Howerton, wearing a warmup jacket and clutching a small white-haired dog in a cluttered apartment that stank of urine, was becoming senile and struggled to carry on a conversation. After an awkward interval, I thanked him for seeing me and got ready to leave. "Please don't go," he begged. So I put away my tape recorder, which seemed to make him relax, and listened as he led me through a Field of Dreams soliloquy.

He reminisced about his career and some of the legends of baseball, Carl Erskine, a Hall of Fame pitcher for the old Brooklyn Dodgers, among them. "The count was three balls and two strikes and I knew a fastball was coming. Hit that sunovabitch right out of the park," Howerton said. Of Ted Williams, he said: "Borrowed his pants once. We were playing in Florida (during spring training) and my (uniform) pants weren't on the truck. He and I were the same size, so he lent me some pants." Jackie Robinson: "Probably the best ball player I ever saw." When I told Howerton my younger daughter was a pretty good baseball player, he said: "Good for her. Hope she sticks with it." It was one of the best afternoons of my life. Regrettably, I never wrote about it until now.

In the movie classic "Field of Dreams," an Iowa farmer builds a baseball diamond in his cornfield and some long-dead legends of the game, including Shoeless Joe Jackson, return from the afterlife and play. Thanks to President Bush senior, I first saw that movie in the White House theater. Lynn and I were invited to the residence one Friday night for a social evening, something only a few people ever experience. With Bush as our tour guide, we got to see the family quarters, including the

Lincoln Bedroom. Best described as an elegant apartment with high ceilings and a magnificent view of the Washington Monument, the family quarters are on the second floor of the Executive Mansion. There are 16 rooms and 6 bathrooms. The centerpiece of the apartment is the Yellow Oval Room, a spacious living room that opens onto the Truman Balcony, a large portico overlooking the White House South Lawn.

The Lincoln Bedroom is just two doors down the hall from the sitting room on the south side of the building. It was simply furnished, with just a bed with a horsehair mattress and a table with a handwritten copy of the Gettysburg Address atop it. Historians doubt Lincoln ever slept in the bed; several other presidents did, including Theodore Roosevelt and Woodrow Wilson. Bush invited Lynn and me to try it out. The mattress was hard as a rock. It was bizarre: there we were, stretched out on Lincoln's bed with the president of the United States looming above us. Perhaps the most bizarre moment was what he then said: "Does either of you need to use the Lincoln bathroom before we see the movie?"

Traveling with Bush when he was vice president was even more interesting than his presidential trips. There were never more than five or six journalists and perhaps three dozen aides and Secret Service bodyguards. So it was a much more intimate group. During a vice presidential trip to the Middle East, we landed and took off from the aircraft carrier U.S.S. Enterprise, a "trap" and "cat shot" in carrier parlance, aboard a 16-passenger aircraft called a COD (Carrier Onboard Delivery). Landing on an aircraft carrier is not for the faint-hearted: you first see the warship far off in the distance as a tiny speck in the ocean. It get larger and larger, and suddenly you're roaring down the deck until you come to a halt with a huge thump as the tail-hook catches an arresting cable.

Pilots told us the takeoff would be even more exciting: a steam catapult pushes the plane from a standing stop to a takeoff speed of more than 125 MPH in a few seconds, literally hurling it into the sky. As we awaited the launch, I was terrified. In the event there was nothing to it. It briefly felt like we were being flung by a rubber band and then we were flying.

We'd left our carry-on bags on the plane while on the carrier and just before takeoff, a press colleague asked a crewman to get his for him. The noise on a carrier conducting flight operations is deafening, so during all this both men were shouting. "Sir, your bag is in the locker with all the other bags. I'd never be able to find it right now," the sailor yelled. "Of course you could. It's a Louis Vuitton," the reporter responded. Talk about people speaking two different languages!

That trip included a two-day stop in Yemen highlighted by Bush's dedication of a U.S.-built oil refinery near Marib, purportedly the ancient capital of the fabled Queen of Sheba. The president of Yemen joined Bush there, arriving in an armored limousine trailed by several pickup trucks armed with anti-aircraft guns. It was a jarring glimpse of the nature of politics in the Middle East. Just about everyone in Yemen was heavily armed. In fact, when some gun-toting Yemini "journalists" tried to join us in the press van, one Secret Service agent yelled to another, "Hey, tell these guys American press only. Get their guns and grenades and shit outa here!." I made a photo that's almost comical showing Bush walking through the souk in Sa'nna wearing a pin-stripe suit and running shoes. It's sobering to know Yemen later became one of the most terrorist infested countries on earth.

Perhaps the most frightening place I've ever been is Auschwitz, the World War Two Nazi death camp in Poland where more than one million people were murdered, most of them European Jews. From the sign in German at the entrance, "Abeit Macht Frei" (Work Will Make You Free), to the ruins of the ovens at Birkenau, the place reeks of unspeakable evil. The first thing you see are the railroad tracks. Then row upon row of brick buildings that now house belongings of Hitler's victims – piles of suitcases, eyeglasses and, most chilling of all, human hair. There's still more horror though: the place where Maximillan Kolbe died. He was a Polish priest who gave his life to save another man. The site of his death shows the demonic cruelty of the Nazis. Several people were jammed into a sealed cell the size of a broom closet, where they quickly started to suffocate. They frantically clawed their way through a thick wooden door only to find an inch-thick steel plate on the other side. Writer Peter Matthiessen captures the grimness of Auschwitz all these years later in his novel _In Paradise_. In it, he tells the story of a spiritual retreat on the killing ground. It was the last book Matthiessen wrote before he died. Its' tone suggests he didn't believe in paradise. Neither, alas, do I.

Though people tend to forget it, public figures are human beings. Constantly having to tamp down one's emotions and put on a happy face is something I could never do. Yet we expect it of our leaders and the people around them – or at least we used to. After Auschwitz, the Bushes visited a children's cancer hospital in Krakow. It had to be extremely painful: their daughter Robin died of leukemia when she was just shy of four years old. There was no news coverage. Later the same day, we went on to Germany. Mrs. Bush joined some of my colleagues and in the rear of the plane during part of the trip, and the conversation at one point turned to the hospital visit. I noticed Mrs. Bush's eyes fill with tears and saw her quickly blink them away. The moment struck me. Had she shown her feelings, it would have been noted in that day's press coverage. It seems people like her aren't allowed to cry.

In _A Grief Observed,_ a book about the death of his wife, author C.S. Lewis writes that the loss of a loved one "gives life a permanently provisional feeling." When I was 12, my mother gave birth to the sister my brothers and I craved. My parents named her Mary. There were childbirth complications that today would be readily fixed; the baby lived for less than 24 hours. To this day I can still picture her tiny white coffin and recall how cold she was when I kissed her for the first and last time. There was a Roman Catholic "Mass of the Angels" that was supposed to sweep away sorrow, and the hasty purchase of a gravesite in rural Moscow PA where my parents now rest beside their lost child. I feared at the time I was somehow to blame; for some reason, I'd misbehaved frequently during the latter stages of my mother's pregnancy.

A month or so after Mary died, my mother told us she'd thrown up blood. Even at my age, I knew what that meant: a pulmonary embolism, at a time when a blood clot in the lung was almost always fatal. She'd had two previous embolisms after the birth of my brother Charlie and her survival then was considered miraculous; her medical history was family lore. Moreover, I followed Major League Baseball closely. So I knew all that Harry Agganis, a 26-year old Boston Red Sox infielder widely expected to be named Rookie of Year, had suddenly died of a pulmonary embolism a few days before my mother's terrifying announcement.

An ambulance was summoned. My mother was hospitalized all summer, hovering between life and death. Twice she received the last rites of the Catholic Church, its prayers for the dying. Those twin experiences in the summer of 1955 might have kindled an empathy I fear too few journalists seem to share. Ever since, I've never fully trusted the good fortune I've enjoyed. Like Garp's son in the eponymous John Irving novel,

I live in dread of the "under-toad," the knowledge that just when one is happiest, terrible sadness is likely to snatch joy away.

***

Threaded throughout my long association with the Bushes are memories of Maine. He spent the month of August there during each of his four years in office. My family and I rented a house in Cape Porpoise not far from the Bushes in Kennebunkport. It was fun for the kids. A couple of times they got a ride in the president's speedboat "Fidelity." (He wasn't at the helm.) I had to churn out stories whether there was news or not, which was hard for my family to understand. Most of the time it was mundane stuff, Bush golf outings, fishing expeditions and so forth. Sometimes bombshell events occurred such as an abortive 1991 coup in Russia when communist hardliners briefly detained Soviet President Mikhail Gorbachev. Bush went back to Washington during the crisis, then resumed his vacation when the coup attempt collapsed.

On my birthday one year, Lynn and I were invited to an informal lobster bake honoring British Prime Minister John Major and his wife Norma, the Bush's house guests. It took place at the Kennebunk River Club, a private social and recreational gathering place a hundred yards or so down the road from Bush's home. After a typical Maine picnic dinner of boiled lobster, corn on the cob and strawberry-rhubarb pie, we were treated to a performance of "Forever Plaid," a goofy off-Broadway musical revue featuring the tunes of popular all-male quartets in the 1940s and '50s. The evening was decidedly preppy and great fun.

During stays in Maine, I had occasional dealings with future President George W. Bush, who struck me as a smart aleck. On one occasion, I asked the elder Bush's oldest son about his father's schedule the next day; having the information would make coverage planning easier. "If I told you I'd have to kill you," he said. I thought it was a sophomoric comment from a man in his 40s. My daughter Becky disliked the younger Bush because he unjustly accused her of feeding the family pooch a hot dog at a picnic for the press at their Walker's Point estate. Becky was a Miss Goodie Two-Shoes. She'd never dream of doing any such thing. No-one was more surprised than I was when George W. became governor of Texas and then 43d president of the United States.

On the final day of Bush senior's 1992 reelection campaign, he spoke at a rally in Glenolden PA, a suburb of Philadelphia; flew to Akron OH for an airport rally, went from there to Louisville and then on to Baton Rouge LA before a windup rally at the Houston Astrodome in his adopted Texas hometown. My Reuters colleague that day, Larry McQuillan, was clearly exhausted. We'd been traveling non-stop for a couple of weeks. Beyond that, this was a day that was going to demand banging out stories quickly – each stop would require a "new top," newsroom jargon for a three or four paragraph update -- and Larry was not the most facile writer. So I told him to take the Air Force One pool while I flew on the press plane and did most of the filing. To keep our bosses happy, I suggested he write a story about the mood in the Bush camp on the eve of the election.

Things at that point did not look good. Bush trailed in the polls and Clinton appeared to be surging. What Larry produced was accurate but probably overwritten: as newsroom critics might put it, he picked his teeth with a sledge-hammer. Larry metaphorically depicted Bush as a punch drunk fighter sagging against the ropes, his knees buckling as he struggled to keep from sinking to the canvas. I first became aware of the story when National Security Adviser Brent Scowcroft approached me at the Baton Rouge rally and asked more in sorrow than anger if such a story was really necessary. Shortly thereafter, another top Bush aide approached me –it was press secretary Marlin Fitzwater if I recall correctly – and asked if I could switch out with Larry on Air Force One. When I asked why, I was told George W. Bush was furious about the story and was storming about the plane, threatening to go back to the press cabin and punch Larry in the face. I declined, saying the president's son's anger wasn't my problem. Imagine how different history might have been if "W" had carried out his threat.

I did take the Air Force One pool when Bush flew back to Washington two days later. It was a somber trip. Even the Air Force One stewards blinked back tears, crusty senior enlisted men though they were. The Bush family was much loved by the people who served them at the White House, the ushers, cooks, custodial staff etc. Why? Because they were unfailingly considerate of others. They would remain at the White House for Thanksgiving and Christmas so members of the vast presidential entourage wouldn't have to be away from their families during the holidays. Once or twice each summer, Bush would gather up a couple of household employees with menial jobs and take them to a baseball game with him. Everyone around "41" and Mrs. Bush had a story about some sort of kindness.

Bush's fall from political grace is still hard to fathom. At the end of the 1991 Gulf war, his job approval rating was stratospheric. Had he spent some of the political capital he enjoyed then, leading the country on some bold domestic initiative, maybe he might have generated the kind of public enthusiasm he needed to win reelection. Hubert Humphrey used to speak of the need to give the American people "the lift of a driving dream." The national atmosphere was electric in the immediate post-Gulf war period: stores and shops in my neighborhood were decked out in red, white and blue bunting, and the same was true throughout the country.

Former British Prime Minister Margaret Thatcher visited Washington during this time, and in an interview I conducted with her heaped praise on the United States and its citizens. "Just listen to you," I teased. "If King George III could hear you, he'd be turning over in his grave." The Iron Lady would have none of it. Waving off the very idea that Britain and its onetime colony were ever estranged, she said in her distinctive, plummy tone: "Oh, he wouldn't mind at all. All that (the differences that led to the American Revolution) was a long time ago."

Lest I seem bent on hero worship in my treatment of Bush, I should note that he, like most politicians I've known, had a political split personality. He governed poetically, but his electioneering often demeaned him. During the 1988 presidential campaign, he castigated Democratic opponent Michael Dukakis as "a card carrying liberal," espousing the right wing canard that to be a liberal is to be un-American. In truth, he and Dukakis were on the same page on most important issues of the day. He sent a coded message to racists that he was on their side with controversial campaign commercial that suggested Dukakis enabled African-American convict Willy Horton to rape and murder a white woman. (To be fair, the ad was aired by a political group supposedly independent of the Bush campaign. But it was the kind of wink-and-nod disassociation all too common in American politics.) Bush also played a pseudo-patriotic card by promising to push for a constitutional amendment making it a crime to burn or otherwise misuse the American flag. This was in response to a U.S. Supreme Court ruling that flag burning, a tactic sometimes used by protestors to attract attention but hardly a national problem, was a protected form of free speech.

None of this reflected the real Bush but he went along with it. His efforts to later disassociate himself from the political hardball played on his behalf embittered some of his underlings. Republican campaign strategist Mark Goodin told me the Bushes regarded folks like him as household help: there to do the dirty work but not part of the same social group.

A few months after Bush entered, I saw firsthand the hypocrisy involved in one of his campaign issues. I was interviewing William Kristol, then Vice President Dan Quayle's chief of staff, subsequently a prominent conservative commentator, in Kristol's office when Quayle called him. As I sat there dumbfounded, Kristol briefed his boss on that morning's White House senior staff meeting. The meeting had turned into a 50th birthday party for White House chief of staff John Sununu, he said, highlighted by the antics of budget director Dick Darman who mischievously dropped trousers, revealing his American flag underpants. "That was all off the record, of course," Kristol told me as he finished the call. Too quickly, I replied, "Of course."

I instantly regretted what I'd done. Under the unwritten ground rules in effect at the time, there was no such thing as "Off the record" after the fact. I knew that, and Kristol knew that. Still, I'd given my word. I wrestled with my conscience for a good part of the day and finally decided I'd try to get the story independently of the overheard conversation, albeit knowing beforehand exactly what I was looking for.

My stratagem worked and I filed a story. But I included a message to the editors saying I needed to discuss it with Reuters Washington Bureau Chief Rodney Pinder before the story was sent out to clients. When he and I spoke, he chastised me for my misguided promise to Kristol but was prepared to go ahead and release my scoop. When I warned him of the likely consequence, however -- White House retaliation, subtle or overt, intended to punish Reuters economically, he had second thoughts and killed the story. Such are the ways of journalism's sausage-making.

Like most of America's one-term vice presidents, the name Dan Quayle is not a household word nowadays. As Bush's understudy, he was seen as a lightweight, a characterization that was oversimplified and unfair. Quayle himself was partly to blame for his poor public image; he exemplified how, in a television-driven age, first impressions are hard to shake. Bush stunned the political world when he chose the junior Indiana senator as his running mate at the Republican Convention in New Orleans in 1988, and Quayle didn't help himself by hopping around like an excited puppy during his introduction to a national audience.

Bush announced his choice of a running mate aboard a Mississippi paddle-wheeler, the Nachez, before the start of the 1988 Republican Convention in New Orleans. Quayle had trouble getting there: his car got stuck in traffic. Once there, he literally jumped with joy at the prospect of running for national office. "Let's go get them! All right! You got it?" he shouted to the crowd of party activists invited to the event.

Quayle's inauspicious debut worsened when the first round of national news stories about him played up the fact that he'd served in the National Guard during the Vietnam War. The Guard was then widely seen as a haven for young men with political connections who wished to avoid fighting in Vietnam. The issue triggered a media feeding frenzy at Quayle's first post-convention appearance that I felt reflected badly on many of my colleagues. A photograph in one of the news magazines showed the boyish-looking Quayle surrounded by a crowd of aggressive journalists at a campaign rally in his hometown of Huntington, Indiana. He looked like a newborn lamb being attacked by wolves.

It was one of the first battles of a culture war that still smoldered three decades later. Quayle exemplified a Vietnam-era generational cleavage that writer Myra MacPherson aptly described in a Washington Post article.

"For the first time, it was chic and righteous in influential circles not to go to war. Approximately 60 percent of draft-age males who did not serve took positive steps to avoid it, through legal and illegal means. Millions clung to student deferments. Doctors willingly wrote letters attesting to enough physical and psychological problems as to suggest a whole generation of weak, halt and lame. Although Republicans defensively infer that criticism of Quayle's actions amounts to a criticism of the patriotism of Guardsmen, the Guard of Quayle's youth was a privileged sanctuary. By the time Quayle joined, (President) Lyndon Johnson, determined not to incur the wrath of the privileged, had virtually made certain that Guardsmen would not be called up," MacPherson said.

Because of my deployment to Korea, the Army waived the requirement that after active duty I spend six years in the Reserves. I was subject to call-up only to meet the needs of the service. So I spent two weeks as a filler in a National Guard unit in 1968. Members of the lily-white unit clearly had friends in high places and were there to avoid the real military.

Nevertheless, I thought it ironic that many of Quayle's news media critics hadn't served either. But the controversy set the tone for his four years in office. Quayle became a lightning rod; missteps that would have been quickly forgotten if they befell others, such as Quayle's misspelling of "potato," became his trademark. I viewed Quayle as a decent, affable guy, not an intellectual giant but not the dummy he was seen as either. Some of Bush's advisors saw him as a political liability and wanted him dumped from the Republican ticket in 1992. But Bush, ever the loyalist, would have none of that.

I traveled Chile with Quayle to for the inauguration of Patrico Aylwin as that country's president in 1990. Alywin was Chile's first democratically elected leader after 17 years of military dictatorship under General Augusto Pinochet. Before the inauguration, Quayle paid a courtesy call on Pinochet at his home in a posh residential section of Santiago. As the two met, about a dozen well-dressed women, presumably Pinochet's neighbors, gathered outside and started chanting in Spanish. We thought it was some sort of welcome until a Spanish speaker told us what they were saying. "Hey Gringos, listen up: get the fuck outa here!" was how the chant went.

I stayed in touch with President Bush senior when he returned to private life and saw him on numerous occasions. In a 1993 Washingtonian magazine interview, he called me a friend, a distinction I'll always value. I'll always remember his call after Lynn died. Another fond memory is a visit my second wife Becky and I had with him and Mrs. Bush several months before we married. I told the former president I was thinking of proposing and said I needed a character reference. He said Becky should "go for it." But she was deep in conversation with Mrs. Bush and missed the recommendation. When I asked her to be my wife a week or so later, fortunately she said yes. We were married in Charleston in 2016.

Through the years, Bush occasionally corresponded with me. In a handwritten note dated 3-25-93 — a little over two months after he left office, he thanked me for a message I'd sent wishing him and Mrs. Bush much happiness in private life:

Dear Gene,

    To say I was touched by your kind & caring note of
March 21 would be a gross Understatement. There's a lot
about Washington I don't miss; but I do miss The guys your
letter describes: the USSS, the people in the White House; and
I miss the decent and kind and honorable ones in the press.
That's where you come in. Many, many thanks. We're going
to be all right.

Sincerely, George Bush

I got another note after my son Sean graduated from Colby College
in Maine. Bush was the commencement speaker; his nephew Billy, who
later gained notoriety as the interlocutor in a recording that confirmed
Donald Trump's contempt for women, was in the graduating class.
Lynn and the kids and I saw the former president briefly after the
ceremony. He posed for a picture with Sean and promised to spend
some time with us at the graduation luncheon. That never happened.
Lynn and the kids had to catch a flight out of Portland so we left
before the luncheon began. It was just as well. A few weeks later, I
got a handwritten note from Walker's Point, Bush's seaside estate in
Kennebunkport:

Dear Gene,

    I had only one regret about the Colby graduation and that
was I never got to visit with you and your son. I thought I'd see
you at lunch but we were whisked away to some inner sanctum.
Thanks for the note.

Warm regards,
George Bush
6-4-94

Perhaps my favorite note from Bush is one I received after I left
Reuters to become one of the founding editors of a news website
called *Stateline*, which was funded by the Pew Charitable Trusts
and focused on state government, a sadly neglected story in the
television age. I wrote Bush telling him of my career move. This was
his response:

Dear Gene,

Your July 7 (note) card was just great. Good luck at Pew Foundation. You're a good man and everyone knows it!

GB

I later learned the highest praise a member of Yale University's secret society Skull & Bones can bestow on someone is to call them "a good man." Bush was a Bonesman. I cherish the accolade.

I'll also always cherish his call about Lynn. Bush asked me what happened and then listened patiently as I told him at length about all her good works. We talked some about Maine. He told me a lot of the grandkids were there, creating a lot of commotion. That was all. I found it very comforting. It was very much in character for George Bush.

Chapter Five
The Comeback Kid

___

ILL CLINTON WAS easily the most intellectually and politically gifted of the presidents I covered. He seemed to know even the most minor details of government policies on almost every major issue. He was keenly aware of what was happening throughout the country and around the world. Once, a minute or so into a State of the Union Address to Congress, he realized his staff had loaded the wrong version of his speech into the Teleprompter. So he extemporized, never missing a beat. Neither his live audience nor the millions watching on television were any the wiser. He complemented this genius with a winning personality. Clinton could charm a snake out of a tree.

Though I admired these gifts and shared many of his political convictions, I didn't care much for the man. With some notable exceptions such as Mike McCurry and Leon Panetta, I disliked his staff even more. I thought them self-important and second rate. Clinton and his team were openly disrespectful of what I regarded as basic good manners, such as dressing appropriately instead of wearing jeans in the Oval Office as many White House aides often did, being deferential to elders and showing up on time. I thought they reduced presidential campaigning to the lowest common denominator (before Donald Trump) by calling their campaign nerve center "The War Room" and elevating the importance of television gasbags like Larry King and Arsenio Hall. I found Clinton himself long-winded and undisciplined. He was chronically late and couldn't seem to make cut-and-dried decisions.

The disdain was apparently mutual. Eight months after Clinton's inauguration, *Vanity Fair* published an article by Jacob Weisberg, a writer known to be friendly toward him, titled "Clinton vs. the White House press corps." It described me as a "mastodon," a long-extinct prehistoric animal. The article also said that after Clinton stumbled in his first weeks in office, I helped him recover his footing with journalists because of the necktie I wore to his first prime time news conference.

"When (Clinton) called on Gene Gibbons of Reuters, one of those with whom he has had testy relations, he complimented Gibbons on the Mickey Mouse necktie he was wearing. 'I'm sorry. That's a great tie. I just lost it for a moment. I wish the American people could see that tie," the magazine article quoted him as saying. *"After the questions ended and Clinton left the room, (White House press secretary Dee Dee) Myers got the tie from Gibbons. Clinton returned wearing it, to be photographed with the former owner. The next day Mickey Mouse ties sold out from the three- for- $10 vendors on K Street near the White House."*

I was deeply embarrassed. I still cling to the old-fashioned notion that reporters should never become part of the story, and I failed to uphold that standard – my necktie was the most talked-about part of the news conference.

What *Vanity Fair* reported is not exactly what happened, though. When Clinton made a fuss over the tie, I responded with a wisecrack. "Well, Mr. President," I said. "Mickey Mouse is what some people think the White House Press Corps is all about." I was using the term in its military slang sense of "stupid" or "senseless." As soon as I uttered the words, I sensed I'd made a mistake. Mouthing off to the president of the United States on national television is not a good career move.

When the news conference ended, I sought out Myers and asked her to give my tie to the president. I meant the gesture as a peace offering, to show I meant no disrespect. Canny political operative that he was, Clinton instantly saw an opening. Senate Republican leader Bob Dole was at that moment on all the networks responding to Clinton's news conference comments. When Clinton returned to the East Room wearing my tie, the networks cut away from Dole and put him back on the air, letting him steal the show politically.

A few weeks after that news conference, the arrogance then pervading the Clinton White House led to a scandal that reverberated throughout the entire eight years of Clinton's presidency. It was a trivial matter to the rest of the country and largely unknown to the rest of the world. But the firing of the White House Travel Office Staff arguably was a serious abuse of presidential power that probably contributed to the suicide of White House lawyer Vince Foster and fueled a widespread belief that the Clintons would crush anyone who got in their way.

I'm not sure the president himself was initially involved. Mrs. Clinton's role remains a mystery. On May 19, 1993 – ironically, Clinton's 100th day in office – my White House press corps colleagues and I were summoned to a briefing at which it was announced that the White House Travel Office was being reorganized and its seven employees terminated. If memory serves, White House Press Secretary Dee Dee Myers conducted the briefing, assisted by White House Administration Director David Watkins. The move was initially described as a good government initiative. The Clinton White House had a flashy name for it: Reinventing Government, or REGO. I believe Myers or Watkins also mentioned that an outside audit had turned up financial irregularities.

The White House announcement sparked an immediate outcry in the press room. White House Travel Office Director Billy Dale and his staff were friends. They'd handled press travel arrangements for years and were all known to us as honest, decent people. We thought they were being shabbily treated. All were retired military enlisted men. They served at the pleasure of the president and thus could be thanked for their service and told to find employment elsewhere. My press corps colleagues and I felt it was grossly unjust to imply they had somehow done wrong, which would make it hard for them to get new jobs.

We also suspected the Clintonites simply didn't understand the White House culture. Yes, there was a travel office slush fund. But it wasn't government money; it came from the news organizations that covered the White House. Our employers paid for airline charters, lodging and other costs of having us on presidential trips. The slush fund was for incidentals: tipping hotel baggage handlers, bribing customs officials and others who could expedite or delay our movements in foreign countries and paying for other essential if unpleasant aspects of group travel. There was also another element: United Press International was bankrupt, and other news organizations, for sentimental as well as practical reasons, were quietly chipping in to keep UPI's redoubtable Helen Thomas and her colleagues on the road.

A day or two after the controversy erupted, I obtained a copy of an explosive White House memo. Written by Catherine Cornelius, a Clinton cousin who was a low-level presidential aide, it undercut the publicly-stated explanation for the travel office staff's dismissal. The Cornelius memo said Dale and his staff were "too close to the press" and that the jobs they held were valuable political plums. It also indicated some of the president's Arkansas friends could benefit financially from travel office business. Cornelius herself wanted to become travel office director.

The memo was dated February, 1993 – well before the "reorganization" occurred. My sources also gave a copy of the memo to CNN producer Wendy Walker, who passed it on to Wolf Blitzer, an affable man whose incredible gift of gab compensates for an enormous brainpower deficit. On our way to confront White House Communications Director George Stephanopoulos with the document, Wolf turned to me anxiously and asked: "They couldn't accuse us of stealing this, could they?" I assured him that if the Clinton White House was that stupid, we'd have an even better story than what we already had.

I did most of the talking in the meeting. Stephanopoulos confirmed the memo was authentic but insisted it was pure coincidence that what Cornelius urged in February transpired -- for very different reasons, according to the White House - in May. I assured him I'd quote his explanation word for word, in the second paragraph of my story. But my lede was certain to be embarrassing. At one point, I warned him that Clinton's team should be very careful about using the awesome police powers of government to go after people for political reasons. It wasn't really my place to do that. But it worried me then and it worries me now. Our system of government is a fragile thing. If its powers are misused, it can make life hell on Earth for any of us.

Reuters and CNN simultaneously broke the travel office story at 11 AM the next day. It immediately ignited a political firestorm. I found the reaction of my colleagues interesting. Brit Hume, then White House correspondent for ABC News, begged me to give him the memo so he could match the story. So did the Wall Street Journal's White House correspondent, and others. I thought the most professional response came from my toughest competitor, Associated Press White House Correspondent Terence Hunt. Acknowledging his respect for my scoop, he simply said: "Clean kill, Gibbons."

The White House response was bewildering. After several postponements of the daily news briefing, always a sign the president's team is scrambling to contain a crisis, Stephanopoulos released the Cornelius memo to everyone and announced that the FBI would investigate travel office operations. So much for my warning about misusing police power. Therein lay the seeds, I'm convinced, of doubts about President and Mrs. Clinton's belief in fair play that cling to them to this day.

My sources told me the FBI investigation was unwarranted and that there was a lot of internal resistance within the bureau. To my undying regret, I didn't pursue the story as aggressively as I should have. Why? Because I knew an FBI power struggle was underway and I feared becoming a pawn in the game. FBI Director William Sessions was nearing the end of his term and hoped to be reappointed. Some of his enemies in the bureau wanted to prevent that. They told me Sessions was doing what the White House wanted to curry favor even though there was no grounds for an investigation. Other sources insisted travel office mismanagement was real and appeared to involve a degree of corruption. I threw up my hands and backed off to keep from being used by one side or the other. I wish now I hadn't done that. But the episode illustrates how the news media can unwittingly serve someone's agenda when our only goal is to inform the public. It's very much like what often happens in a police state or a military occupation: people inform on their neighbors to gain an advantage or retaliate for a long-forgotten offense.

The investigation ended with Billy Dale's indictment on embezzlement charges. Sam Donaldson of ABC News and Los Angeles Times Washington bureau chief Jack Nelson were among those who testified in his defense. Dale was exonerated after jury deliberations lasting less than 30 minutes; I knew and trusted Dale and regarded his prosecution as a gross miscarriage of justice. The FBI found no grounds for prosecuting any of the six others. But I saw the toll the investigation took. John McSweeney, a decent, hardworking man I liked very much, died of cancer soon after the probe began, arguably hastened to his grave by the pressure. Others became nervous wrecks. All ran up huge legal bills. Ironically, the Clinton administration wound up putting several of the men in other government jobs, and Congress eventually passed legislation reimbursing everyone for their legal expenses.

What came to be known as Travelgate was disturbing. But in my opinion it was an aberration from Clinton's governance. During his eight years in office, Clinton made a serious effort to provide health care for every American, improve race relations in the United States and put the country on a sounder financial footing. In these and other initiatives he encountered some resistance from fellow Democrats and got little or no cooperation from congressional Republicans. The Republican Right was shrill and vicious in its opposition. One of the back-of-the-book ads in a right-wing weekly advertised anti-Clinton bumper stickers that said: IMPEACH HIM, HELL – LET'S GET A ROPE. Knowing the kind of antagonism he faced from a substantial minority of the American people, I can't understand to this day why Clinton empowered the fanatical fringe in this sexually straight-laced country by ignoring the norms of proper behavior.

My biggest personal difference with Clinton was that he hadn't served in the military. Indeed, he maneuvered shamelessly to avoid service (as did many of his contemporaries). Serving one's country in uniform was – and is – a big deal for me even though none of my children served.

From my childhood on there was never any doubt I'd be in uniform. I was embarrassed that my dad didn't served in World War Two. He had a legitimate reason – he suffered from morbidly high blood pressure. – Still he was the only dad in my circle of friends who hadn't been in the Armed Forces. As quaint a notion as it seems today, I saw myself as redeeming the family honor by becoming an infantry officer. While I like to think of my two years in the army as being noble, fortunately for me it was largely an extended adolescence.

Unlike now, military service in the 1960s was a rite of passage, a ticket to be punched on the way to full adulthood. The Cold War raged between the United States and Russia, sparking periodic international crises, and every draft-age young man expected to spend time in uniform. Two years of military training was compulsory at the University of Scranton but I planned from the start to spend a full four years in the ROTC (Reserve Officer Training Corps) program and graduate as an army lieutenant.

I'm glad I did. My two years of active duty expanded my horizons immensely. I came in contact with people very different from me and traveled abroad for the first time. I was trained in the use of firearms and learned small unit tactics on a battlefield. Although a very junior officer, I was held to high standards that reinforced what I'd learned at home: own up to mistakes, always tell the truth and be scrupulously honest financially. I still keep $2,000 in a savings account linked to my checking to assure I'll never bounce a check. If I give someone my word, I feel duty-bound to keep it. I'm convinced the United States would be a lot better off if business and political leaders lived up to the military standard that "Officers Eat Last." While I had no use for gung-ho fellow soldiers (known at the time as "war lovers"), I hoped I'd meet the test bravely if I wound up in combat and my life was on the line.

Today it's taken for granted that nobody but career soldiers defend the country. To me, that's a problem. The armed forces by and large are isolated socially from the rest of the country, which is always dangerous. Think of how many democracies plunged into military dictatorships when some of the generals and colonels decided civilian leaders were heading in the wrong direction: Greece and Chile immediately come to mind. Equally important, I think by not having compulsory national service it contributes to the partisan divisions that might yet doom our country. In a multi-racial and multi-ethnic, pluralistic society such as ours, the armed forces used to be the ultimate melting pot. I didn't know a single black person growing up; there were few African-Americans in Scranton. It wasn't until I was in the army that I first ate a meal with a person of color.

My acceptance of blacks as fully equal didn't occur on an emotional level until I hurt myself on a patrol in South Korea one night and two black soldiers carried me on a stretcher over rocky terrain for more than a mile. My injury wasn't anything heroic. While waiting for darkness before setting off on what amounted to a training exercise, I was throwing a football around with some of my troops. Jumping to catch a pass, I landed the wrong way and broke my ankle. The stretcher bearers went out of their way to avoid jostling me, knowing every bump would be painful. By the time I got to a military hospital, I literally loved those guys. Today few Americans enjoy the bonding that the common experience of soldiering brings. I believe it helps explain why our country is so divided.

I spent 13 months of my two years as a soldier in South Korea. Along with Berlin, it was a tense frontline in the Cold War, a potential flashpoint for World War Three. Although the country was under the dictatorial rule of General Park Chung-hee, a leader not quite as despotic as North Korea's Kim Il Sung, it was "Freedom's Frontier" to the American people and we who served there. I met Park a few weeks before I went to Korea. He was in Washington for a state visit with President Lyndon B. Johnson and spoke a National Press Club luncheon. John Cosgrove, a relative who helped me greatly early in my career, arranged for me to attend the luncheon and introduced me to the general at a VIP reception beforehand.

After a mind-numbing flight from Travis Air Force Base California on a chartered commercial jet, I arrived in Seoul and plunged into another world with strange sights, smells and cacophonous noise. I can still picture my first glimpse of Asia from an army bus inching out of Kimpo Airport on a bumpy dirt road amid military trucks, jeeps and crowds of people. Old papasans with wispy white beards and black stovepipe hats. Plump mamasans, cloth-covered bundles atop their heads. South Korean soldiers on foot, alone and in groups, unarmed and clearly off-duty. Hordes of laughing and crying children. Colorfully dressed *josans*, eager for business. (It was quickly apparent who the working women were.)

After a couple of days at a dusty, dingy complex of wooden barracks and one-story buildings known as the "repple-depple" – army-speak for Replacement Depot -- I was assigned to Second Battalion of the 7th Cavalry, an outfit with a romantic if ignominious past: under the command of Colonel George Custer, it was massacred by native Americans led by Sitting Bull in the Battle of Little Bighorn in what was then Montana Territory.

Soldiers in the Second of the Seventh greeted each other with the battle cry "Garry Owen," an Irish marching tune dating to Custer's time. The shoulder patch of our parent outfit, the 1st Cavalry Division, was (and is) distinctive: a black horsehead and diagonal line on a yellow background. Soldiers in other units liked to taunt us that "the horse is the horse that's never been rode, the line is the line that's never been crossed -- and yellow is the reason why." I wore that patch only briefly -- during my stay in Korea, we were re-designated as the 2nd Infantry Division. The 1st Cavalry colors were assigned to an outfit then based at Fort Benning GA before it deployed to Vietnam and became one of the best-known outfits there.

I was stationed about 30 miles north of Seoul near the DMZ, a 150-mile long no-man's- land separating South Korea and the communist North. There were no paved roads in the barren, land-mine studded countryside. Indeed, there was little or no vegetation, just yellowish dirt. Villages in the region consisted of primitive tin-roofed huts alongside roadside ditches that doubled as sewers. In the summertime, small unpotty-trained children played in the roads, naked from the waist down, dodging a constant stream of traffic.

Every few miles, there was an army outpost surrounded by barbed wire enclosing a cluster of Quonset Huts – "hooches" in military parlance. The cantonments bristled with tanks, artillery pieces and other weapons. Seoul was a metropolis but a primitive one. The capital city boasted few wide boulevards lined mostly with ramshackle buildings. Only two four star hotels catered to visitors, the Bando and the Chosun. Many GIs preferred the Oriental Hotel, the home of a popular massage parlor. Eighth Army headquarters in an area called Yongsan was the most modern installation in the city. Now an office, commercial and residential center, Yeongdeungpo in the southwest section of Seoul was in my time the Red Light District. A two lane road known as MSR (Main Supply Road) One ran north from the city to the DMZ, passing a Korean National Police checkpoint where vehicles were required to switch to blackout drive at night.

The two Koreas then were in the thirteenth year of a shaky truce and the Vietnam War was heating up in Southeast Asia, so there were scary moments when wailing sirens signaled an alert. That warbling sound caused instant chills and put us a state of readiness known as DEFCON (Defense Condition) 2 -- one step short of preparing to launch or repel an attack. We picked up our weapons and ammunition, formed up into companies and headed out to defensive positions known as the MB (Main Battle Position). There were few alerts while I was in South Korea for some reason. Things changed soon after I left: there was heightened tension for years following the North Korean seizure of a U.S Navy spy ship, the U.S.S. Pueblo, and the capture of its 83 crewmen in 1968. The crew was released 11 months later. The ship is still in North Korea, where it has become a showplace of "imperialist wickedness."

That incident was followed by the North Korean downing of a U.S. Navy reconnaissance plane over the Sea of Japan in 1969. Thirty-one Americans died, the greatest single loss of aircrew during the Cold War. Six years later two U.S. Army officers – CAPT Arthur Bonifas and First Lieutenant Mark Barrett – were brutally murdered by axe-wielding North Korean soldiers in the truce village of Panmunjom. The United

States and South Korea responded with a massive show of force and the world held its breath, fearing another outbreak of the Korean War.

Every few nights, we went out on patrol, always with the same gung ho mission: kill or capture communist infiltrators. None ever turned up during operations I led. We'd typically go by truck to a staging area, establish a base camp and fan out from there to set up ambush positions along the south bank of the Imjun River. Lying prone in the dark in an abandoned rice paddy waiting for bad guys, home seemingly a million miles away, every shadow seemed menacing at first. But after an hour it was hard to stay awake.

Once in a while, we heard the sound of gunfire along or near the DMZ, but I was never even close to a firefight. I could often hear the enemy though: giant loudspeakers on the North Korean side of the DMZ blared incessant propaganda about the wonders of socialism and issued blood-curdling threats sometimes directed at American soldiers by name.

U.S. and South Korean forces were greatly outnumbered by the tiny troops in brown uniforms we occasionally saw far off in the distance. But we had an ace in the hole – nuclear-tipped rockets and artillery shells deployed far forward enough that if the North Koreans attacked, we would either use this weaponry or lose it. Many armchair generals in Washington undoubtedly would have been dumbstruck and terrified had they known about the nuclear hair-trigger that existed in such a tinderbox. I found it comforting because it gave me and my comrades a fighting chance if the North Korean army attacked. When Jimmy Carter became president 10 years later, he ordered the nukes removed.

The semi-combat footing we were on notwithstanding, being an army lieutenant far from home was almost pleasant. Yes, there was training. Not as much of it as I'd expected. In our off-duty hours, my comrades and I did just what you'd expect of young men with time on their hands: a lot of drinking and hell-raising. Beer was two bucks a case and getting laid was a cinch: Korean women on the make, called "mooses" in GI lingo (a shorthand version of the Korean word for "little sister") were hard to avoid, not that many G.I.s tried.

Some of the camp followers were prostitutes; some wanted to marry a soldier and make their way to the U.S. good life; some merely wanted access to the attractive array of merchandise available cheap at the Post Exchange. Fraternizing with women "from the vill" – the shantytowns outside the fence of each of our bases -- was only for enlisted men. For the officers there were two popular, quasi-sanctioned brothels in Seoul: the Ranch House and the Green Door. The going rate to spend the night with a "josan" was $10.

South Korea in the 1960s was the Wild West and we were the cowboys; subsistence-level economic conditions existing there then gave GIs enormous purchasing power and allowed us to buy almost anything we wanted. A popular politically incorrect barracks ditty captured the anything goes, give-a-shit bravado we faked: "When the ice is on the rice along the Imjun, and Joe Chink comes slipping softly through the snow; You can bet your ass I will not be with you. I'll be shacked up with my moose in Yonju-gol."

The 50,000 U.S. troops in South Korea in my time weren't an occupying army. We were there ostensibly to protect the populace from their communist neighbors and help the country rebuild. But a casual racism and the testosterone-charged attitude almost endemic among heavily armed young men in their late teens and early twenties was ever present in our dealings with the people. We routinely referred to our allies as "Gooks" or "Slopes" or "Dinks" and treated them brutally on occasion.

One incident I was involved in of has haunted me all my life. Several of us were returning to our compound late one night after a beer-soaked evening of drinking and playing pool with officers of a neighboring battalion when we overtook a Korean man bicycling along the road. Piled high fore and aft on his bike were hundreds of beer cans. It was amazing how artfully the beer cans were stacked and how the man maintained his balance. This was a not uncommon sight in Korea. Lots of people made a living transforming our trash into cigarette lighters and other souvenirs. As our jeep came abreast of the man, one of my comrades jammed a pool cue into the spokes of the bike, sending the man flying as his beer cans spilled all over. We laughed and laughed as we went on our way. It was racist and cruel.

There were other moments of compassion and kindness. My uncle John Cotter told me that during World War Two, he'd quickly become hardened to the suffering of civilian adults but could never ignore the children. So it was when we were in the field. Whenever the chow lines opened, crowds of villagers would gather around, hoping for the scrapings from our mess kits. It was always the kids who got them. Our battalion supported a nearby orphanage with food, medicine and money and many of the troops went there often to teach English and play with the kids. Many troops also went home with Korean brides, establishing a lifelong kinship with the country. But I've always regarded the bicycle incident as a sobering reminder of how young people in uniform too often behave when deployed in foreign lands. How I wish our political leaders would take a lesson from it before they casually propose to put "boots on the ground" somewhere. But since few politicians know what it's like to serve these days, I probably wish in vain.

I spent just six months as a platoon leader near the DMZ. Truth be told, I wasn't very good at the job. The occasional alerts always scared hell out of me and I'm afraid my nerves showed, when I should have been showing self-confidence and a can-do spirit to the troops. My next job was serving as assistant public affairs officer at division headquarters. In that role I helped put out a weekly newspaper for the troops and dealt with press inquiries, which usually arose when a village was placed off-limits because of unacceptable venereal disease rates. These actions would always prompt howls of outrage from Korean newspapers because it was an economic blow for the local populace.

There were some comic moments during my tour of duty on the frontlines. I was battalion duty officer one night, sort of an after-hours caretaker, when a coded message from Eighth Army headquarters arrived. This was serious business. Eighth Army was the supreme command in South Korea. But we had only one officer trained to handle coded messages and it took me 20 minutes to find him. It too him another 20 minutes to do the decoding. The message said two North Korean infiltrators had been spotted at such and such coordinates and ordered us to intercept them. By the time we had this order in hand the infiltrators were undoubtedly halfway to Seoul.

Another night I was hobbling around on crutches recovering from a broken ankle, when the alert sirens went off. I pleaded to go to the trench line, crutches and all. Our fighting positions were almost a mile to the rear of our compound; if I stayed where I was and a North Korean attack was coming, I'd likely be one of the first Americans captured or killed. My pleas were fruitless. The battalion commander, who probably knew the alert was only a drill, put me in charge of compound security. I armed myself with a couple of weapons and lots of ammunition and started hobbling toward the headquarters building. It took me awhile to get there because the weight of all the ammo I had in my pockets kept pulling my pants down. By the time I arrived, the alert was over. It was false alarm.

My thirteen month tour in Korea included one unusual sidelight – a week with an Air Force fighter-bomber squadron at Osan Air Force Base south of Seoul. During that familiarization assignment, I got the ride of my life in the backseat of a T-33 jet trainer flown by a Korean pilot. It was exhilarating. As we taxied out to the runway, the pilot told me in crisp, clear English that if I became airsick, I should tell him immediately.

"I'll get down to 10,000 feet and fly straight and level. Take off your oxygen mask, remove your helmet and throw up in it. Under no circumstances are you to get vomit on my airplane, Lieutenant," he said. What followed was sheer ecstasy, one of the most exciting times of my life. For more than an hour, we danced on the wind, swooping, soaring, twisting and turning. Everything happened so fast I had no chance to get frightened.

Years later, I had a chance to fly in the backseat of a carrier-based Navy F-14 Tomcat. An admiral then the Navy's chief public information officer arranged for me to spend two days at Oceana Naval Air Station near Virginia Beach and get a taste of one of the hottest fighter planes in the world. Before I could fly however, I had to undergo a few hours of training. This included showing I could extricate myself from a Dilbert Dunker, which would have involved calmly getting myself out of an upside down mockup cockpit several feet underwater and swimming to the surface. All my life I've had a fear of the water. This frightened me. I chickened out, and have regretted it ever since.

Being sent to South Korea turned out to be a godsend. It was the first time I was ever that far away from home; the first time I ever left Scranton for any extended period, in fact, was when I was in the army. So it expanded my horizons. It also exposed me to another country and culture, creating a thirst for foreign travel that has lasted ever since. More importantly, it might have prolonged my life. The Vietnam War was still a brushfire when I began active duty. Some American military advisors were serving in the war zone but that was about it. In the summer of 1965, just after I joined my battalion close to the DMZ, President Lyndon Johnson massively escalated the war and U.S. troops began pouring into Southeast Asia. Two of my friends died there, people I knew from Fort Benning's Infantry School. Tom Grant was one of the sharpest soldiers I ever encountered. Jim Gardner wanted to see action. Their names are now chiseled on the Vietnam Wall. As an infantry platoon leader, I might have shared their fate.

I went back to South Korea on presidential trips with Reagan, Bush and Clinton. My first return amazed me. Gone was the war-ravaged, ramshackle country I'd known. In the place of tin-roofed shacks were shiny glass and chromium high rise buildings. The streets were crowded with well-stocked shops and well-dressed people. Instead of defending an 18-mile-wide invasion route into South Korea known as "The Bowling Alley," one company of U.S. troops was stationed on the DMZ. All the rest were South Korean.

On each subsequent visit, the changes were even more dramatic. But when Clinton went, there was a vivid reminder of how much the United States had also changed. Using a pair of binoculars, he looked out at enemy positions on the northern side of the DMZ but neglected to remove the lens caps – a mistake no-one with any military experience would make.

To his credit, Clinton did go out to the Bridge of No Return, a tiny one lane bridge a few hundred yards northwest of the truce village of Panmunjom. That probably made him the first president since Abraham Lincoln to set foot on a military frontline. The Bridge of No Return became famous at the time of the Korean War armistice in 1953 when photographs of returning U.S. and allied prisoners of war pouring across it were on newspaper front pages for days.

I also have another sense of it. As the division's assistant public information officer, one of my duties one day was escorting a television correspondent and his crew to the bridge to film a report. I was unarmed and worried about the assignment – North Korean troops stationed in and around Panmunjom were notorious for creating provocative incidents. This was made to order for one. Nevertheless, I took the TV guy and his crew out to the bridge and stood by nervously as he positioned himself less than 50 yards away from a North Korean sentry post. "IS THAT A GUN???" he asked dramatically as the camera rolled. "No, it's binoculars. They're as interested in looking at us as we are at them," he went on in a slightly less anxious tone. The man continued his narrative and finally signed off. But he wasn't satisfied with his performance. Take after take followed. I got more and more jumpy. By the time we finished I was a nervous wreck.

Fortunately for us the North Koreans apparently weren't up to making mischief that day.

Clinton's election as president marked the end of the post-World War Two era when military service was almost a prerequisite for national leadership. Nowhere was this more evident than at the big fancy-dress Washington galas, such as the annual dinner of the White House Correspondents' Association. Until the 1990s, it was traditional for the U.S. Marine Band to play a medley of military service marches at these events As each service's march was played, veterans of that service would rise and stand at attention. When the music ended, there'd be prolonged applause, after which the nation's political and media elite would resume socializing, warmed by the afterglow of shared remembrance of their time in the armed forces.

One year my guest at the correspondent's dinner was General Colin Powell, then Chairman of the military Joint Chiefs of Staff. As the band played, there I was, a former Army lieutenant with two years of peacetime service to my credit, being hailed as a veteran alongside a battle-tested four star general resplendent in full dress uniform. It was, and is, a moment I savor.

Starting in the '90s, fewer and fewer civilians stood. Many who attained prominence, people like Clinton, Newt Gingrich, Rush Limbaugh and Donald Trump, dodged the draft during the Vietnam War. Clinton had a series of student deferments. Gingrich married his high school math teacher (and got a divorce as she recovered from cancer surgery). Limbaugh was medically deferred because of a persistent boil on his buttocks. Trump was 4F because of bone spurs. At one glittering gathering of the nation's elite late in Clinton's presidency, not a single person at the head table stood for the service songs – in fact, the band could barely be heard above the din of conversation.

Clinton had a rocky relationship with the military, driven not so much by his lack of service as it was by his "Don't Ask, Don't Tell" policy toward gay people serving in uniform. While he was jogging one day at Fort McNair, an army installation in southeast Washington where a lot of the high-ranking officers stationed at the Pentagon live, I overheard a general in civilian clothes remark to a fellow general, "We oughta hold up a sign saying 'No queers!" They weren't the exceptions. When Clinton visited the aircraft carrier Theodore Roosevelt off the coast of Virginia, there was further evidence of military hostility toward his gay-friendly policy. Out of his sight but in full view of the press, two Marines danced with each other, declaring they were in love.

A 1993 military peacekeeping mission to Somalia that ended badly hurt Clinton further. Nineteen American servicemen died, 73 were wounded and an army helicopter pilot was captured when a raid to capture Somali warlord Mohammed Aidid went badly awry.

To me Clinton's worst failure as commander-in-chief was his clumsy response to terrorist bombings of the U.S, Embassies in Tanzania and Kenya, attacks that killed more than 200 people. He ordered a barrage of cruise missile strikes on terrorist camps in Afghanistan and, inexplicably, a pharmaceutical plant in Sudan. Critics called it life imitating art. Theatres across America were then showing a movie then called "Wag the Dog." It was about a fictional president ordering military operations to divert public attention from a sex scandal. The movie cast a shadow on the missile strikes because the Monica Lewinsky Scandal had just burst into the headlines.

Clinton's adulterous relationship with the 22-year-old White House intern was reckless for many reasons. But there was a little-known sub-plot illustrating the dark undercurrents, generated for the most part by the far right, sweeping through American politics. Lucianne Goldberg, a New York book agent, was figuratively gunning for Clinton. When she learned of Lewinsky's dalliance though Washington friend Linda Tripp whom Lewinsky saw as a kind of big sister, she pounced. She advised her friend on ways to get evidence of the illicit affair and even arranged for a courier service owned by one of her relatives to deliver messages between Lewinsky and the president.

I knew Lucianne Goldberg from way back when as one of the most odious creatures I've ever encountered. During the 1972 presidential campaign, she was a regular on the McGovern press plane, ostensibly a magazine writer. (Sen. George McGovern of South Dakota was Republican president Richard Nixon's challenger). The Watergate Scandal that drove Nixon from office revealed her for what she really was: an informant for the Nixon campaign traveling with McGovern to gather dirt on him. She was also on the lookout for anything that would discredit the news people covering the Democratic presidential nominee. Once, when she was invited to join a group going to see *Deep Throat*, a porno movie then the rage among supposed sophisticates, she said she had to work but asked who was going to the movie. The names were reported to the Nixon campaign. Thankfully I wasn't one of them.

I cannot understand why responsible journalists scoffed at Hillary Clinton's claim that there was "a vast right-wing conspiracy" to destroy her husband and her. To me it was obvious. Goldberg clearly was one of the masterminds. Another was Richard Mellon Scaife, a billionaire crackpot who published the Pittsburgh Tribune-Review, a right-wing newspaper forever critical of Clinton. Ironically, I warned White House Press Secretary Mike McCurry about Goldberg several months before the Monica Lewinsky Scandal broke. He seemed to shrug her off as one of the countless cranks every president encounters.

As I mentioned previously, while at Harvard on a fellowship, I researched and wrote a scholarly paper about how the American far right, financed by a shadowy group of ultra-conservative billionaires, was using the Internet to poison the nation's information bloodstream. I tried to interest news media colleagues in what I'd found but had no takers. I wrote a story about it for *Neiman Reports*, a professional magazine for journalists. Still my findings were ignored by the mainstream media. It's little wonder that misinformation and propaganda are widespread now.

Actually what I found was child's play. We now know that in 2016 Russia helped put Donald Trump in the White House by sowing Facebook, Twitter and other social media with phony material meant to create dissention and division. It was a classic disinformation campaign. Yet the American public still seems to generally dismiss this grave threat to our democracy, viewing it as just more politics as usual.

In *Our Man*, a brilliant book that uses the life of Richard Holbrooke, a brash, abrasive U.S. diplomat, to frame American foreign policy from the Vietnam War onward, writer George Packer writes that the Lewinsky scandal was a much bigger deal than anyone recognized when it broke in 1998 "Imagine a president careless enough to stumble into his enemies' trap and expend his power on a blue dress. Imagine a superpower so confident of perpetual peace and prosperity that it felt able to waste a whole year on Oval Office cocksucking," he wrote.

"Not even Al Qaeda, which blew up two American embassies in East Africa that August, could get our serious attention," Packer said. "Clinton's response, a bunch of Tomahawks, was derided left and right for following the script of DeNiro's *Wag the Dog*."

Clinton's carelessness with his professional life will, I believe, resonate for a generation or more. With his political skills, he might have put the United States on path that rivalled the legacy of Franklin Delano Roosevelt. Instead, he helped pave the way for Trump, whose presidential bid might have been cut short by the disclosure of his perverse sexual antics had the American people not been desensitized by Clinton's behavior.

Monica Lewinsky almost certainly wasn't Clinton's only extracurricular activity. There was a blonde middle age woman with an ambiguous job in the West Wing; the standing joke was that she headed the Office of Presidential Pleasure. Once I saw firsthand the sexual tensions in the Clinton White House. On my last flight on Air Force One, I was invited to ride up front with President and Mrs. Clinton. Clinton put on a show of the multitasking he was famous for, playing gin rummy with White House aide Bruce Lindsay, working a crossword and talking to me – all at the same time. Mrs. Clinton and I reminisced about some of her trips I covered, and she invited me to a 30th birthday for Kelly Craighead, her personal assistant.

The party was at a Martha's Vineyard nightclub called "Hot Tin Roof" owned by songstress Carly Simon. I was uneasy from the moment I arrived. One of the perils of covering the White House is getting too close to the people you're covering and this was way too close for comfort. Clinton, who seldom drank, seemed to be a little tipsy. He and Carly Simon, who was provocatively dressed, seemed to be flirting. The birthday girl was in a corner crying. Mrs. Clinton was nowhere to be seen. I excused myself and left. It was almost too strange to be believed.

Other social events were more rewarding. Take, for example, a White House State Dinner honoring Mary Robinson, the president of Ireland. Clinton called the evening "the largest gathering of Irish-Americans since the last Notre Dame football game." The dinner took place in a gigantic white tent set up on the South Lawn of the White House. To my surprise and delight, I was seated at the head table with Presidents Clinton and Robinson. The other head table guests were Massachusetts Sen. Ted Kennedy, Carolyn Kennedy Schlossberg, the daughter of JFK; the wife of AFl-CIO President John Sweeney and a woman who was an Ohio state legislator. "With the White House gardens ablaze with fairy lights on the trees and the Washington Monument and the Lincoln Memorial visible ... in the balmy evening, it was an unforgettable occasion," *The Irish Times* enthused.

Lynn was seated at another table with New York developer Mort Zuckerman, whom she later confessed bored her to death. I had little conversation with the two presidents: Senator Kennedy and I talked about sailing and the Civil War. Kennedy was a doting uncle. As the evening ended, he told Carolyn to be sure to get her dinner menu signed by the presidents. I was too bashful to request such a souvenir.

There's always a fine line to walk when you socialize with people you're supposed to be holding accountable. I sometimes crossed it. In 1992 I arranged an internship for my son Sean in Vice President Quayle's press office. That wasn't all: Quayle gave Sean a lift back to college aboard Air Force Two. The vice president was traveling to New Hampshire and took my oldest son as far as Manchester, just a short bus ride away from Colby College in Waterville Maine. Looking back, that was clearly a conflict of interest. My only defense is others did the same thing.

A larger problem for folks in my line of work is that is it's hard to be dispassionate about news makers and news sources you know and like. There's a tendency to be too easy or too harsh. In a controversial *New Yorker* magazine article, Janet Malcolm framed the problem facing a true professional. "Every journalist who is not too stupid or full of himself to notice what is going on knows that what he does is morally indefensible," she said. He is a kind of confidence man, preying on people's vanity, ignorance or loneliness, gaining their trust and betraying them without remorse."

Colleagues like David Hoffman of the Washington Post held the view that reporters should never party with people they cover to avoid even the appearance of being compromised. As I saw it, meeting important people in a polite setting was a means of gaining access, of unlocking information. Still, a White House social event was a pretty heady experience.

The first State Dinner Lynn and I attended was hosted by President Bush. It honored Nicaraguan President Violeta Chamorro. State Dinners were then the mother of all social events, a mix-and-mingle with so many notables you wind up name-dropping friends nuts. At a reception before the dinner we made small talk with major league baseball pitcher Dennis

Martinez, who'd just completed a perfect game. Lynn's dinner tablemates included Vice President Dan Quayle and actor Sylvester Stallone.

I was seated with Barbara Carrera, a glamorous Nicaraguan-American movie actress who played the villain in a James Bond movie, and a grouchy Kentucky senator named Mitch McConnell, who went on to become Senate Republican leader. It was truly pinch-me-I'm-dreaming time: men in tuxes and the women in evening gowns enjoying a gourmet meal in the magnificence of the White House State Dining Room, under the gaze of a portrait of Abraham Lincoln. Crooner Johnny Mathis, whose love songs were the theme music of our youthful romances, provided the after-dinner entertainment. Lynn and I were so excited afterwards we didn't sleep that night.

Almost as exciting was taking my beloved Aunt Trudy, whom my brothers and I regarded as our second mother, to a White House Christmas Party. It was Lynn's idea. The two people closest to my aunt – my mother and their Jesuit priest-brother Joe – had recently died. It had been a tough year for her. The Yuletide White House is a study in elegance, its holiday decorations breathtaking. President and Mrs. Clinton couldn't have been kinder when they greeted us in the receiving line. "I know who you are," Mrs. Clinton told my aunt, because I had in fact told the first lady about her.

During the evening, I introduced her to people she'd seen on television or read about. Dancing in the East Room to the music of the U.S. Marine Band, Aunt Trudy told me it was the best evening of her life. It was one of the most rewarding moments of my life.

Another eerier occasion was an evening lecture at the White House by Harvard historian Bernard Bailyn, an expert on early American political life. The Clintons were firm believers in intellectual self-improvement; they regularly attended invitation-only Renaissance Weekend gatherings of influential people held each autumn at Hilton Head SC. For some reason, Lynn wasn't invited to the lecture, just me. It took place a just few days after the Monica Lewinsky Scandal broke, so there was air of tension, a sense of the White House being under siege as Bailyn took the podium. He talked about the rough-and-tumble politics that shaped our country, how what we think of as the gentle good-mannered courtliness of the Founding Fathers was in reality a sharp-elbowed, dog-eat-dog world.

A stand-up buffet dinner followed the talk, and at one point I found myself standing next to Mrs. Clinton. We began talking about the books we were reading. I'd just finished "_The Deep Green Sea_" by novelist Robert Olen Butler, a haunting story about a Vietnam veteran who returns to Vietnam 25 years after the war and falls in love with an orphaned young woman, only to realize she might be his daughter. I started to tell Mrs. Clinton about it, thinking she'd be intrigued. But I quickly backed off, given the prevailing circumstances.

Then came a dilemma: it's considered bad manners to leave a White House social event before the president bids farewell, but the evening was still going strong and was nearing the closing time of the garage where my car was parked. As I tried to discreetly sneak away, Clinton intercepted me and excitedly told me about a new campaign finance reform plan he'd just learned about. He really was (and undoubtedly still is) a policy wonk. Mercifully, he soon moved on to another guest and I was able to sneak out the door and get to my car before the parking garage closed its doors for the night.

*****

While I didn't care much for her husband, I was, and am, a big admirer of Hillary Clinton. Time and again, I saw her use her position to make life better for others. I also enjoyed her wicked sense of humor. I found her to be someone with whom you could talk, someone who would listen to opposing arguments. In my experience, she was anything but the cold hearted bitch she's been portrayed as; she was warm, friendly and human.

Yet she was never excused any error or human frailty. Because she was a strong woman who espoused policies anathema to the Republican right and religious zealots (often one and the same), policies that would empower women and accord the poor preferential treatment, she generated a lot of outright hatred. Like the widespread lack of respect for the courage and decency of President George H.W. Bush, I found Hatred of Hillary hard to understand.

I saw her compassion firsthand on a trip to Romania in 1996. It was six years after the despotic regime of Nicolae Ceausescu came to a violent end, the communist dictator and his wife Elana executed in a hail of machine gun bullets. In the last years of Ceausescu's reign, the country's blood supply became contaminated with the HIV virus, causing thousands to die of AIDS and thousands of HIV positive children left behind. During the trip, Mrs. Clinton visited an orphanage in Bucharest and a little girl of three or four was selected to greet her. Frightened by the hustle and bustle as the first lady's entourage arrived, the little girl became ill and threw up all over herself. Embarrassed orphanage staffers tried to hustle the crying child away. But Mrs. Clinton rushed to her side and hugged her, soiling her own clothes in the process. This at a time when most people blanched at the thought of contact with an AIDS patient's bodily fluids, believing the disease could be transmitted this way. No television cameras recorded the moment. Just a print reporter – me.

In yet another admirable moment, I saw Mrs. Clinton fairy dust the lives of Untouchable Bangladeshi women excited that the "Queen of America" would visit Moishahati, a tiny village about 150 miles from the capital of Dhaka. "Do you have a cow in your house?" one woman shyly asked her, trying to imagine a life that to poor people was one of unimaginable riches.

To me, it was a graphic example of America's "soft power," our ability to give the world's less fortunate peoples a spiritual uplift just by showing we cared about them. I've always believed in that kind of diplomacy, which addresses Thomas Jefferson's plea that Americans show "a decent respect for the opinions of Mankind." Sadly, our nation in recent years has all too often shown a penurious, belligerent face to the world.

On the next-to-last leg of Mrs. Clinton's South Asian trip, I got violently ill for the first and only time in all my years of traveling with the White House. It happened at Chitwan National Park in south central Nepal, a jungle habitat for rhinoceroses, Bengal tigers and other exotic animals.

To get there, we flew aboard a two engine prop plane from the Nepali capitol of Kathmandu to a grassy airstrip near the park and traveled by Land Rover to a nearby river. There we boarded dugout canoes for the river crossing. Waiting on the other side was a herd of elephants to carry us to a jungle resort.

At dinner that night, I suddenly felt like I needed fresh air even though we were eating in a screen-enclosed mess hall. On my way out the door, my legs suddenly felt rubbery and I looked for a place to sit down. The next thing I knew I was regaining consciousness as a White House doctor and Secret Service medic hovered over me. I never found out whether I was sickened by food poisoning or dehydration. By the next morning I was fine. A Secret Service agent on the trip who got sick at the same time wasn't as lucky. He required 13 liters of fluid administered intravenously to get him back on his feet.

On the 22-hour flight home a few days later, I had an extraordinary conversation with Mrs. Clinton, the kind of *tete de tete* that rarely occurs between newsman and newmaker. I awoke from a sound sleep and got up to go to the bathroom. When I came out I found Mrs. Clinton in the galley, looking for saltine crackers to calm a mildly upset stomach. Dressed in a sweat suit and wearing thick eyeglasses, her hair piled up in a bun, she looked downright dowdy, nothing like her public persona. We engaged in polite chit-chat at first but then she shared some of her fears and frustrations. She told me of the physical risks she and her family worried about every day and talked about her impatience with the inaccuracy and frivolousness of much of the news coverage of her.

She shared with me a concern only a mother could have: during our visit to India, her daughter Chelsea, then 15, had been invited to lunch with the prime minister's granddaughter. Not to accept risked offending the Indian leader. But the Secret Service feared the food might make Chelsea ill. Mrs. Clinton decided to gamble: her daughter had lunch with the granddaughter. A diplomatic incident was avoided. Fortunately it all worked out.

Over the years there's been much speculation about the nature of the relationship between Bill and Hillary Clinton. One exchange I was privy to might shed some light. Or maybe not. We were in Istanbul, where Mrs. Clinton met Patriarch Bartholomew, the Greek Orthodox equivalent of the Pope, and convened a gathering of Christian, Jewish and Muslim clerics to try to help dampen the endlessly troublesome religious strife in the region.

Mrs. Clinton's schedule that day also included a boat ride on the Bosporus, after which the entire entourage – her, Chelsea, the first lady's staff, Secret Service bodyguards and traveling press, would go to a restaurant for dinner. I had to file a story. So I begged off the boat ride and went back to the hotel to work, promising to rejoin the group later on.

As luck would have it, I finished filing sooner than I thought I would and went down to the lobby to buy a newspaper. When I got off the elevator, Mrs. Clinton was walking out to her motorcade, heading off to the boat. She urged me to join her, but it took me a full 15 minutes to grab my coat and get out to the street. No matter. Everything was lined up and waiting for me to get my act together and once I climbed aboard a vehicle off we went.

After the boat ride, Mrs. Clinton, her chief of staff Melanne Verveer and I were walking back to the cars when an aide approached with a mobile phone. He said the president was calling from New York. "Tell him I'm busy. I'll call him back later," Mrs. Clinton said. A sign of marital discord? Perhaps. But ask yourself this: what spouse has dropped everything when their partner called to talk to him or her? Maybe Mrs. Clinton wanted more privacy when she and her husband spoke. In this case, it didn't matter why she didn't take the call because I didn't report it. But in so many matters large and small, the news media and a large segment of the American public almost never gave her the benefit of the doubt.

Clinton outmaneuvered his political opponents again and again and arguably did a lot of good for the country. Among other things he was the first president to balance the budget in my adult lifetime. Congressional Republicans gave him little if any help in this and many fellow Democrats went along only grudgingly. He supported and obtained legislative approval of stringent new work requirements for welfare recipients, an achievement that led two senior administration officials to resign in protest. He obtained legislative approval of the North American Free Trade Agreement (NAFTA), an accomplishment that that ironically drove millions of working class voters in the northeast and Midwestern industrial states into Republican ranks. Many of these individuals went for Donald Trump over his wife Hillary in the 2016 presidential race, costing Mrs. Clinton the Electoral College votes that would have boosted her into the White House.

In terms of foreign policy, Clinton's greatest achievements probably were two peace agreements: one in Bosnia, the other in Northern Ireland. He launched a high stakes effort to achieve peace in the Middle East late in his presidency but the effort collapsed and probably only made things worse in the long run.

I accompanied Clinton on a grueling trip to Israel for the funeral of Prime Minister Yitzak Rabin, who was assassinated by a right-wing Jewish extremist in 1995. We didn't spend the night: it was an out and back trip. After the funeral on Jerusalem's Mount Hebron, I walked with several colleagues to the hotel where our press center was located. To my surprise, we were approached several times by young Israelis who told us they disliked their country and wanted to leave. I've since wondered if they sensed something I did not at the time: that Israel was fast becoming a right wing theocracy with enmity verging on hatred for its Arab citizens and Palestinian neighbors.

An iconic photo of Clinton's presidency shows him presiding over a handshake between Rabin and PLO leader Yasser Arafat. The image was made at a White House ceremony in 1993 at which the onetime enemies signed the Oslo Accords, a framework for peace that has never been realized. Clinton said later that getting that handshake was difficult; until a few minutes before the ceremony Rabin adamantly refused to do it. He finally relented when Clinton argued that a signing without a handshake would be terrible optics: the agreement to work for peace would look forced. "All right, I'll do it. But no kissing," Clinton quoted the Israeli leader as saying.

Clinton made 54 international trips to 72 countries as president. I was on many of them. Foreign travel is usually a good way for U.S. presidents to get good press but Clinton was often dogged by scandal. A summit with Russian President Boris Yeltsin four months after he was inaugurated wound up a reminder of Clinton's reputation as a skirt-chaser when word leaked out that he'd met during the parlay with Hollywood's Sharon Stone, an actress known for her sexy roles.

The big news of a trip to Ukraine, Russia, Belarus and Switzerland in 1994 was Clinton's reluctant agreement to the appointment of a special prosecutor to look into questionable land dealings in Arkansas – the Whitewater affair – in which he and his wife were involved. During a trip to France, Netherlands in Britain in 1997, a U.S. federal court ruled that Arkansas state employee Paula Jones could sue him for sexual harassment when he was the state's governor. That suit was the genesis of Clinton's impeachment by the Republican-controlled U.S. House of Representatives in 1998. The Senate, where Democrats were in the majority, voted to acquit him but he wound up being disbarred. Losing one's license is professional death for a lawyer.

Perhaps the most unusual presidential trip I ever made was accompanying the Clintons – Bill, Hillary and Chelsea – to my hometown of Scranton in 1995. It was a trip I at first tried to avoid, showing how jaundiced one becomes if you cover the White House too long. I was at my desk in the press room of the West Wing one day when April Mellody, a White House aide who was also from Scranton, came back to tell me the Clintons planned to travel there for a family baptism. It would be a private visit but a press pool would tag along. When she told me the trip was set for the following Sunday, I replied, "Oh hell, I hate to work on weekends," and let the matter drop.

A few minutes later, Deputy Press Secretary Ginny Terzano was at my desk. "Gibbons, you lazy good-for-nothing. You won't go to your hometown with the President of the United States? We were even planning to have Gibbons Beer on Air Force One," she said. She knew the brand because the press office staff and members of the White House press corps had a beer party several days earlier and I'd brought a six-pac of Gibbons along. Call it bribery but the promise of drinking my grandfather's beer *on the president's plane* talked me into the trip. I arranged for my brother Joe and his family to have their picture taken with the Clintons at the airport arrival ceremony, a boon known in political circles as a "grip 'n grin," making the trip even sweeter.

Joe, his wife Mary Ellen and children Doug and Liz were on the rope line when we arrived. "I'm so embarrassed I nearly didn't come here today," my brother told me. The problem was a story in the local newspaper implying that Joe and the president were bosom buddies. It went on to say Clinton's old pal planned to greet him with a case of Gibbons Beer.

The story had nuggets of truth. My brother brought the beer to the airport with him as a favor to the president's advance team. They'd asked where they could buy it when they called to get the information they needed to clear him and his family for the grip 'n grin. Joe had told a friend about this who told a reporter, who never bother bothered to check with the primary source of the information. Thus the embarrassing story.

Joe was more upset about it than I was. But there was a funny end to the episode on the flight home. When an Air Force steward came around taking drink orders I asked for a Gibbons Beer. I about thought my dad and granddad somewhere in the Great Beyond beaming about the heights the family beer had reached.

When the steward told me the only options were Schlitz or Budweiser, I said I thought a case of Gibbons was also aboard the plane.

"There is, Sir," he replied. "That's the president's beer. We're not serving it to everyone."

My take on the Clinton presidency: enormous opportunity squandered. The man was brilliant, a truly gifted politician. There was so much he could have accomplished beyond the considerable amount he actually did. But he didn't think the standards leaders should live by applied to him and thus gave his enemies, who were numerous and vicious, the ammunition to nearly take him down. Clinton, in my opinion, was too clever by half: he wasn't known as "Slick Willy" for nothing. And I think his extracurricular activities, which were stupid, almost laughable and not ever closely comparable to Donald Trump's antics, helped pave the way for Trump.

Overlooking Korean DMZ. North Korea
in background. (author photo)

1980 Democratic National Convention,
New York City. (author photo)

Lynn Weingarten Gibbons,
July 5, 1947–July 13, 2012 (author photo)

Jimmy Carter's Hometown,
1976. (author photo)

Aboard Reagan Campaign Charter, 1980.
Nancy Reagan in foreground. (author photo)

Mount Saint Helen's Volcano,
1980. (author photo)

1976 Democratic National Convention. With
NH delegate Chris Spirou (author photo)

Interviewing President Reagan,
1983. (author photo)

With President Bush in Oval Office, 1991.
(White House photo, used with permission)

At Walker's Point with "41." Lynn, Jennie
and Jennie's friend. (author photo)

Jogging Timeout on Martha's
Vineyard. (author photo)

Reminiscing with Hillary Clinton
about 1995 India Trip. (White House
photo. Used with permission.)

Flying to Bosnia with songstress Sheryl
Crowe aboard USAF C-17. (author photo)

With President Clinton and NBC's
Brian Williams aboard Air Force
One. (White House photo.)

With Margaret Thatcher and Reuters'
Debbie Zabarenko, 1991. (author photo)

Visiting President and Mrs. Carter,
Plains GA, 2015 (author photo)

At the helm of CS-40 "Winsome."
(author photo)

Visiting President and Mrs. Bush,
Kennebunkport, 2015. (author photo)

Marine One arriving on White House
South Lawn. (author photo)

Reagan Ranch, Santa Barbara
CA (author photo)

Rebecca Turberville Gibbons (author photo)

Chapter Six

Jimmy Who?

PLAINS, GEORGIA, POPULATION 755 or thereabouts, is a geographical flyspeck, a tiny Southern town in the middle of nowhere. Railroad tracks and a two-lane highway designated U.S. Route 280 parallel the town's Main Street. The business district is one block long with eight – count 'em, eight -- one and two story shops lining the sidewalk. Peanut products, old comic books and mementos of the 1950s and '60s seem the only items for sale. Across the highway on one of the side streets is a building that was once a public school. Now it's a museum celebrating the accomplishments of a student who became the town's best known citizen. Across the street is Plains Baptist Church. Though there are other churches in town, this is, or was, the principal place of local worship. Right around the corner is Billy's Gas Station, once owned by one of Plains' most colorful characters. A few blocks west, in a fenced-in compound on Woodland Drive, is the modest middle class home of the 39th President of the United States.

I know Plains intimately. It hasn't changed much since I spent a lot of time there in the mid to late 1970s covering Jimmy Carter. It amazed me then and it amazes me now that this rural, sunbaked south Georgia town could be the wellspring of someone who for a time was the most powerful man on earth.

Carter owed his ascent to a rare alignment of historical forces. America was war weary after the Vietnam War and still recovering from a constitutional crisis brought on by political crimes that drove President

Richard Nixon from office. He was a fresh face, earnest and devoutly religious, with an appealing promise: "I'll never lie to you."

A U.S. Naval Academy graduate turned peanut farmer whose only previous political experience was two terms in the Georgia state senate and one term as governor, Carter was the first president I covered extensively. He wasn't particularly likeable once you got to know him. He spoke almost exclusively about serious matters in a soft Southern drawl, using a vast vocabulary of unusual words to explain what he was trying to say. He was easily angered, and those who stirred his wrath often found themselves fixed with what aides and reporters called "the icy blue-eyed stare."

Carter came from a family unique for its time and place; his mother "Miss Lillian" served in the Peace Corps in India at age 68; his sister Ruth was a Christian evangelist; his sister Gloria rode motorcycles; and his brother Billy prided himself on being a redneck. While there were accomplishments during his presidency, most notably the Panama Canal treaties and the Camp David accords between Egypt and Israel, Carter is remembered today largely as a failure, a man who led the United States during a time of national vexation at home and abroad.

Though he never actually used the word, Carter's best-known presidential address became known as the "malaise" speech. In it he seemed to scold the public for not adjusting better to the trials and tribulations the country was then experiencing. Reading the speech today makes Carter seem prescient, identifying problems that have since grown exponentially. Had many of the goals and policies he pursued become part of the fabric of life – energy conservation, peace and stability in the Middle East, worldwide support of human rights – our country might now be better off. Carter exemplified what "Christians" claim to believe. Love thy neighbor. Look after the poor, the sick, the weak. His repudiation speaks volumes about the hypocrisy of millions of those who profess America's most practiced religion.

I first set foot in Carter's hometown a few days after the 1976 Democratic Convention and, except for a few weeks of home leave and a few weeks traveling with Republican Gerald Ford during the fall presidential campaign, lived there until the day before Carter's inauguration on January 20, 1977. I remember the Democratic convention well. My mother and dad babysat Sean and Jennie, our only children then, and Lynn came along to the political gathering, which took place at New York City's Madison Square Garden.

She'd attended Barnard College and loved Manhattan. I wasn't a big fan. On our last day in the city, Lynn was victimized by a pickpocket, who stole some irreplaceable pictures of the children and everything else in her wallet. Another distasteful memory of that convention is a professional one: a group of pre-teen schoolkids were playing journalists at the convention and publishing a daily account of what they saw and heard called *Children's Express*. To my chagrin and that of my colleagues, the kids scooped the world with news that Minnesota Sen. Walter Mondale would be Carter's vice presidential running mate.

Mondale was one of the few Democrats in the U.S. Senate who wasn't a candidate in the party's presidential primaries. Carter's strongest opponents were Sen. Henry "Scoop" Jackson of Washington, Sen. Hubert Humphrey of Minnesota and Sen. Frank Church of Idaho. Every four years in those days, a group of about three dozen political writers traveled from one primary battleground state to another, starting in Iowa and traipsing back and forth across the country. I shudder now at what then seemed an exciting existence: living out of a suitcase for weeks at a time, far from family and friends, consumed by developments in a rarified political world most people were only dimly aware of and very few cared about.

Sometimes the outside world intruded. I was in Cleveland the last weekend of the 1976 primary season when I got a call from the UPI newsdesk in New York ordering me to get to Idaho as soon as possible. An earthen dam had collapsed near Twin Falls, sending a wall of water down a river valley. Hundreds of people were feared drowned.

I quickly arranged to fly out with Sen. Church, who was returning to his home state to assess the damage. But a baggage truck backed into his chartered plane, forcing him to transfer to a small executive jet. There wasn't room for me, so I flew commercial from Cleveland to Pocatello, with plane changes in Milwaukee, Denver and Salt Lake City. After purchasing a pair of cowboy boots in Pocatello (in case of snakes), I drove north into the flood area.

The damage was extensive — some small towns were almost completely destroyed -- but, miraculously, only 11 people died in the catastrophe. At the end of my first full day on the ground, the New York news desk decided the story wasn't as big as the editors expected and ordered me to move on. Go to California and help cover primary returns, they said. So I drove back to Pocatello, boarded a plane for Las Vegas and changed there to a flight to Los Angeles. When I got there, I went directly to the UPI bureau and worked until well after midnight. Totally spent, having had only about six hours sleep in 72 hours, I went to my hotel to go to bed. When I got there, I found hundreds of people standing outside: my hotel was on fire! Such was life on the road in an election year.

In Plains after the convention, I joined some three dozen press colleagues headquartered at a shabby Americus GA motel. UPI and AP were represented as were the New York Times, the Washington Post and three or four other major newspapers. The news magazines also sent reporters, as did ABC, CBS and NBC. The so-called national press was a small world then. There were no cable news organizations or social media outlets. We scrambled to cobble together stories each day, usually relying on Carter campaign aides for tidbits of information. In the evenings, we reporters and occasionally some Carter staffers would sit around the motel pool drinking beer and swapping stories. Once we commissioned Randy Lewis, at 19 the youngest member of Carter's staff, to reconnoiter the motel bar. "Not worth a visit," he reported back. "The place is filled with 40-year widows – all of whose husbands were killed in bar fights."

In those days, the presidential campaign didn't begin in earnest until Labor Day. But Carter made a couple of day trips during the long hot summer and we all went along. On a trip to New York City, Faye West, the proprietor of a small barbeque restaurant where we often ate, came with us. We took her to the famed Manhattan restaurant "21" for lunch and ordered hamburger steak, which was on the menu for $22. Faye said she'd sell the same thing "for a buck and a half – and throw in a baked potato."

On one summer daytrip there was a Washington stopover, allowing me to take Sean, then four years old, back to Georgia with me aboard Carter's plane. Lynn and Jennie flew down commercially to join me the next day. During the flight, I got up to get coffee, and when I returned to my seat there was Carter, deep in conversation with my son. A photo taken during their talk quickly went up on the wall of the press room in Plains, complete with some wiseacre dialogue. "I got the window first and I'm keeping it!" Sean was telling the future president.

A noteworthy incident occurred while Lynn and the kids were visiting. The summer of '76 was a summer of softball. Nearly every night, Carter would assemble the brawniest, most athletic members of his Secret Service protective detail and take on the press and his brother Billy in a game of softball on the high school field. He always pitched. He and his team always won by a lopsided score. Carter was an intense competitor who loudly challenged every call that went against him. The games became grudge matches. There was nothing my colleagues and I enjoyed more than beating him on a close play.

Carter's team was at bat and I was out in center field one night when there was an explosion behind me and a column of smoke rose from Billy's gas station. Everyone ran toward the blast, Carter included. When we got there, we saw a gasoline tank truck in front of the station enveloped in flames. In one of the most heroic, foolhardy acts I've ever witnessed, a local man jumped into the cab and drove the truck west away from the center of town. Billy was being restrained from getting closer to the scene. "Let it go, Billy. Let it go," Carter called out. "No! It's the only damn thing I have in this world," his brother sobbed.

As things turned out, the damage was minimal. A spark from a soda machine ignited fumes as the gasoline truck finished filling the station's storage tanks. But all the valves were closed and the flames were quickly extinguished. During the excitement, Lynn gathered up all the children around her, including the Carter's 12-year old daughter Amy and moved them off in the other direction. In retrospect, she was probably the only adult there showing any sense. Though domestic terrorism was far from anyone's mind in 1976, the incident might well have been an attack. Lynn was the only one with the presence of mind to think of people's personal safety.

That wasn't the only time I saw the Secret Service lose track of a person they were supposed to protect in a potentially dangerous environment. During a visit to Istanbul, I lingered behind on a tour of the Topkapi Palace museum to inspect an exhibit more closely when Chelsea Clinton tugged on my sleeve. She said she'd become separated from her mother and asked me to help her get back to her. We had to wade through a crowd to get to the building Mrs. Clinton was in, so swinging my elbows I led Chelsea through until she and her mother were reunited.

Some 22 miles northeast of Plains is Andersonville, a place out of time notorious for what happened there during the Civil War. It was a Confederate prisoner-of-war camp, a stinking brutal hellhole where nearly a third of the 45,000 Union soldiers held in captivity died. Most perished of disease and starvation, some at the hands of guards or fellow prisoners. Captain Henry Wirz, the camp commandant, was later accused of war crimes, tried and hung.

Having read MacKinlay Kantor's haunting novel "Andersonville," I went there often during the time I spent in Carter's hometown. It was usually deserted and I liked the solitude, being alone with my thoughts. I thought of the place as an American Auschwitz. When I returned nearly 40 years later, I was dismayed by the changes. The old POW camp had been transformed into a well-manicured national park, with lots of exhibits and recreated relics of the past. I believe something more real was lost in the process.

I felt something vaguely mystical whenever I visited Andersonville. It was almost as if the place were haunted and spirits of the dead were still there. I can't explain it. Nor can I explain a few other mystical events I've experienced since Lynn died. I've read dozens of books about spiritual mattters but I'm deeply suspicious of the subject.

An element of Carter's character foreign to me and most of my colleagues was his spirituality, his deep commitment to his born-again Christian religion. Carter often taught Sunday School, a practice he has clung to for the rest of his life; indeed, his bible teaching was often the grist of our news reports from Plains. "His faith and his explicit expression of it were novel for most politicians and most reporters. I am not at all certain we succeeded either for ourselves or our audiences in learning and communicating the essence of the man who became president," UPI's Wes Pippert wrote.

Within a few weeks of his election, Carter's close association with the Plains Baptist Church was tested when Clennon King, a part-time minister and black activist from nearby Albany GA applied for membership. There were unproven allegations that a right-wing Albany businessman was behind it; whatever the cause, it attracted a lot of attention. So as not to embarrass the town's favorite son, the congregation voted to desegregate. The day King first showed up to worship was a media circus. Television cameras everywhere. Exasperated parishioners. Tempers flaring. "I want to worship my Lord and Savior Jesus Christ and you news people won't let me," said one man as he walked out of the service, tears streaming down his face. The affair caused divisions within the church that forced the pastor to leave and continue to this day, leading Carter and many other townspeople to worship at a new church, Maranatha Baptist, about a half-mile away.

I was with Jimmy Carter in Warm Springs GA, site of Franklin Delano Roosevelt's "Little White House," when he launched his fall campaign. It was where FDR often recuperated from the effects of polio and where he died in 1945. In a speech that was surprisingly brief and free of any eloquent soundbites, Carter said the country was "stagnant, divided and drifting."

"It is time for leadership. We must be united and strong, and we must get our country moving again," he said. Later the same day we went to a stock car race in Darlington SC and wound up that evening in Richmond, VA. There were large welcoming crowds everywhere we went that fall. Carter's trademark toothy grin became a front-page staple of the nation's newspapers. Working press arrangements were another story. Strange as it seems now when instantaneous communications are taken for granted, those of us covering the campaign toted portable typewriters – ultra-light Italian-made Olivettis were the models of choice – and we filed our stories by telephone or telex.

During the first few weeks of Carter's bid for the presidency, there was often no time to send in a story after a major speech. Or there was filing time but not enough telephones to go around. It was maddening trying to explain to one's bosses why my campaign coverage was so thin.

Things finally came to a head at a big airport rally somewhere in the U.S. rural Midwestern heartland where Carter unveiled his farm policy. Strange as it might seem now, presidential candidates in those days actually talked about what they would do if elected instead of simply attacking their opponent. More than enough telephones were on hand for us to report the news to the country. The problem was only a few of them worked.

I was boiling mad when I got back on the plane. I'd been unable to file and feared my job might be in jeopardy. When I got to my seat there was a pamphlet on it: "What You Should Know About VD." Another reporter found one that said: "How To Get Rid of Lice." And so on. It was the work of Jim King, a mischievous Carter political operative. His stunt got everyone laughing, which put everything in better perspective. It was a screw-up, yes, but the campaign logistics would soon be fixed – and were. One thing that never did get fixed was the tendency of high school bands throughout the country to greet Carter with rousing renditions of "Marching Through Georgia." They apparently didn't realize the song celebrated General William Sherman's march to the sea during the U.S. Civil War, when much of Carter's home state was devastated.

The rest of the 1976 campaign is pretty much a blur, except for an incident in Illinois, where Carter addressed an enormous crowd at a lunchtime rally on the state university campus in Champaign. With him on the podium were an array of Illinois politicians, Democrats all, including reform Gov. Dan Walker, Sen. Adlai Stevenson III and gubernatorial candidate Michael J. Howlett. The latter was a Chicago machine-backed political hack who had successfully challenged Walker in the primary. Everyone got a round of applause except for Howlett, who was loudly booed.

Flying to Chicago afterward, the pilot of Carter's plane made an announcement, listing the names of all the dignitaries aboard. Back in the press cabin, we lustily cheered each name until he got to Howlett, whereupon we booed and hooted. It was meant in good fun but Howlett didn't take it as such. His face beet red with anger, he burst through the curtain separating the personages from the peons. "FUCK YOUSE! FUCK YOUSE ALL!" he bellowed, using both hands to give us the middle finger. In the next morning's editions, the Chicago Tribune printed the F-bomb for the first time.

Tracing the trajectory of his presidency, I was also with Carter on Election Night, on his flight to Washington for the inauguration and on his flight home. We awaited the returns at an Atlanta hotel and the outcome of his battle with President Gerald Ford was in doubt until 3:30 AM the next morning. Carter won, carrying 23 states with a total of 297 electoral votes; Ford carried 27 states with 240 electoral votes.

When Mississippi finally put him over the top, making him the first person from the Deep South to be elected president since Zachary Taylor in 1848, Carter wanted to go home. He wanted to leave us newshounds behind, but press secretary Jody Powell and other cooler heads prevailed. So he waited at the airport fuming while we filed our stories. I was one of the first reporters to finally board his campaign plane, a chartered United Airlines Boeing 727, and found Carter near the entranceway. "Congratulations Mr. President!" I said, using the honorific a bit prematurely. "Thank you. Close the door!" he replied in a short-tempered tone of voice.

The flight to Washington two months later was more celebratory. Though Ford had given Carter the use of one of the planes in the presidential fleet during the transition of power, we were aboard a chartered Delta jetliner for the inaugural flight. Carter roamed the aisles in shirtsleeves, in buoyant good humor and grinning broadly, as Misty Melarky, the family cat, leaped from seat to seat. Amy and Mrs. Carter traded chit-chat with us. Carter's mother Miss Lillian was also aboard, beaming with pride and anticipation.

I waited for hours before going home, hoping in vain to get an advance text of Carter's inaugural speech. It was bitter cold: the Potomac had frozen for the first time in years. But Washington's new subway system was operating, making it easy to get around. It was bright and sunny on Inauguration Day. After the swearing in ceremony, President and Mrs. Carter walked most of the way from the U.S. Capitol to the White House, waving to cheering crowds along Pennsylvania Avenue. Their walk established an enduring tradition. Most of Carter's successors have done the same, at least in spirit, walking a block or two along the parade route.

I covered the Inaugural balls that night. My wife Lynn went to one with my brother Joe, still single then, who'd been a pro-Carter Pennsylvania delegate at the aforementioned Democratic convention in New York. The cold weather and the ostentatious nature of the celebration caused many women ball-goers to wear furs. (This was before PETA – People for the Ethical Treatment of Animals – made it politically incorrect and sometimes downright hazardous to be seen in such attire.) In an inauspicious omen of graver difficulties down the road, cloakrooms at many of ball venues were badly managed and an embarrassing number of furs were misplaced or stolen.

From the start of his presidency, Carter was politically whipsawed between opposition Republicans and liberal Democrats suspicious of his Southern roots. His style of leadership was also problematic. Carter campaigned and governed as an outsider. "He was not a coalition builder and he was not comfortable with Congress as an institution, nor with many of its members, because he did not see either them or their institution as 'trustees' for the public interest. He saw himself, as President, as a 'trustee' for the public good," political scientist Erwin Hargrove observed.

A story made the rounds in Washington that Democratic House Speaker Thomas "Tip" O'Neill asked top presidential adviser Hamilton

Jordan if he pronounced his name "Jordan" or "Jerden." "My friends call me Jerden but you can call me Jordan," the Carter aide supposedly replied. That exchange might have been apocryphal, but the Carter White House was often at odds with the Washington political culture.

The political headwinds started days after the man from Georgia entered the Oval Office, a time when most presidents enjoy a political honeymoon, particularly those whose parties controlled Congress with commanding majorities His first setback came when he was forced to withdraw his nomination of Theodore Sorensen, the JFK speechwriter who authored Kennedy's famed "Ask not what you can do for yourself, ask what you can do for your country" inaugural speech, to be CIA director. Senate opposition centered around Sorensen's status as a conscientious objector during World War Two. How strange that objection seems today, given the fact that Presidents Clinton and Trump dodged the draft during the Vietnam War.

Carter seemed snakebit after the Sorensen matter. There was the Bert Lance Affair, a controversy over the Carter budget director's pre-government practices as a small town banker – including the use of a corporate plane to attend University of Georgia football games. It forced Lance to resign after eight months in office. I remember him as a colorful, sleepy-eyed bear of a man who didn't resent his critics, saying "bitterness breeds destruction." Lance was also the person who originated an axiom that's become part of the language: "If it ain't broke, don't fix it."

Lance had no sooner left Washington than Carter's brother Billy came under fire for a series of misadventures that culminated in a scandal dubbed "Billy-gate." In a fit of colossal bad judgment, he registered as a foreign agent and accepted a $220,000 loan from the government of Libya, which was then friendly to the United States. The move probably reflected Billy's lack of sophistication. His "good ol' boy" persona wasn't an act. Indeed, in a picture taken at a Plains softball game that hangs in my home, Billy is wearing a T-shirt imprinted with the words "Redneck Power."

Nevertheless, disclosure of the Libya loan forced Carter to basically disown his brother. "I am deeply concerned that Billy has received funds from Libya and that he may be under obligation to Libya. These facts will govern my relationship with Libya as long as I am president. Billy has had no influence on U.S. policy or actions concerning Libya in the past, and he will have no influence in the future," he said.

Some of the wounds were self-inflicted. Take the "Killer Rabbit" story, which syndicated columnist Dave Barry described as the single most memorable event of Carter's presidency. During Carter's time in the White House, a nearby bar called "The Class Reunion" was a popular hangout for the White House press office staff and the White House press corps.

One evening, while having a nightcap with Brooks Jackson of the Associated Press, press secretary Jody Powell recounted an unusual incident. He said that while Carter was fishing by himself during a visit to Plains, he had to use an oar to fend off a large rabbit which swam toward his boat, hissing and gnashing its teeth. The resulting story moved on the AP newswire under the headline, "Bunny Goes Bugs: Rabbit attacks President." The timing couldn't have been worse from Carter's standpoint: when the story appeared, movie theaters around the country were screening a comedy called "Monty Python and the Holy Grail." It included a scene in which a rampaging rabbit attacked and killed people, not the kind of optic Carter needed or wanted.

"Carter, who'd grown up in the country, calmly used his paddle to splash water at the critter and scare it away. But a photo of the encounter that the White House unwisely released to the press made the president look somewhat comical and small. How was a guy who let a rabbit get the drop on him supposed to guard the U.S. from attack by the Soviet Union?" public radio's WNYC said in a commentary.

Less than two months later, Carter's public image took another hit. While competing in a 10 kilometer race in Maryland's Catoctin Mountains near the Camp David presidential retreat, he pushed himself too hard and collapsed from heat exhaustion. Photographs of him sagging into the arms of his Secret Service protectors were splashed across the front pages of the nation's newspapers, a deadly development for a president fighting perceptions of political weakness.

Arguably, Carter's most towering achievement was Senate ratification of the Panama Canal Treaties, which ceded control of the U.S.-built waterway to the Panamanians. He also established two Cabinet agencies, the Departments of Energy and Education and deregulated the U.S. airline industry. The latter move made air travel less expensive, transforming it into the mass transportation it is today.

I traveled to Panama with Carter for a ceremonial signing of the canal treaties, which gave the United States a perpetual right to protect the canal – a legalism that proved useful when President Bush senior sent U.S. troops into the Central American isthmus in 1979 to oust dictator Manuel Noriega from power. At a huge rally in Panama City to celebrate Carter's arrival, Panamanian strongman Omar Torrijos chose an unflattering metaphor to praise his guest's political courage, comparing him to a man who jumps from a plane without a parachute. Fortunately for Carter, Torrijos spoke in Spanish so his comment was lost on most U.S. reporters.

Torrijos had it right: Carter took on an unpopular cause in fighting for the treaties in the face of stiff opposition from conservative Republicans and politically timid Democrats. Ronald Reagan led the fight, claiming the Panama Canal was U.S. property. "We bought it. We paid for it. It's ours, and we're going to keep it," was his battle-cry.

History has upheld the soundness of Carter's judgement. If the treaties had not been approved, American troops probably would have faced a guerrilla war in Panama that easily might have spread throughout Latin America, causing major security problems for the United States in our own backyard. Indeed, Torrijos later revealed that Panamanian troops had infiltrated the U.S-administered Canal Zone and were prepared to sabotage locks and other vital installations had the Senate rejected the treaties.

Carter was lucky that bipartisanship was still alive and well when he was in office. On issues of major national interest, especially security issues, most responsible Republicans and Democrats still subscribed to Wisconsin Republican Sen. Arthur Vandenberg's rule: "Politics stops at the water's edge." One of Carter's chief allies in the treaty battle was Howard Baker of Tennessee, the Senate Republican leader, In today's climate, where radio and television rabble rousers like Rush Limbaugh, Bill O'Reilly and Sean Hannity are more interested in ego gratification and financial enrichment than they are in the national interest, I doubt the Panama Canal Treaties would even come to a vote, much less win Senate approval.

Less than a month after the Panama trip I traveled with Carter to what was then West Germany, where he attended a summit of leaders of the world's seven major industrial powers: The United States, Britain, France, West Germany, Italy, Canada and Japan. The summit took place in the federal republic's capital city of Bonn. But we also visited West

Berlin and gazed across the Berlin Wall at a pile of rubble that had been
Adolf Hitler's bunker.

It was customary at the time for the White House to put two or
three American reporters on the U.S. guest list for foreign state dinners.
So it was that I got invited to the social event of the trip: Chancellor
Helmut Schmidt's dinner for President and Mrs. Carter. The black-tie
fete took place at Schloss Augustusburg, an ornately furnished 18th
Century rococo palace not far from Bonn and Cologne. Words almost
can't describe it: the evening had fairybook, Teutonic, even faintly Nazi
overtones. After arriving at the palace by limousine provided by the
German government, I walked to the entranceway through an honor
guard of German soldiers standing at rigid attention, holding flaming
torches.

The scene inside was straight out of a movie: ornately furnished
rooms illuminated by beautiful chandeliers; a chamber music ensemble
playing softly in the background; men and women in evening dress, a
cardinal of the Roman Catholic Church in bright red cap and flowing
robes, generals with chests full of medals in dress uniforms dripped
with braid, the leaders of two world powers – and me. I remember
meeting Helmut Kohl, who as chancellor several years later presided over
the reunification of Germany. He was an opposition leader then. The
dinner the splendor magnified: elaborately decorated tables, stately and
attentive waiters and a five course meal centered around roast venison,
washed down with some of the finest wine I've ever enjoyed. It was all
very heady stuff.

Six years later, I found myself back in the same setting. It was, in
Yogi Berra's immortal words, "déjà vu all over again." Ronald Reagan
was visiting Germany, and by the luck of the draw I was once again on
the guest list for the state dinner in his honor. The scene was the same:
German soldiers with torches, a glittering cast with whom to mix: I even
recognized most of my tablemates as people I'd dined with at the dinner
with Carter.

There was one enormous difference. A media firestorm had erupted
shortly before Reagan's visit, sparked by his plan to lay a wreath at a
German military cemetery in Bitburg. The ceremony was Kohl's idea
and was meant to symbolize the post-World War Two reconciliation of
the American and German peoples.

The problem was that some of those buried at the cemetery were members of the hated and feared Waffen SS, which was responsible for many atrocities including the murder of 84 American prisoners at a crossroads near Malmady, Belgium during the Battle of the Bulge in the closing days of World War Two. The controversy embarrassed and infuriated the Germans. In the eyes of my German dinner companions, I was one of those responsible for the furor. So they effectively shunned me, speaking only Deutsche though I knew they were all fluent in English. It made for a distinctly uncomfortable evening.

Carter's foreign travels probably were a welcome respite from having to deal with gasoline lines, hyper-inflation and other domestic problems. But a visit to Tehran on December 31, 1977 might have helped doom his presidency. In a New Year's Eve toast, Carter toasted his host with some ill-chosen words. "Iran, because of the great leadership of the Shah, is an island of stability in one of the more troubled areas of the world," he said.

It was anything but, and the United States deserved much of the blame. In 1953, the U.S. Central Intelligence Agency engineered a coup that ousted Iran's democratically elected Prime Minister Mohammad Mossaddegh from power. He was in Washington's gunsights because he'd moved to nationalize U.S. and British-owned oil companies.

Shah Mohammad Reza Pahlavi's ensuing rule became more and more despotic and cruel. Less than 12 months after Carter's visit, a revolution led by a fundamentalist Muslim cleric, the Ayatollah Khomeini, forced the Shah and his family to flee Iran. Soon thereafter, student radicals stormed the U.S. embassy and took 52 American diplomats and citizens hostage. Their ordeal continued for 444 days, ending only when Ronald Reagan took office. The crisis made Carter look powerless, an optic worsened by an abortive military rescue effort that led to the resignation of Secretary of State Cyrus Vance. He was further victimized by irresponsible television news gimmickry that inflames rather than enlightens the public.

The instigator was a supposed shining example of everything good and noble in journalism, CBS anchorman Walter Cronkite. Throughout the ordeal, Cronkite signed off his evening news broadcast by saying, "And that's the way it is on (whatever) day of captivity for the American hostages in Iran. It was a gratuitous daily editorial hammer blow to Carter, who worked assiduously to get the hostages back alive while avoiding shedding innocent blood. Imagine the outcry from the Republican right if TV newsreaders ended their evening broadcasts during George W. Bush's presidency by observing it was "the umpteenth day that Osama Bin Laden, murderer of nearly 3,000 Americans, remains at large." The 9/11 attacks happened on Bush's watch and he failed to get the perpetrator. But he wasn't held accountable the way Carter was.

Beset by the hostage crisis and serious U.S. economic headaches, Carter found himself the target of a challenge from within his own Democratic Party that severely dampened his chances of reelection. Even the leader of the insurgency couldn't explain it. When asked by CBS correspondent Roger Mudd in an interview why he was running for president, Massachusetts Sen. Ted Kennedy had no answer.

There were all sorts of tragi-comic aspects to the Democratic infighting. One of the silliest was early test of political strength between Kennedy and Carter in Florida. Seeking to expand their influence and generate some national publicity, state Democratic leaders scheduled non-binding party caucuses that supposedly would provide the first indication whether voters preferred Kennedy or Carter. There was only one polling place in each county, and the caucuses took place on a weekday morning. Most folks were working. Florida is also a haven for the elderly. So it was really a logistical exercise: corner the market on charter busses to bring retirees to the polls.

Carter won the caucuses handily. But commentators thought he should have won by a larger margin since he had the power of incumbency. Carter bested Kennedy in 36 of the 48 Democratic primaries that followed and was easily nominated for a second term. But Kennedy remained recalcitrant to the end. At the Democratic Convention, he embarrassed his rival on what was billed party unity night, moving elusively around the speaker's platform as Carter chased him, knowing the news media expected a handshake photo. My other takeaway from that event was country music superstar Willie Nelson smoking marijuana behind the podium.

My fondest memory of the Carter-Kennedy tussle is of what amounted to a boondoggle. During the Texas primary, Kennedy visited Mexico City, a move designed to appeal to Hispanic voters. I went along on the trip, and spent part of my time sightseeing. Early one morning, I went to the Mayan pyramids at Teothihuacan. Except for my driver, I was by myself. It was eerie to point of being almost mystical to climb to the top of the ancient stone monuments where human sacrifices often occurred and wander along a broad promenade known as the Avenue of the Dead. Later that day I visited the Basilica of Our Lady of Guadalupe, according to Wikipedia the most visited Roman Catholic pilgrimage shrine in the world. The church stands on a site where the Virgin Mary is said to have appeared several times to a Mexican peasant named Juan Diego. On display there is an image of the Virgin supposedly imprinted miraculously on Juan Diego's cloak. Most scholars, and indeed many Catholic authorities, doubt its authenticity.

Two weeks before he left office, Carter flew to Georgia to lay the groundwork for his return to private life. Most of the White House press corps was already focused on Ronald Reagan, so only about a dozen of us went with him. Someone suggested we invite Carter and his wife Rosalynn to join us for dinner at a local restaurant. To our surprise they accepted, giving me the best expense account item of my career: *Share, dinner with news source (President of United States) $60.* (Even in 1981, this was cheap. There was no such thing as an expensive restaurant in South Georgia).

The dinner conversation was off-the-record, meaning nothing the Carters said or did could be reported in any form. Even under those ground rules, the outgoing president was remarkably candid in his comments about other world leaders and U.S. political figures. One of his more interesting observations was that the French president had more raw power than any other world leader. I don't know why he thought that, and he didn't explain. At one point, Carter said his daughter Amy was interested in becoming a journalist, "but of course she's very young." Mrs. Carter acidly remarked toward the end of the meal that if any of us were to find ourselves in Plains in the future, she and Jimmy would be glad to see us. "We'll treat you with class," she said. That was a pointed reference to a Time Magazine column by Hugh Sidey, a president-watcher known for his Republican leanings, asserting the Reagans would restore class to the White House.

The only thing that immediately leaked into print about this remarkable evening was a Carter wisecrack as we said our farewells. He said he wished two things for his successor: that Menachem Begin continue to be prime minister of Israel and that Sam Donaldson stay on the White House beat. Begin, a prickly hardliner determined to restore Israel to its Biblical greatness, had been nearly impossible for Carter to deal with, and the obstreperous Donaldson, who started the practice of shouting questions at presidents, was also a thorn in Carter's side.

When Carter returned to Plains for good on January 20, 1981, I was part of the small contingent of reporters and photographers – the press "pool" – that went with him. It was a surreal experience: seeing presidential power evaporate in the blink of an eye was like watching Cinderella's coach turn into a pumpkin.

Unlike the jubilant atmosphere on the flight to Washington four years earlier, there was a palpable sense of defeat and exhaustion on the trip home. Carter had been up all night leading end-game negotiations to free the hostages in Iran. Although it appeared by daybreak agreement had been achieved, their fate still hung in the balance at the start of the Inaugural ceremony at the U.S. Capitol. Just before the proceedings started, there was a television news flash that the hostages' chartered Swissair jetliner was finally airborne. It wasn't accurate. In a final insult to Carter, authorities in Tehran waited until Reagan was sworn in to let the plane take off for Germany, the first stop on the hostages' journey to freedom

The first sign of Carter's diminished status appeared as he left the Capitol for Andrews Air Force Base. Instead of the highly polished armored black Cadillac limousine he rode in as president, the vehicle awaiting him as a former president was a plain brown Chrysler sedan that closely resembled a family car. As his four or five car motorcade wended its way through southeast Washington, small knots of African-Americans stood outside the housing projects waving goodbye. One black woman held up a homemade sign made out of the lid of a pizza box. "Thank you, Jimmy," it said. I thought it a magnificent tribute to a white man from the Deep South.

At the airbase was the big blue and white Boeing 707 that had flown Carter around the world. Because he was no longer president, its radio call sign was no longer Air Force One. "Special Air Mission Twenty Seven Thousand" (27000 was the plane's tail number) was its Air Traffic Control designator for Carter's homeward journey.

Once the jet was airborne, it flew low and slow over the White House and dipped a wing, Most of Carter's aides were in tears during the farewell pass (he and his family were out of sight in the front cabin), but Phil Wise, a young Georgian who'd been Cabinet secretary, yelled out: "Free at last, free at last. Thank God Almighty, we're free at last!" That, of course, was a line from Dr. Martin Luther King's famous "I have a Dream" Lincoln Memorial speech.

Later, at Warner-Robbins Air Force Base outside Macon GA, Carter spent about 10 minutes shaking hands with well-wishers before boarding a Marine helicopter to travel that final few miles of his homeward journey. He had fractured his collar bone in a cross country skiing accident at Camp David a few days earlier, so he used his left hand as he worked the rope-line, apologizing to people for not offering proper handshakes.

In Plains, a crowd far outnumbering the town's population stood shoulder to shoulder at a Welcome Home party. Carter's homecoming gift was a set of woodworking tools. It rained during the ceremony. As I left the party, I found yet another sign of the transfer of power: bare spots on the wall of Carter's hometown press office. Hours before, there'd been telephones there connected to the White House switchboard.

There was a nice grace note to the final act of Carter's remarkable political rise and fall. Using the presidential jet that brought him home courtesy of his presidential successor, Carter flew to Germany the next day to greet the returning hostages. I wanted to go too but UPI, then my employer, said no.

Carter is often described as the best ex-president America has ever had. His humanitarian work at home and abroad, is a shining example of a Biblical verse he quoted often, from the prophet Micah: "Act justly, love mercy and walk humbly with God." Among other things, he led a successful battle to eradicate Guinea Worm Disease, once a leading cause of pain and disability in remote parts of Africa. There were an estimated 3.5 million cases of the disease in 1986; by 2019 there were only 54 known cases. Well into their 90s, Carter and his wife Rosalynn were wielding hammers and other hand tools to help Habitat for Humanity build or restore decent, affordable housing for poor people in the United States and throughout the world. According to the Carter Center, they personally assisted more than 4,000 families in the nearly 35 years they were associated with the program.

In 2002, Carter was awarded the Nobel Peace Prize "for his decades of untiring effort to find peaceful solutions to international conflicts, to advance democracy and human rights and to promote economic and social development." In his acceptance speech, a powerful testament of his deep spiritual convictions well worth reading, he recalled the admonition of Miss Julia Coleman, his favorite high school teacher: "We must adjust to changing times and still hold to unchanging principles."

In a 2011 interview with The Guardian, a British newspaper, Carter reflected on his presidency. "We kept our country at peace. We never went to war. We never dropped a bomb. We never fired a bullet. But still we achieved our international goals," he said.

In <u>The Other Side of the Story</u>, a book published in 1984, Press Secretary Jody Powell bitterly reflected on why the news media treated Carter so harshly when he was in the White House "Most journalists are convinced that no one makes it very far in politics without selling a sizable chunk of his soul. But here was a guy who not only claimed to have done it differently, but who clearly was of the opinion that politics as usual was wrong," he wrote. "To make things even worse, this guy was setting himself up to be not only better than most politicians, but also better than most journalists. There was an implicit challenge involved, or at least many journalists thought there was, to prove that Carter was at least as rotten as all the rest."

Jody died of a heart attack in 2009, just shy of his 66th birthday. He was one of the finest of the 10 White House press secretaries I dealt with, the others being Marlin Fitzwater and Mike McCurry. Jody told the truth and didn't take himself seriously. For some reason I no longer recall, just the two of us wound up drinking one evening at a bar in Portland during the 1976 Oregon primary campaign. A drunk on a nearby bar stool picked up on Jody's Southern drawl and engaged him in conversation. "You sound like Jimmy Carter," the drunk observed, adding that he didn't like Carter. By the time the conversation ended, the drunk was convinced Jody WAS Carter and was a convert to the cause. I still wonder if the guy went to the polls and voted.

My wife Becky and I visited Plains in 2015, sat in a front row at Carter's Sunday School class and visited briefly with the former president and Mrs. Carter after services at Marantha Baptist Church. Carter, then 90, said he remembered me. I believe he probably did.

Carter's hometown hadn't changed much. We stayed in a bed & breakfast on Main Street that used to be a hardware store owned by Carter's cousin Hugh, who sold "Bricks From Hospital Where Jimmy Was Born" for five bucks each. We saw the old ballfield where we played softball and, after a search, located the Pond House, a family retreat a few miles from Plains where Carter often held meetings during the Summer of '76. The only new addition was the Carter family farm in nearby Archer where Jimmy grew up, now restored and administered by the National Park Service. Carter's presidential library is in Atlanta.

For me, the visit was bittersweet. It was nice to return to what seemed a simpler time in my life but there were reminders of so many people I miss: Billy Carter; who became a friend; Jody; and Lynn, who was in Plains only once. During her visit, Carter hosted a fish fry at his peanut warehouse. Sean, age four, and Jennie, age two, were charmed by him. When it came time for the family to head home, Sean told Carter's daughter Amy, then age 7, "I have to go back to America."

Billy Carter was only 51 when he died. He sold Pabst Blue Ribbon beer at his filling station, evading Georgia blue laws by giving it away on Sundays. You could help yourself to a six-pac and pay him the next day. Jody died too young too. At Jody's funeral, his former boss reminisced how the two of them traveled together in the early days of the 1976 presidential campaign, often sharing a motel room.

Carter said he always tried to get to sleep early because Powell snored. That was usually easy because his lieutenant often went out after dinner for a beer or two, carousing with some of the locals. On one occasion, the former president recalled, Powell returned and awakened him with good news: he'd snared a local television appearance for his boss the next morning. This was good news indeed – TV was the gold standard of free publicity at this stage of his campaign. Carter said that as they drove to the station Powell asked him to think of a favorite recipe and then told him he'd have to wear a toque. His TV appearance was a cooking show!

As president, Carter tried to eliminate the regal trappings of the office. He carried his own suitcase and, for a time, stopped the playing of "Hail to the Chief" to herald his arrival at an event. He also sold the presidential yacht *Sequoia*, deeming it an unnecessary extravagance. His daughter Amy went to public school. His efforts to deglamorize the presidency were a dismal flop. As Ronald Reagan later demonstrated, showmanship is an essential element of politics in an age of visual information delivery -- what the TV cameras show is more important than policy.

During the 1980 presidential campaign, I spent more time covering Ronald Reagan than I did covering Carter. It was hard to believe that a former actor who'd starred in a movie about a monkey called *"Bedtime for Bonzo"* would defeat the incumbent but the results weren't even close. Reagan won by a landslide, carrying 44 states and winning 50.7% of the popular vote. A botched military effort to free the hostages in Iran was one of the contributing factors. There were only two presidential debates: Carter fared poorly in each. At one point he mentioned discussing nuclear proliferation with daughter Amy, then 13, a remark that prompted post-debate ridicule.

Lynn and I were at Carter's last White House Christmas Party for the press. It was not a happy occasion. Carter was clearly very uncomfortable and left the receiving line before greeting all the guests. It was later reported that the reason for his discomfort was that he was suffering from hemorrhoids. An ignominious ending to a well-intended but problem-filled presidency.

Showing the difference between then and now, we parked our car, a Volvo sedan that was always breaking down, on the driveway adjacent to the south entrance of the White House. Because of the threat of terrorism, today it's impossible to bring a private vehicle within blocks of the White House grounds. When we left the party, I jokingly told Lynn it would be nice for once if our car wouldn't start. Imagine summoning a tow truck to the Executive Mansion!

On a lovely afternoon in late autumn of 2020, I climbed into my car and went off to take pictures along country roads near my wife Becky's home in rural South Carolina. It was harvest time in Cotton Country and the snow-white fields covered with cotton plants were a thing of beauty. It reminded me of all the time I'd spent in Plains more than four decades earlier. I was on my own and having fun, churning out news stories and spending off-hours with my journo chums. Around me was the rural South, a starker region than what I was used to but somehow mesmerizing. Meantime Lynn was back in a Washington suburb keeping the home fires burning, raising the children, waiting for my return. As I drove along, I wondered what she thought about all that. Was it fair, her side of the marriage? Hell, no! I'm amazed and gratified beyond measure that our relationship survived and, once I retired, flourished.

Chapter Seven

Jerry Ford and Tricky Dick

LYNDON JOHNSON ONCE said Jerry Ford was "so dumb he can't fart and chew gum at the same time." It was cruel and unfair. Ford was a graduate of the University of Michigan and Yale Law School. He played football at Michigan and was one of the stars of a championship team. He was perhaps not as wily a politician as LBJ, but he was a solid, likeable, gentle man. As president, Ford modestly described himself as "A Ford, not a Lincoln," a clever play on words that also boosted auto manufacturing, his home state's signature industry. Although he had a penchant for getting himself into klutzy situations that tended to reinforce his public image as a clumsy oaf, I believe he deserves more credit than he gets for a pretty good record as president. He had an excellent Cabinet and his policies were progressive. One of his first acts was to announce a conditional amnesty for those who evaded the draft or deserted during the Vietnam War. Indeed, he'd probably be regarded as a bit to the left of a liberal Democrat today. His pardon of Richard Nixon for any crimes Nixon might have committed as president tainted Ford's occupancy of the Oval Office and might have foredoomed his bid to be elected president in his own right in 1976. I believed then and still am convinced it was a gutsy decision that spared the country years of anguish and turmoil.

I first met Ford when he was a Michigan Congressman serving as House Republican Leader. He didn't make a good first impression.

While he was affable enough, he sometimes plunged into the political fever swamps. He once led a crusade to impeach liberal U.S. Supreme Court Justice William O. Douglas on flimsy charges that included publishing an article in <u>Evergreen Review</u>, in a magazine whose pages also included several pictures of bare-breasted women. It was a ridiculous waste of time and Ford himself sometimes seemed a little embarrassed pursuing it. But it was raw meat for the Republican right.

While not as glamorous as being assigned to the White House, the Congressional beat was a lot more stimulating. Potentially there were 535 reliable sources of information about what was going on in the government – 435 House members and 100 senators – as well as a few thousand House and Senate staff members. There were also at least a dozen real characters. These included William "Fishbait" Miller, longtime doorkeeper of the House of Representatives who had a lucrative sideline: a monopoly on sanitary product sales in ladies rooms on the House side of the U.S. Capitol; Congresswoman Bella Abzug, who told a congressional aide "Go fuck yourself" when informed she couldn't wear her trademark hat on the floor of the House; and Senator Russell Long of Louisiana, who was often said to be "in high spirits" during legislative debates, meaning he was drunk.

The atmosphere of the Halls of Congress was far different from what it is today. These were serious people – men mostly, in my day – doing serious business. There were sharp partisan differences to be sure, but at the end of the day the lawmakers almost always found common ground. There wasn't the personal enmity verging on hatred that characterizes so much of American politics these days. I think one of the reasons for the collegiality that once prevailed was that so many members of Congress were veterans of World War Two.

The dozen years I spent on Capitol Hill were difficult, lonely ones for me. They had to be harder for Lynn. She was isolated, with small children demanding constant attention. I was a UPI Audio reporter then and I often worked far into the night recording stories for morning drive time, reading the same forty second snippet again and again until I was certain it couldn't be further improved. Meantime, Lynn was at home being mother and father to the kids and waiting for me to get home. She sometimes must have been desperate for companionship. My success as a journalist was paramount.

Once when she was late-stage pregnant with Sean, our oldest child, I used her shamelessly to get my first big front page byline. Let me explain: while I was on the radio, heard all over the country on independent stations that purchased UPI services, writing for the newspapers that were UPI clients was much more prestigious than doing radio reports. So doing so-called print reports it was something I did whenever I could.

Backed by the Nixon administration, the U.S. aviation industry led by corporate giants Boeing and General Electric was pushing for government subsidies to build a supersonic transport plane. Environmentalists and other liberal groups saw the program as a wasteful, destructive boondoggle. After a nasty fight in the U.S. Senate, SST foes succeed in killing it. For all intents and purposes, the program was dead. Or so the opponents thought.

A week or so after the battle ended, Lynn and I were at a Washington dinner party. In an unguarded moment, a senior White House official spoke of a plan to resurrect the issue. When I pressed him for more information he clammed up. As we wound up the evening over coffee and cordials my teetotaler wife, exhausted from carrying our unborn child, nodded off.

Her pregnancy was not how I explained her slumber when I made a series of late night telephone calls to other dinner party guests after we got home, however. I said I was mortified that Lynn obviously had too much to drink and was calling to apologize. I then asked more questions about what was afoot with the SST. Armed with just enough information to ferret out the backstage maneuvering, I went into work early the next day – a Saturday, one of my days off – and put together a breaking news story that played on the front pages of Sunday newspapers. Lynn was gracious about how I'd used her. She had the front page of the Sunday edition of the *Washington Star* with my byline framed, and it hung in our family room for years.

Ford became vice president when Nixon underling Spiro Agnew became embroiled in scandal and abruptly resigned. The separate Watergate scandal was threatening to take down Nixon as well and conventional wisdom was that Ford got the nod because he would make his president impeachment proof. LBJ's brutal description was political gospel: Ford just wasn't smart enough to occupy the Oval Office. But he adroitly walked a fine line as Nixon's legal troubles mounted, not saying or doing anything to undercut his boss while avoiding the kind of defense that would destroy his own credibility.

That whole era was an unnerving time. Nixon was "Vietnamizing" the Vietnam War but thousands of U.S. troops were still fighting and dying. There was a constant fear of Russian or Chinese intervention, igniting a thermonuclear Third World War. The Middle East was another flashpoint. Israel was surprised and nearly defeated in the 1973 Middle East War. In the aftermath, Washington and Moscow went on nuclear alert. Cuba was still another national security nightmare. Would it again be a base for Russian nuclear missiles 90 miles from our shores?

Add to all this widespread domestic unrest: there were antiwar protests around the country. Ohio National Guard troops shot and killed four unarmed college students demonstrating against the war at Kent State University. Some of the biggest demonstrations took place in Washington. It wasn't unusual to see the White House ringed by rented busses parked bumper to bumper to keep dissenters at bay. From the perspective of the 1970s, most of today's security issues seem minor. Nevertheless, the American people, who lived through worse, seem to frightened as never before. I blame the info-tainment industry. If current events were seen within the context of history – a BIG if, since so many "journalists" have no knowledge of history and no desire to learn it – perhaps unscrupulous politicians would be less able to peddle fear to so many voters.

I didn't get to the White House much during Richard Nixon's presidency. I made only two trips with him: one to New York, where he delivered an address at the United Nations and one to Maryland, where he spoke at a political event. I was on the road extensively during the 1972 presidential race but always covering the Democrats. I traveled with George McGovern throughout the fall campaign but never covered the Republican side. I don't know why that was: it was standard practice to switch back and forth between the candidates in order to get a better perspective on how the race was going. Lynn and I bought our first home that fall and I must have declined some campaign assignments because of my preoccupation with moving.

My only personal encounter with Nixon was embarrassing and unprofessional. I was filling in at the White House – someone was out sick or on vacation and I got sent over to substitute – when the press office announced a snap news conference. Things like that happened often before television became all powerful and the information flow from the White House became a reality show: the president would decide he wanted to see the press and everyone would file into the Oval Office and ask questions. No television cameras. It was pretty routine.

Except it was anything but routine to novice reporters like me. I'd seen the Oval Office once before. When I was in college a distant cousin and his wife invited me to come to Washington for a few days and surprised me with a Saturday morning visit to the White House. The visit included a brief meeting with George Reedy, President Johnson's press secretary. He took me to the door of the presidential office, which was empty that day, and pointed to some scuff marks on the floor. Reedy said the marks had been made by President Eisenhower, who sometimes entered the room wearing golf spikes. Ike installed a putting green on the White House South Lawn in1954. It fell into disuse after he left office but President George H.W. Bush had another one built when he was in charge.

On the day I first actually set foot in the Oval Office I was in the back of the group crowding around the president's desk and could neither see or be seen by Nixon. Someone asked a question about a congressional issue. As he finished his answer, I jumped in. "Mr. President – on another congressional issue?" I shouted. "Yes," he replied, cueing me to step forward.

Suddenly I was staring across the desk of the most powerful man in the world. Framed in the window behind him was the Washington Monument. The American flag and flags of the nation's armed forces with dozens of battle streamers draped around them added to the majestic setting. It was overwhelming. Somehow I managed to ask my question. It was a question that put Nixon on the spot.

"I didn't hear the first part of your question. Would you mind repeating it?" he asked.

At that point I succumbed completely to my surroundings and became completely tongue-tied. No, that doesn't begin to describe it: I became a blithering idiot, stammering and blushing and making no sense at all. Nixon seized the moment to talk about something he wanted to talk about, using me as a foil to deliver his message. The transcript of the news conference made me look foolish. Thankfully I was not identified. I felt like I had no business playing in that sort of league.

I was never that hopelessly outclassed again – but I've never felt I had the upper hand in an encounter with a powerful politician either. Most are masters at dissembling. The few who try to tell it straight: Ford, Jimmy Carter and George H.W. Bush come to mind – generally have a short shelf life at the political pinnacle.

Nixon's downfall was long and drawn out. I covered the Senate Watergate hearings from start to finish. Just as a dramatic 1958 professional football championship game between the Baltimore Colts and the New York Giants launched the National Football League toward the television sports dominance it enjoys today, those hearings, which played out over much of the summer of 1973, arguably laid the groundwork for the ubiquitous presence of cable news. It was great entertainment with colorful characters such as North Carolina Sen. Sam Ervin, who chaired the proceedings, and dramatic developments that included disclosure that there were tape recordings of relevant White House meetings. As the hearings unfolded, a parallel investigation went on in the federal courts. This proceeded out of the public eye but was no less meaningful. Nixon lost ground at every step. Steadily his political support peeled away.

The Ervin Hearings provided momentum for a drive to impeach Nixon, which thrust the House of Representatives into the political spotlight. For the first time since Andrew Johnson's impeachment more than a century earlier there was a real possibility the President would be ousted from office.

Covering the House Judiciary Committee's impeachment inquiry was the toughest three months of my life in journalism. Lynn often said it was the toughest three months of our marriage. Jennie was born in February 1974. The impeachment inquiry started in earnest in May and concluded in late July. Unlike the political kangaroo court proceeding against President Clinton in 1998, the inquiry was bipartisan.

In its initial phase, the committee held closed door hearings in the Rayburn House Office Building. We reporters would wait outside and buttonhole members when they emerged for lunch or go to the House floor to cast votes. Seldom did we get any real news. The hearings often lasted well into the evening. Afterwards, we'd "run the traps," visiting members' offices to seek inside information. There were few, if any, significant leaks. Jennie was a colicky baby. I'd often get home late at night and have to walk with her in my arms until she fell asleep before I'd finally get to bed. I was stressed out and cranky, not much fun to be around.

In late June or early July, the committee made public thousands of pages of transcripts of White House tapes. The tapes were recordings of nearly every word uttered in the Oval Office during Nixon's presidency. They were released in stages under embargo, which usually gave us 10 or 12 hours to read through them, find the most important parts and write it up as news. What was most sensational was Nixon's language. "I don't give a shit what happens. I want you all to stonewall it," he told aides at one point, ordering a cover-up of the criminal activity that ultimately cost him the presidency --a White House-sanctioned burglary of the Democratic Party's national headquarters.

It was Nixon's paranoia that led to the burglary. He was convinced, wrongly, that the Democrats had damaging information that could cause him to be denied reelection. Soon after the committee finished its work, voting to charge him with obstruction of justice, abuse of power and contempt of Congress, Nixon resigned.

In assuming the presidency, Jerry Ford declared: "Our long national nightmare is over." A year later, I interviewed the chairman of the House Judiciary Committee, New Jersey Democratic Congressman Peter Rodino. He told me that after the first article of impeachment was voted, he went back to his office and cried.

"I recall that there were those that wanted to interview me ... and I just couldn't at the time talk to anyone. I excused myself – said I had to make a telephone call," Rodino told me during a half-hour broadcast that aired on the first anniversary of Nixon's departure. "I called my wife and I broke down and was overcome with emotion."

During the broadcast I also interviewed California Republican Charles Wiggins, a House Judiciary Committee member who'd been a diehard Nixon supporter. He told me he was okay with the ultimate outcome.

"It was necessary that Richard Nixon's presidency be terminated for the good of the country. The fact of the matter is the (American people were) simply fed up with Watergate. They were convinced, I think, of Richard Nixon's personal involvement in it and it would have been very difficult for him to provide moral leadership to the country given this reality," Wiggins said.

I anchored the UPI Audio broadcast of Nixon's resignation speech from the National Press Building two blocks from the White House and heard his off-the-record comments to the people with him in the Oval Office before he went on the air. Bizarre doesn't begin to describe them. He first ordered the Secret Service agent with him to leave the room. When the agent said he couldn't do that, Nixon relented. But he then told official White House photographer Ollie Atkins to get out. "He's always trying to catch me picking my nose," Nixon said. I'm sure he was joking to break the tension, but it was a pathetic coda to his political career.

Nixon's speech was brief and to the point. "I shall resign the presidency at noon tomorrow. Vice President Ford will be sworn in as president at that hour in this office," he said. After bidding farewell to his staff at a White House East Room ceremony early the next morning in a maudlin speech that included the line "My mother was a saint," he and his family departed for their home in California. "President Nixon looked just awful," future President George H.W. Bush wrote in his diary. "He used glasses – the first time I ever saw them. Close to breaking down – understandably. Everyone in the room in tears ... I remember Lt. Col. Brennan, who has been with him for so long – Marine – standing proudly but with tears running down his face... The Nixon speech was masterful. In spite of his inability to totally resist a dig at the press, that argument about hating – only if you hate do you join the haters." Bush was then chairman of the Republican National Committee.

Ford and his family waited several days before moving into the White House. So there I was at about 6:30 AM on the first full day of his presidency, camped outside his suburban Alexandria VA home with 50 or 60 other reporters and television crews when Ford, in baby blue shorty pajamas, came out on his front porch to fetch the morning newspaper. It was his first real taste of the white hot media spotlight that's an accoutrement of the presidency. Ford's honeymoon with the press and public ended abruptly about a month later when he preemptively gave Nixon a blanket pardon for any crimes he might have committed as president.

"The facts, as I see them, are that a former President of the United States, instead of enjoying equal treatment with any other citizen accused of violating the law, would be cruelly and excessively penalized either in preserving the presumption of his innocence or I obtaining a speedy determination of his guilt in order to repay a legal debt to society.

"During this long period of delay and potential litigation, ugly passions would again be aroused. And our people would again be polarized in their opinions. And the credibility of our free institutions of government would again be challenged at home and abroad," Ford said in a televised speech to the nation.

In retrospect, Ford's decision served the nation well: the distraction of a disgraced former president in the dock would not have been in the public interest at a time when America faced serious domestic and foreign challenges. But White House Press Secretary Jerry TerHorst, a highly respected former Detroit News reporter, resigned on the spot and Congress was in an uproar. In an unprecedented blurring of the separation of powers decreed by the Constitution, Ford testified about his decision on Capitol Hill. But his approval rating nose-dived, and the Nixon pardon might have been the decisive issue in the 1976 presidential campaign, when he sought election in his own right.

Still, his was a reassuring presence after years of Watergate turmoil. Perhaps because he was America's first unelected president or maybe just because of his Midwestern roots, he was unassuming and down to earth. He smoked a pipe, liked a martini or two in the evening and followed sports. His wife Betty underwent breast cancer surgery and talked openly about it, removing the stigma from a health problem that afflicted millions of women. To the dismay of her four young adult children, she also spoke openly about problems of adolescence such as smoking marijuana and premarital sex.

Staffers who followed Ford to the White House from Capitol Hill were like him, likeable people. Even Dick Cheney, who evolved into a dour, suspicious Darth Vader-like figure as George W. Bush's vice president, was a regular guy when he was Ford's chief of staff. On one occasion, Cheney joined in a prank targeting Newsweek White House correspondent Thomas DeFrank.

As a proud, outspoken graduate of Texas A&M, DeFrank was constantly teased by colleagues about being a farm boy. With Cheney's connivance, DeFrank's tormentors arranged to put a sheep in his hotel room during a presidential visit to Cleveland. The frightened animal ran amok, causing several hundred dollars in damages. A collection was taken up to pay the bill. I don't know if Cheney contributed.

Ford himself often suffered embarrassments. He twice stumbled on the airplane steps while boarding and disembarking from Air Force One, and the clips were endlessly replayed on television. A political rally in Oklahoma offered another comic moment. A large crowd flocked to the airport to greet Ford, and during the welcoming ceremony he was given a University of Oklahoma football helmet as a memento of the Sooner's annual game with the University of Texas, which he planned to attend the next day.

Nearly everyone within eyeshot could see the helmet was a child-size model meant as a desk ornament. But genial Jerry tried to put it on. Suddenly there he was, leader of the Free World, with is ears pushed out and a ridiculous miniature helmet stuck on his head. As he struggled to remove it, his grunts carried across the airfield on a powerful rock concert sound system set up for his speech. The football helmet finally came off, but we reporters were howling with laughter by the time it did. Ford's staff was not amused.

Undoubtedly the funniest incident the 38th president found himself in occurred during a 1976 campaign visit to a Wisconsin dairy farm. As he strolled through the barnyard with farmer Peter Senn, a cow lifted its tail and sprayed him with feces. New York Times reporter James Naughton wrote that Ford had "an encounter with an incontinent cow." I was there. The cow was more than incontinent. I euphemistically reported that Ford "got a bit of the barnyard on his suit." White House aides weren't unhappy this time; they felt it would help Ford with the farm vote.

Though I wasn't assigned full-time to the White House then, I accompanied Ford to Puerto Rico for a summit of the world's major industrial countries in 1976. On that trip I nearly drowned. I was swimming by myself in the surf behind my hotel and got caught in a riptide. Fighting panic – I've never been a strong swimmer – I rode with the current until it dumped me back on the beach a few hundred yards from where I'd been. As I climbed out of the water, I saw a crowd gathered nearby. In the center was the dead body of someone who wasn't as lucky as me.

I was also lucky in another way that shows how Washington works sometimes. After I knew I'd be covering the summit, I was playing tennis with a White House aide and complained that I'd be over my head because I didn't know much about economics. The aide told me to come by his office and he'd brief me on the issues involved. When I took him up on his invitation, he was on the phone but handed me a classified document. I quickly recognized it was the president's briefing book, complete with talking points on U.S. objectives at the summit, and frantically started taking notes on its contents.

"I can't copy that for you, but if you can bring it back in an hour, be my guest," my friend said as he hung up the phone. I rushed back to my office, made a copy, and returned the document with time to spare. That was the extent of my pre-summit briefing.

Days later I was in San Juan and Alan Greenspan, then chairman of the President's Council of Economic Advisors, was holding a news conference after the first summit session. Two giants of economic reporting, Hobart Rowen of the Washington Post and Edwin Dale of the New York Times, were leading the questioning and the ever-enigmatic Greenspan wasn't being very informative. There I was, presidential briefing book in hand (which I shielded from the view of the other reporters); I had a pretty good idea of what had transpired. My advantage seemed so ridiculous I nearly burst out laughing.

During Ford's presidency, I started going to the annual dinner of the White House Correspondents Association, which in recent years has become an egregious example of everything wrong with American journalism. The black tie dinner in the immense ballroom of the Washington Hilton hotel was one of the highlights of the spring social season for news people and newsmakers, along with the Radio-Television Correspondents Association dinner and the elite Gridiron Club dinner. It was a chance for politicians, lobbyists, the military and the media to mingle and schmooze over a meal and a drink or two. I liked to joke the event also let a bunch of New York corporate executives go back to Scarsdale and boast about dining with the president (them and 2,300 other people.) It was all good fun and more or less harmless.

In the late 1980s and early 1990s, however, the complexion of the dinner started to change. It began when Michael Kelly of the Baltimore Sun invited a young woman named Fawn Hall to be his guest. Kelly, who later died in Iraq during the second Gulf War, was out to attract some attention. His guest, a low level White House employee, barely met the criteria for being at the dinner – being a news source. She'd been in the news only because of a minor, titillating aspect of a Reagan White House scandal: she'd hidden some sensitive documents in her underwear.

Thereafter, led by the television networks, news organizations started trying to one-up each other by inviting people in the news unconnected to government, the more outrageous the better. Thus Paula Jones, the plaintiff in a sordid, politically motivated sexual harassment lawsuit against President Clinton, paraded about the dinner in a fancy low-cut ball gown one year, an in-your-face insult to the president and his wife, both of whom were also there. What had been largely an inside-the-Washington-beltway party turned into a vulgar Hollywood on the Potomac celebrity-fest at which working journalists are vastly outnumbered. Reflecting the sophomoric antics that more and more were the norm, the affair is now called "the nerd prom." In my opinion, the dinner has become an embarrassing outrage with which no news organization worthy of the name should wish to be associated.

In the interest of full disclosure, I should note I was a member of the board of the White House Correspondents Association for two years and president of the Radio-Television Correspondents Association for one year before that. A few days before the RTCA dinner at which I was to assume the presidency, my mother died. Her funeral was the morning after. There was no way I could attend the dinner in Washington and be back in Scranton PA in time for the funeral. I'd be seated at the head table between President and Mrs. Reagan. My name would be in all the newspapers. My mother was gone, so I decided to go to the dinner. For the first and only time in our 41 years of marriage, Lynn threatened me with divorce – and meant it. "Your brothers need you. Your children need you to set an example, to show them what's really important. If you go back to Washington, I will leave you," she said – and meant it. Lynn was right. I was way off base. I'd completely lost sight of what life is all about. I've regretted it ever since.

Years after Ford left the White House, I saw him at a luncheon after the dedication of President George H.W. Bush's presidential library at Texas A&M University. I walked over and introduced myself. "Yes, I remember you Gene. Why don't I ever hear you on the radio anymore?" he said. It had been more than 10 years since I worked for UPI Audio. I shouldn't have been surprised by Ford's remarkable memory. I'd accompanied him to Grand Rapids MI for a homecoming ceremony after he was sworn in as vice president. More than 2,000 people shuffled through a receiving line after the ceremony and he greeted nearly every one of them by name. It was an impressive performance.

While I covered Ford as president only sporadically, I made my first flight on Air Force One during his watch. It was a trip to Norfolk VA for the commissioning of an aircraft carrier. I flew on the presidential aircraft scores of times thereafter. One of these was the inaugural flight of the Boeing 747 that most people think of as Air Force One on September 6 1990. (Whatever aircraft the president is aboard uses the call sign "Air Force One." Several smaller planes were also used to transport the president when I covered the White House, including a McDonnell Douglas DC-9 and a couple of Gulfstream executive jets.)

Despite his reassuring conduct of the presidency after taking over from Nixon in 1974, Ford had to beat back a strong challenge from former California Governor Ronald Reagan to win his party's nomination for the job in his own right in 1976. He seemed to be winning the fight until Reagan scored an upset in the North Carolina primary. After that, the battle went on all the way to the Republican National Convention in Kansas City, a boisterous affair that demonstrated the fading influence of the party's moderate wing. Ford was forced to dump moderate Vice President Nelson Rockefeller as his running mate in favor of more conservative Kansas Senator Robert Dole; even then it took some deft last-minute maneuvering to keep Reagan from stampeding the delegates.

Rockefeller, who was pictured during the convention giving the finger to his right-wing critics, died at age 70 less than three years later, ostensibly of a heart attack while working on his art collection in his Manhattan office. The cause of death announced by longtime spokesman Hugh Morrow was accurate. The circumstances weren't. Word quickly leaked out that the former veep was stricken fatally during an intimate interlude with a woman 45 years younger than him, giving rise to a much-repeated newsroom wisecrack that in Rockefeller was "coming and going" in his final moments.

Besides the encounters with a dairy cow in Wisconsin and a football helmet in Oklahoma, another of Ford's campaign trips that year bears mentioning. It started in Louisiana with a riverboat trip down the Mississippi to New Orleans aboard the SS Nachez. (The same riverboat on which Dan Quayle made his inauspicious debut as George H.W. Bush's running mate in 1988.) Ford and wife Betty attended a Tulane-Boston College football game that evening. The next day Ford embarked on a day-long bus trip that featured rallies in several Mississippi and Alabama cities along the Gulf Coast. Among Ford's traveling companions were some prominent Southern Democrats who were supporting him, including former Mississippi Governor John Bell Williams and Mississippi Congressman William Colmer. Both were notorious racists.

Williams introduced Ford at the first few stops. As we rolled toward the next one, White House Press Secretary Ron Nessen announced that Colmer would be taking over the introductory chores. "What happened to John Bell Williams?" someone in the back of the bus shouted. Almost reflexively I muttered to myself: "He had to go to a lynching."

Stan Cloud of Time Magazine, who was sitting next to me, overheard the remark and burst out laughing. He'd just taken a sip of coffee which he spit all over the seat in front of him. Everyone wanted to know what caused the commotion. Stan, who was almost in tears laughing, repeated my remark. Nessen was not amused. It probably shows how far we've come on the racial issues that today my comment would not be considered humorous.

During his brief stay in the White House, Ford chose an African-American, William Coleman, to be Secretary of Transportation. Coleman was only the second black to serve in the Cabinet and the first in a Republican administration. University of Chicago President Edward Levi gave up that job to become Ford's attorney general. George H.W. Bush was his CIA Director and Brent Scowcroft became his national security advisor, the same role he played in Bush's presidency.

Ford and Carter had three debates during the 1976 presidential campaign. Their face-to-face encounters took on added importance because they were the first debates since Nixon and Kennedy squared off in 1960. I covered all of them. The first, in Philadelphia, was delayed for 27 minutes at one point as technicians scrambled to fix a microphone problem. During the second one, which took place in San Francisco, Ford inexplicably declared: "There is no Soviet domination of Eastern Europe," a statement that plunged his campaign aides into days of damage control.

I'll never forget how Ford tried to explain what he meant. He used a White House hand-held radio, known in those days as a "walkie-talkie" to broadcast a statement to the reporters covering him as we sat on a press bus in a Los Angeles suburb. It was a patchwork effort to manage a mess that seemed almost hilarious at the time because it comported with the image of clumsiness that unfairly dogged him.

"If it hadn't been for the debates, I would have lost (the election). They established me as competent on foreign and domestic affairs and gave the viewers reason to think that Jimmy Carter had something to offer," Carter said later.

Carter opened his inaugural address with a tribute to Ford. "For myself and for our nation, I want to thank my predecessor for all he has done to heal our land," he said. The onetime rivals became close friends after both were back in private life. Carter arranged monthly briefings for Ford during his presidency and their friendship blossomed when they traveled to Egypt together for the funeral of that country's assassinated president, Anwar Sadat.

As a former president, Ford was sometimes accused of cashing in on the job he once held by serving on corporate boards and drawing directors' fees. But he also remained engaged in civic life. Among other things, he opposed efforts to overturn an affirmative action admissions policy at his alma mater, the University of Michigan, a move that upset many fellow conservatives.

In a New York Times op ed article published in 1999, Ford wrote: "Times of change are times of challenge. It is estimated that by 2030, 40 percent of all Americans will belong to various racial minorities. Already the global economy requires unprecedented grasp of diverse viewpoints and cultural traditions. I don't want future college students to suffer the cultural and social impoverishment that afflicted my generation. If history has taught us anything in this remarkable century, it is the notion of America as a work in progress."

Ford died the day after Christmas in 2006 at his home in Rancho Mirage CA. At his funeral, President Bush senior delivered one of the eulogies. "To know Jerry was to know a Norman Rockwell painting come to life. An avuncular figure, quick to smile, frequently with a pipe in his mouth. He could be tough. He could be tough as nails when the situation warranted. But he also had a heart as big and open as the Midwestern plains on which he was born. And he imbued every life he touched with understated gentility," Bush said.

It was an apt epitaph.

Chapter Eight

In the Presence of Sainthood and Nature's Fury

POPE JOHN PAUL II's first visit to the United States in 1979 was headline-making from start to finish. The man now known to Roman Catholics as Saint John Paul the Great was the first non-Italian pontiff since Pope Adrian VI, a Dutchman who ruled over the Holy See for just one year early in the 16th Century. Karol Jozep Wojtyla had been a Polish cardinal, an ethnicity that made him a hero to millions of American Poles, and he was expected to bring a new breeze to the archaic institution he led. When I was assigned to cover the visit, my devout Irish Catholic mother rejoiced. She was confident my proximity to the successor to Saint Peter, the man Catholics called "the vicar of Christ," would bring me back into the fold I'd drifted away from after leaving home. It did nothing of the sort.

The pope visited six cities during his week-long trip: Boston, Philadelphia, New York, Des Moines, Chicago and Washington. I traveled with him on his chartered airliner, which had the papal coat of arms painted on its nose along with the name "Shepherd One." As someone used to the irreverent, freewheeling atmosphere of presidential campaign trips, I was quickly turned off by the rigid, heel-clicking authoritarianism that surrounded John Paul. Men in cassocks and Roman collars were forever scurrying to and fro, enforcing strict, often silly *diktats* about what reporters like me could and couldn't do. Their dogmatic approach to everything was reinforced and attenuated by the pope's U.S. Secret Service bodyguards, many of them devout Irish Catholics who saw themselves on a holy mission.

My apostasy often showed. During a live broadcast of the pope's arrival in Boston, I noted that he was dedicating his first Mass to the youth of America. Drawing on my altar boy background, I went on to say that a priest declared at the beginning of the liturgical rite, "I will go to the altar of God, God the joy of my youth." The late Cokie Roberts, an author and commentator then with National Public Radio, kicked me in the shin and said: "That's the old Latin Mass. The Mass is in English now!"

Sometimes there were comic moments. The pope ended his stay in New York by conducting an outdoor religious ceremony in a driving rainstorm, leaving us all soaking wet as we boarded his plane for a flight to Des Moines. Someone hung John Paul's pure white cassock up to dry on the curtain rod dividing his first class cabin from those of us in economy, and it bounced up and down like a cartoonish Caspar the Friendly Ghost as the jet climbed to cruising altitude through significant turbulence.

In Chicago I was part of a pool covering the pope's arrival by helicopter at the residence of Cardinal John Cody, an arch-conservative with considerable influence in American politics. His scheduled arrival time came and went; the pope was running late. Nevertheless, the clerics in charge directed us back to the bus. The other reporters, all members of the Vatican Press Corps, complied obediently. Although I was told I wouldn't be allowed back on the bus if I didn't comply, I ignored the warning.

John Paul finally arrived, and as he walked to his car a young man jumped the fence surrounding the landing field and ran toward the pontiff. He didn't get very far before he was tackled by Secret Service agents and pinned to the ground. Apparently sensing that the miscreant was not a threat but a simply a believer overcome by emotion, the pope motioned to the agents to bring the man to him. The two hugged, and each went on his way. When I got back to the bus, I shouldered my way on, insisting I'd done what I was there for and covered a news-making aspect of the pope's itinerary. The clerics felt otherwise: I'd been defiant and disobedient. One guy in a Roman collar said it was obvious I was "a fallen-away Catholic." I told the pope's handlers to go to hell. I'd about had it with the church I was raised in by then.

My alienation undoubtedly had something to do with a joke I played on Lynn as the trip ended in Washington. My UPI employers at the time told me to stay with the traveling entourage instead of going home. Millions were expected to attend the final public event of John Paul's visit – a Mass on the Mall – and my bosses feared I wouldn't be able to get back into the city from my home in the Virginia suburbs. So Lynn came into town to meet me for dinner. The pope was staying at the Papal Legation on Washington's Embassy Row, but the rest of the traveling party was staying at a hotel on Thomas Circle, then the heart of the capital's Red Light District. When Lynn arrived, the hotel lobby was filled with clergymen, an unnerving sight for someone not of the faith. Once I saw her obvious unease, I couldn't resist pulling her leg. "Fifty dollars! No, I won't pay that much," I said in a loud voice. Lynn didn't think it was funny.

Members of the traveling press were granted an audience with the pope before he flew back to Rome. I didn't go. John Paul was to meet and greet us in the backyard of the Papal Legation, but we waited and waited and it was cold. So I finally decided to skip it and got back on the bus. Little did I know then that I'd passed up a chance to be blessed by a saint – not that it bothers me. Pope John Paul II was canonized in 2014, nine years after his death.

I saw the Polish Pope twice more after that. He and President Reagan met in Fairbanks, Alaska in 1984 when Reagan was on the homeward leg of a trip to China. I saw him again when he and President Clinton met in Denver in 1993. In neither case was I anywhere near as close to him as I was when I covered his 1979 visit. There was an unfortunate incident during the Denver visit. When some Catholic prelates tried to crowd into a photograph with the pope and the president, a young Clinton aide cried out, "Hey, get the fuck outa there!" The young man was fired for the outburst.

As the product of a parochial grade school and Jesuit high school and college, I was thoroughly indoctrinated in the Catholic faith. The schooling didn't take; early on, I had problems with how the Church of Rome represented itself as the "divinely inspired one true religion." How, then, to explain the billions of people on Earth who worshipped differently? Or the Borgia popes, who presided over a Vatican drenched in financial corruption and sexual licentiousness? Or the Inquisition? Or the church's persecution of Galileo and other truth seekers? Or its role in rapacious European colonialism?

Not that I can recall in my 16 years of Catholic education were any of these issues ever addressed. Nor was the Vatican's moral squalor in dealing the Spanish Civil War or Hitler's Nazi Germany during World War Two. My coverage of American politics deepened my disenchantment: time after time I saw the Catholic hierarchy align itself with the most reactionary forces in politics. This unholy alliance existed even before the U.S. Supreme Court legalized abortion in 1973 which put the church's political activities on steroids. I can recall as a child constant preachments against "godless Communism" which caused church leaders to join forces with such scoundrels as Richard Nixon and Senator Joseph McCarthy.

I was long gone from the faith by the time the church's horrific sex abuse scandal exploded as a result of a *Boston Globe* investigation in 2001-2002. The Pulitzer Prize winning journalism was led by Walter Robinson, whom I knew well, and amply documented in the motion picture "Spotlight," which won an Academy Award for Best Picture in 2016. Robbie and his team uncovered priestly misconduct and the Catholic hierarchy's continued cover-up by pouring through records and knocking on doors for months, dogged legwork unheard of outside of newspapers. Sadly, that kind of investigative journalism is a vanishing practice now because of the financial problems besetting the newspaper industry in the age of the Internet.

My abandoned Catholicism was no impediment to a close relationship with my "Uncle Joe," my mother's Jesuit priest younger brother. From the time I was a little boy, he was one of my favorite people. He was funny and kind, and radiated holiness without being a bore. He loved to spend time with our family when I was a kid, and was a frequent, much welcomed visitor when I had a home of my own. I'll love him always for what to my mind was perhaps one of the most deeply Christian, loving gestures I've ever witnessed. When my father died, Father Joe said the funeral mass and my oldest son Sean was an altar boy. He knew that Sean wasn't even baptized. But when it came time for communion, he nevertheless administered the sacrament to his heathen grand-nephew. If God is love, so was Uncle Joe.

In his old age, my priest uncle struggled with his faith. I don't know the extent of it, but he let me know he was deeply disappointed with the direction of the church. He became the chaplain of pro football's old Baltimore Colts and reveled in that role. He loved that team, and the team loved him. A year or so before he died, he was talking to me one day of his misgivings about his fellow priests and whether his life had been well spent when he suddenly said with great emphasis: "I, for one, NEVER abused a child!"

Whoa, I thought – where did that come from? I didn't press him. But I'm convinced he'd become at least dimly aware of the extent of what was going on and it pierced him to the core. How any institution claiming a link to God could not only tolerate such behavior but actually protect it is something I'll simply never understand.

Equally maddening to me is the U.S. Catholic hierarchy's often pernicious influence on American politics, centering on the issue of abortion. Ever since the U.S. Supreme Court's Roe v. Wade decision legalized the procedure, the church has embraced some of the most heinous politicians I've ever known so long as they opposed abortion. This, my opinion, is a significant factor in the political polarization that bitterly divides our country and a cause of the rise of Donald J. Trump.

In 2006, I was invited to be principal speaker at the Mayor of Scranton's annual prayer breakfast. It was my brother Joe's idea of a cosmic joke. As I told the audience, I wasn't a churchgoer and didn't give a lot of thought to spirituality. The latter wasn't true; all my life I've struggled to understand what life on Earth is all about, why so many are poor, sick and hungry while a few like me have more than we need. In my speech, I talked about the godliness of two people who didn't believe in God, Lynn and one of my squad leaders in South Korea, Sergeant John Lynch.

I recounted how after Lynn and I were married a few years and had managed to save a few thousand dollars, I was startled one day to find our savings account nearly empty. When I angrily confronted Lynn about it, she said she'd loaned the money to a woman who'd done some housework for us. The woman's grandson needed expensive medical treatment and they had no health insurance.

I was furious. I told Lynn what she already knew: that we were saving to put our children through college and it was unlikely we'd ever get the money back. Through her tears she told me that her friend needed the money and we didn't, at least not at that moment. I've since learned that while she wasn't a believer and without knowing it, Lynn was espousing a Judeo-Christian philosophical principle known as "preferential option for the poor:" that through one's words and actions, one must always show compassion for the neediest among us. A footnote to this story is that the woman eventually repaid us every last cent.

Sergeant Lynch's story involved a sick child at an orphanage we supported in the Korean village of Munsan-ni. This little boy had a horrible skin disease that covered much of his body with open sores. Our medics gave the people in charge of the orphanage medicine with which to treat the child. But when he didn't improve, we suspected they were selling it on the black market, not an uncommon occurrence in that place at that time. So Lynch, a hard-bitten, hard-drinking type whom you'd never find in any church, took it upon himself to treat the boy. For several weeks, he went to the orphanage every day to bathe the boy and apply the medicine to his oozing sores. When I congratulated him on it he shrugged it off with a racial slur, saying if the gooks wouldn't do it, someone else had to.

I also talked about Vice President Hubert Horatio Humphrey, a gentle, decent, deeply patriotic man who embodied the word "liberal," a term dripping with negative connotations in modern American politics thanks largely to thinly-veiled racism and the mean-spiritedness of people like Anne Coulter and Rush Limbaugh who've made millions inflaming the public. A few weeks before he died of prostate cancer at age 66, Humphrey's colleagues honored him by inviting him to address a Joint Session of Congress. What he said that day will stick with me until the day I die.

"The test of government," he said," is what it does to make life better for those in the dawn of life – the children; for those in the twilight of life – the elderly; and for those in the shadow of life – the poor, the sick and the disabled." In the late 1970s when Humphrey spoke, his test of government was America's test – there was no real argument about what he said. Republicans and Democrats differed on the details but both parties endorsed public policy aimed at making life better for every citizen, especially the least of us – the most powerless members of our society. It was Richard Nixon who established the Equal Employment Opportunity Commission and the Environmental Protection Agency, the former to combat racist hiring practices and the latter to ensure clean air and water was not just to be found in wealthier communities.

To be sure, there were major distractions – the Vietnam War, Watergate – but the naysayers were on the fringes, largely dismissed as religious zealots or political crackpots. That was then. Now we see an ever-widening gap between rich and poor. A health care program enacted under President Barack Obama that reduced the number of American without access to proper health care by half faced a slow death after he left office instead of being perfected. It's becoming more and more difficult to be poor, sick or disabled in these United States. Our country, which once prided itself as a nation of immigrants, is slamming the door to immigrants and refugees.

How far we've come since Humphrey's time. Here was a man who truly rose from his bootstraps, who vaulted to national prominence from a hardscrabble background. Yet he never forgot from whence he came. His endless quest in life was to make things better for the next generation. Demonstrating that life is unfair, Humphrey was brutalized throughout the 1968 presidential campaign by the very people who supposedly shared his values, the liberal wing of the Democratic Party. It all had to do with the Vietnam War, which Humphrey privately opposed. Everywhere he went he was greeted by chants of "Dump the Hump." He was often spat on while shaking hands along a rope-line. At the Democratic Convention in Chicago, police assaulted peaceful antiwar protestors. Sen. Eugene McCarthy, a fellow Minnesotan and onetime pal who had presidential aspirations of his own, only begrudgingly endorsed Humphrey when it was too late to make much difference.

It was a tumultuous time. Even so, I don't think there was the partisan hatred that divides us today. Certainly there weren't the for-profit talk radio and cable TV hatemongers that dwell among us. A 1968 campaign sidelight comes to mind that illustrates the difference between the practice of politics then and now. Humphrey was walking through the lobby of Philadelphia's old Bellevue Stratford Hotel when he noticed a Republican "Truth Squad" led by Pennsylvania Senator Hugh Scott was holding a news conference in a hotel ballroom. Humphrey playfully invaded the event and engaged in some lighthearted banter with the participants. As he turned to leave, Scott called out to him, "Hubert, whatever happens in November, you're a good man. God bless you!" What a mind-boggling difference with the political rhetoric of today.

A lot of today's smash-mouth politics is the legacy of Lee Atwater, a political operative for President Reagan and President Bush senior.

I knew Lee – he was a guy who believed in winning at all costs, that the end justifies the means. He put a whole new meaning on the word "spin." His shading of the truth started a trend. What most reasonable people would call ought-right lies are now known as "alternative facts." When he was 39 years old, Atwater was diagnosed with brain cancer that quickly killed him. On his deathbed, Atwater publicly apologized to political opponents he demonized, including Michael Dukakis, the 1988 Democratic presidential nominee. His political soliloquy in a 1991 interview published in *Life Magazine* a month before he died is a sobering commentary on the harm he helped inflict on our democracy.

"My illness helped me see that what was missing in society is what was missing in me: a little heart, a lot of brotherhood. The 80's were about acquiring – acquiring wealth, power, prestige. I know," Atwater said. "I acquired more wealth, power and prestige than most. But you can acquire all you want and still feel empty. What power wouldn't I trade for a little more time with my family. What price wouldn't I pay for an evening with friends. It took a deadly illness to put me eye to eye with that truth, but it is a truth that the country, caught up in its ruthless ambitions and moral decay, can learn on my dime."

Atwater died remorseful. But his playbook is still in use. The veiled racism, super patriotism and an incessant drumbeat that it's somehow un-American to want government to devote significant resources to the poor, sick and disabled that were his stock in trade are now on steroids. Humphrey would be sick at heart.

When I was in school, we learned about Congressional figures who loomed large in American history, people like Henry Clay and Daniel Webster. Humphrey deserves such recognition though I doubt many young people today would even recognize his name. Among other things, he was a pioneer in the U.S. civil rights movement. At his party's 1948 convention in Philadelphia, the then-mayor of Minneapolis delivered an impassioned plea for equality for the nation's black citizens. "The time has arrived in America for the Democratic Party to get out of the shadow of States' Rights and to walk forthrightly into the bright sunshine of human rights," he said.

Humphrey's speech triggered a walkout by nearly three dozen convention delegates from Southern states and the formation of the Dixiecrat Party, a political insurrection led by South Carolina Sen. Strom Thurmond that nearly cost Democratic President Harry Truman the election. Humphrey was a pivotal figure in the debate that led to congressional passage of the landmark 1964 Civil Rights Act. Brooklyn Dodger great Jackie Robinson, who broke major league baseball's color barrier in 1948 and is now enshrined in baseball's Hall of Fame, was among African-American leaders who supported his 1988 presidential bid. I was there when Humphrey and Jackie Robinson met at a bank in Harlem during the fall campaign. The two also attended the fourth game of the 1968 World Series, a series that pitted the Detroit Tigers against the Saint Louis Cardinals. I was there but as well my only memory of that event is of Humphrey in the Cardinals' locker room afterwards posing with some of the players.

I was also with President Jimmy Carter when he stopped in Minneapolis while enroute home from a trip to California to give Humphrey a ride back to Washington. Members of Humphrey's family, including his granddaughter Vicky, a Down's Syndrome child, were at the airport to see him off. It was a sad occasion; Humphrey was critically ill and nearly everyone knew it was probably his last journey. Although he had been vice president and a U.S. senator before and after he was veep, the flight to Washington was Humphrey's first time ever on Air Force One.

The 1968 presidential campaign is pastiche of memories. Prominent among them: Robert Kennedy's assassination. We were at the U.S. Air Force Academy on June 5, 1998; Humphrey was giving the commencement address the next day. Together with two other more senior Humphrey campaign aides I'd watched the television coverage of Kennedy's win in the California Democratic primary. We talked briefly about the possibility of a Humphrey-Kennedy ticket in the fall and then I'd gone to bed. Being awakened when Kennedy was shot in Los Angeles. Scrambling to make sense of it all. Spate Drummond, a dashing Air Force lieutenant colonel who was Humphrey's military aide, leaving to fly a fighter to Boston to pick up a neurosurgeon who might save Kennedy's life. Humphrey's speech abandoned, flying back to Washington amid heavy security the next morning. It had seemed like the gloom that covered the country after President Kennedy was taken away was beginning to lift. Now his brother. It was just awful.

The tumultuous Chicago convention was another downer. I argued afterward with my father. He thought the demonstrators deserved the bashing they got. "I WAS THERE," I shouted during an overnight visit with my parents in Pennsylvania. "IT WAS A GODDAMNED DISGRACE!" (Dad subsequently became radicalized by the Vietnam War. My brother Joe once saw him standing beside his car holding up his hand and making the V sign for peace as two antiwar activists were being transferred from Lackawanna County Jail to an arraignment in Harrisburg.)

Another more pleasant take-away from that turbulent time, one that could never happen now: In early October of the 1968 campaign, Humphrey and Nixon agreed on a brief timeout. Both sides would take a breather for two or three days before entering the homestretch of the presidential race. We went to Long Beach Island NJ where Humphrey was to relax at the seaside official residence of the state's Democratic governor. Then, consternation!

After getting a night's sleep, Humphrey decided he needed to return to Washington. There didn't seem to be any good reason but there was no talking him out of it. He agreed to take only one aide and keep the trip quiet. The rest of Humphrey's entourage, including his staff and the entire press corps covering his campaign, enjoyed some time off at the beach. No one was the wiser.

Still another flashback: Humphrey on the campaign's last day, cheered by a sea of people as he rode through downtown Los Angeles in an open car. His campaign, finally, seemed to catch fire. The polls looked good. There was a sense he might win.

I travelled with Humphrey for nearly nine months in 1968. It was a heady experience for a 25-year old. It gave me a glimpse of what goes on at the highest level of U.S. political life. Mine was a fleeting view, however; I knew nothing about the inner workings of the campaign. My job was to tape-record Humphrey's speeches and send out short sound-bites to radio stations throughout the country. I also recorded reports about what he was saying and doing that went to any radio station willing to use them. No one ever checked my work. I was entirely on my own. I can't imagine that happening today. No political campaign at any level would risk letting someone as junior and inexperienced as I was operate on their own.

I deeply respected Humphrey. He was an honest, decent, humble man devoted to improving the lives of his fellow citizens. When Lynn and I married in 1971, he sent us a moving congratulatory letter simply signed "Hubert." I went on to cover seven more presidential races:

Nixon-McGovern in 1972; Carter-Ford in 1976; Carter-Reagan in 1980; Reagan-Mondale in 1984; Bush-Dukakis in 1988; Bush-Clinton in 1992 and Clinton-Dole in 1996. None matched my first taste of what goes into choosing America's leader.

Humphrey told me early in the Watergate uproar that if only President Nixon would acknowledge what he and his people had done, the American people would forgive and forget. I believe he was right. I stopped in to see him at his Senate office shortly before he died. Typical of the man, he was concerned that I had a bad cold. Never mind that he had terminal cancer. The man had a profound influence on me; I think of him often. I try to live by a lesson he claimed his father taught him: pack as much life as possible into every day. You'll get plenty of sleep when you die.

Looking back over three quarters of a century, I marvel about all the others who've also helped shape my life. My mother and dad; my brothers Charlie and Joe; Lynn and Becky; my children; three teachers and a colorful character with whom I worked.

Matthew O'Rourke – we students called him "Mattie" behind his back – was one of the teachers. A professor of English at the University of Scranton, he helped fire in me a love of the language, an essential attribute for anyone who aspires to write. O'Rourke had flair. He dressed and acted the part of an English don, which was probably his single most captivating aspect. He turned us on to really good books and marched us outdoors in the springtime to sit by the side of Lake Scranton and hear him lecture on poetry. One day he announced that the woman he loved was to marry someone else, and dismissed the class. He was enigmatic. I often wonder whatever became of him.

Father Joseph Devlin S.J. was a philosophy teacher. Like many of my fellow students, I saw myself as an intellectual, and read up on Sartre and Kierkegaard, Neitzsche and Kant. All were anathema to the Roman Catholic Church, which added to their allure. But I have to admit philosophy bored me until I took Devlin's class. He made the subject come alive. Logic and ethics were his forte. Burned into my consciousness is his favorite syllogism for demonstrating faulty logic: "All monkeys whistle; The pope whistles; Therefore, the pope is a monkey." My main takeaway from Devlin's teaching was, and is, that the end NEVER justifies the means. It's a shame that many of America's corporate, religious and political leaders were never exposed to this good man. Our country would avoid a lot of grief if we made his chief precept our bedrock principle.

Foremost in my pantheon of personal heroes is Army Lieutenant Colonel George M. Lindsay, who headed the University of Scranton's Reserve Officer Training Program (ROTC). A large, barrel-chested man with a bristling moustache that made him look like a stereotypical officer of a British regiment, Colonel Lindsay epitomized the military credo: duty, honor, country. But he wasn't a West Pointer – far from it.

Lindsay, who never lost his Boston accent, was just eight years old when his father died, leaving his mother with him and several younger children. His mother found work in a psychiatric hospital to support the family. When he was old enough Lindsay joined the Army to help out and fought through the Pacific during World War Two. When the war ended, he finally got his high school diploma and went through college on the GI Bill. He then rejoined the army and climbed through the ranks, finishing his career as a professor of military science. Lindsay's decorations included two Bronze Stars, the Purple Heart and a Combat Infantryman's Badge. He was courageous and outspoken, with no use whatsoever for right wing extremism then embodied in the John Birch Society. Most of all, he was an inspiring leader.

Colonel Lindsay was immensely proud of his brother John, whom I knew as *Newsweek's* chief political writer. In fact, John and I became campaign trail buddies. He himself was a profile in courage. He was terrified of flying – a paralyzing phobia in a profession like ours – and assuaged his fears by drinking too much. He managed to go on the wagon though, and just accepted the air travel as an occupational risk. I often was his teetotaling dining companion to keep him from temptation – most of our colleagues were a hard-drinking bunch who did a lot of imbibing at dinner. Some drank a lot more than others, which led to creation of the so-called Germond Rule: "Eat and drink defensively, because the bill will be shared equally." Its originator was Jack Germond, a political writer for the Baltimore Sun.

In retirement, my old military mentor lived in San Francisco, and when he was in his eighties I tried to call him once a month to tell him what was going on in Washington. He liked that: he once told me the worst side-effect of growing old was becoming irrelevant. "You make me feel relevant again," he said.

Colonel Lindsay was 88 when he died. In the last few years of his life, he got into blogging, writing about his wartime experiences. When a controversy over President Clinton's permissive policy toward gays in the military erupted – a policy known as "Don't Ask, Don't Tell" – the colonel blogged about it, saying there'd always been and always would be gays in the military. He wrote about a gay medic in the Pacific, calling the man one of the most heroic soldiers he ever knew. If someone did their duty and minded their own business, he said, their sexuality should be no big deal. How progressive of someone of his generation, and so typical of one of my most cherished role models.

Another individual who helped shape my life was endlessly interesting but hardly inspiring. At one time, Edward "Pye" Chamberlayne's odd middle name and authoritative baritone voice made him one of America's most recognizable radio newsmen. He counted William Faulkner among his friends. At least he'd met him, having traveled to Oxford, Mississippi while he was a University of Virginia student to visit his favorite novelist. Pye was immensely talented, He had a way with words that enabled him to clearly and briefly explain complex issues, but his inordinate fondness for booze kept him from going as far in his chosen profession as he otherwise might have.

He had a legendary mischievous streak. After three or four double bourbons, his toupee askew, Pye would often do something outrageous that endeared him to colleagues while earning him powerful enemies. One episode involved television diva Barbara Walters, one of that medium's first celebrity journalists. She visited Plains GA soon after Jimmy Carter won the 1976 presidential election to interview the country's incoming leader. The interview became controversial because of its supplicatory tone. "Be good to us, be kind to us," she implored the president-elect at one point as if he were about to become an all-powerful potentate.

Walters and her entourage were sitting in the dining room of the Best Western Motel in Americus GA early one evening when Pye stumbled in, already in his cups but eager for company. Without waiting for an invitation, he pulled up a chair and joined the group, addressing Walters as "my Million Dollar Baby." He was referring to the fact that Walters some weeks earlier had been named co-anchor of ABC Evening News with Harry Reasoner and given a seven figure salary, then an unbelievably lofty sum in the news business. Walters, whose condescension was world class, tried to ignore him. Pye then escalated the assault. "You know,

Barbara, when you're giving the news on television people can see your nipples right through your dress – and I'll tell you, it's dynamite!" he declared loudly and earnestly.

I myself was once victimized by Pye's drink-induced playfulness. We'd finished covering a Democratic Party conference in Philadelphia and were racing to catch the last express train to Washington. As we rushed through the lobby of our hotel, Pye spotted some familiar faces in the bar and suggested we have a quick drink. I demurred and went on the train station.

I'd just stepped away from the ticket counter when I saw Pye enter the station, swaying a bit as he walked. I saw him spot and seize a microphone sitting on a counter and check to assure it was on.

"ATTENTION, ATTENTION," I heard him announce. "THE TRAIN SCHEDULED TO LEAVE FROM TRACK 10 WILL INSTEAD BE LEAVING FROM TRACK 12. THE TRAINS SCHEDULED TO LEAVE FROM TRACKS 13 AND 14 HAVE BEEN CANCELLED. THANK YOU."

Pandemonium ensued as hundreds of conference attendees scrambled to learn what was going on. Then came a second announcement. "ATTENTION, ATTENTION. MR. GENE GIBBONS, PLEASE CALL HOME. IT'S ABOUT YOUR CAT," Pye intoned. Not only did we not then have a cat -- he knew full well I loath cats. At that point a railroad cop ended Pye's fun by threatening him with arrest. The whole episode was so embarrassing I pretended I didn't know him on the train home.

Pye's fondness for the outrageous often emerged in his work. In an interview, he asked California Sen. Alan Cranston about his health, remarking that the senator looked awfully gaunt. Cranston explained that he was an avid runner and liked being thin. "Senator, are you aware that people call you "Shroud of Turin" behind your back?' Chamberlayne proclaimed.

Even more offensive but equally amusing was an interview he did with a roving evangelist named Arthur Blessitt, a fringe candidate on the Democratic ticket in the 1976 New Hampshire presidential primary. Blessitt, whom President George W. Bush later credited with having brought about his religious awakening, campaigned throughout the Granite State on foot carrying a 12-foot wooden cross. At the foot of the cross was a caster, the type of swivel wheel usually found on furniture.

In his inimitable fashion, Pye asked the preacher how often he had to replace the wheel.

Pye was UPI Radio's top banana when I joined the organization. I liked him and he liked me. He taught me a lot about writing and broadcasting. I was probably better at getting the story, but he could take what I uncovered and explain it much better. Soon we were a team: "Pye Chamberlayne and Gene Gibbons on Capitol Hill." We traveled together on several presidential campaigns and socialized with our families when we were home. Pye's excessive drinking eventually drove us apart. I tired of having to placate people he insulted when he was drunk and getting him home or back to a hotel when the night was over. When United Press International ran aground financially, I bailed on the company, joining Voice of America briefly – a job I detested because it wasn't real journalism – and ultimately signed on with Reuters. We had no real contact for several years.

Then Pye called me one day. He was in the hospital, recovering from heart valve replacement surgery. I went to see him. Our friendship seemed poised to resume. I'd left Reuters by then to become co-founding editor of a news website called Stateline. I often hired Pye at a day rate to help edit copy. He did an outstanding job. As far as I knew, he'd kicked the bottle. So I was shocked one morning when his wife Mary called to tell me Pye had died in his sleep. He was only 68. I doubt my career would have flourished as much were it not for my difficult friend. He was everything I was not: brash, outspoken, unreliable, much too fond of alcohol. But he was also a wonderful teacher. Pye hated to be called a journalist. "Journalist," he said, was just a fancy word for a reporter who didn't pay his bills.

II

One of the most memorable stories I ever covered had nothing to do with politics – in May 1980 a mountain blew up with me on it! The presidential campaign was then several months old, and I was in the Pacific Northwest to cover the Oregon primary. But the voting was overshadowed by a massive volcanic eruption.

The day before the eruption occurred, Adam Clymer of the *New York Times* told me he had driven that morning into neighboring Washington for a close-up look at Mount St. Helens, a long-dormant volcano that had come back to life two months earlier. Its activity had consisted of minor vomiting of steam and ash, but geologists were watching a glowing bulge on the mountain's north slope and warned that a major eruption could come anytime. Clymer's trip sounded interesting, so I decided to follow suit and got directions from him. Thus on Sunday, May 18, 1980 at 8:31 AM, I was approaching Cougar, a tiny village on the southwest slope of Mount St. Helens, when the volcano went off like an atomic bomb.

Although an earthquake measuring 5.0 on the Richter Scale preceded the eruption, possibly triggering it, I felt nothing; the motion of my car apparently masked the tremor. Nor did I hear the sonic boom generated by the blast even though it rattled windows nearly 100 miles away in Seattle. Because the blast was a lateral one, the sound waves were deflected away from me.

I undoubtedly would have been frightened had I been aware of the earthquake or the thunderous explosion with which the eruption began. But I didn't realize what was happening until a car a few hundred yards in front of me swerved to the side of the road and stopped. At first I thought the driver was trying to avoid an animal, so I started braking too.

Then I saw it: a gigantic, boiling boulder-shaped mass of dirty gray smoke where the peak of Mount Saint Helens was a moment earlier. I pulled over, and as I stepped from the car, the whole ridgeline seemed to disintegrate. It was awesome – so awesome I watched in fascination rather than terror.

As the volcanic cloud grew, the sky darkened as if a fierce thunderstorm was about to begin. I was getting nervous, but I was also excited about what I had stumbled into. I thought was if this was THE eruption everyone was waiting for, I would scoop the *Associated Press*, my then-employer's chief competitor.

To beat the AP, I had to get to a pay phone. (Cellphones didn't exist then.) I'd seen one at a recreation area a few miles earlier so I jumped back into my car and sped there. While waiting for the Portland UPI bureau to take my call, I wondered if I was overreacting to another routine volcanic sneeze that looked spectacular because I'd never seen one before. A glance at the billowing ash cloud convinced me otherwise, so I used a lot of superlatives as I described the scene. When I finished dictating, the desk man on the other end told me I'd better leave the area. "But would you mind calling the Seattle bureau first?" he asked. I made the call he requested and also called New York to file a radio story. Then, fighting panic, I drove down off the mountain.

I drove well over the speed limit, fearing that some of the ravines I'd crossed earlier might soon be impassable, the girder bridges spanning them knocked down by the volcano's fury. When the last bridge was behind me, I breathed easier and let up on the accelerator. To the south, it was still a sunny, peaceful May morning. But I could no longer see much behind me. The northern sky was pitch black, the peak of Mount Saint Helens completely hidden.

As I neared the safety of the valley floor, a pair of light planes appeared overhead. I figured they belonged to the U.S. Geological Survey, which was monitoring the volcano. Minutes later, when another small plane swooped down across the road and landed in an adjoining field, I had my second lucky break of the day

Don Dexter, the operator of a rural flying service, was piloting the plane. As he rolled to a stop, I caught up with him and asked what he'd seen from the air.

"It's a cataclysm," he said. "The whole top of the mountain is blown away." Saying he was certain air traffic controllers would waive no-fly restrictions that had just been imposed for a news flight, he offered to take me up to see for myself. I'm not a big fan of little airplanes, but I climbed into Dexter's Cessna and soon was approaching Mount Saint Helens again, this time from the air.

From afar, the volcano looked like an inkwell with a towering blue-black plume. As we flew nearer, its monstrous power became frighteningly apparent. It was like looking into the jaws of a massive blast furnace: tongues of lightning arced around the cone and licked at the towering smoke rising from it. It reminded me of a creature of Roman mythology – Vulcan at his forge – and I used the analogy as I taped an ad-libbed radio story. I also had Dexter tape a description and the matter-of-fact word picture he painted was all the more dramatic for its conciseness.

What we didn't know was that hell on earth lay beneath the volcano. The ash cloud blocked our view to the north and west, so we were unaware than thousands of acres of scenic woodland had become a killing ground. Fifty-seven people died that morning, killed by superheated gasses and debris that spilled from the mountain and carved a swath of destruction extending in some places up to 18 miles out from the core.

The dead included 83-year old Harry Truman (no relation to the president), owner of a lodge at the mountain's Spirit Lake who refused to evacuate. The death toll would have been much greater if the eruption occurred less than 18 hours earlier: 50 carloads of Spirit Lake property owners were allowed in to get their belongings the previous afternoon, and another trip was scheduled at 10 that morning.

The National Oceanic and Atmospheric Administration (NOAA) declared Mount St. Helens "the deadliest and most economically destructive volcanic eruption in the history of the United States." But it was slow developing into a national story. A race riot in Miami initially stole the headlines, dashing my hope of scoring a widely celebrated journalistic scoop. Although most of the big western newspapers carried my first-person account and I got on radio newscasts throughout the country, I didn't get a single newspaper byline east of Denver. Cable news was then non-existent and the major TV networks downplayed the eruption; it was strictly a newspaper picture story for the first several days. It wasn't until President Carter flew out to see the volcano several days later that Mount St. Helens got the attention it deserved.

There's a curious footnote to my accidental presence at one of the biggest natural disasters in U.S. history. I spent much of the day the volcano erupted covering Geological Survey briefings in Vancouver WA and got back to Portland after dark. I wrote a dispatch advancing the story for the next afternoon's newspapers, then went out for a drink with several colleagues. I was dead tired by the time I reached my hotel and went to bed, and was almost asleep when I awoke with a jolt. I knew I was safe in Portland, but it was as if I was back on the road near Cougar again, reliving the whole experience. I got out of bed and sat in a chair paralyzed with fear until the flashback ended. I've never had such an episode again nor would I ever want to.

In the course of my work, I crossed paths with a lot of mid-level celebrities, people whose names were household words — at least they were if you followed politics. The ones I remember fondly are, or were, decent and down-to-earth, unaffected by being in the public spotlight. People like Marlin Fitzwater, Lowell Weicker, Pete McClosky and Bob Casey.

Marlin, whom I count as a close friend, is the only individual to have served as White House Press Secretary to two presidents: Ronald Reagan and George H.W. Bush. He set the gold standard for the position

(Jody Powell, the White House Press Secretary under President Carter, and Mike McCurry, who held the job under President Clinton, were close runners-up.) As one of a tiny handful of presidential advisors intimately familiar with his boss's thoughts and actions, he was "in the loop." If he gave someone like me guidance on a news story, it was rock solid – you could take it to the bank. While he wasn't about to talk out of school or go beyond the party line, journalists like myself could always rely on him for one thing that couldn't be said about many White House spokesmen I worked with: he would never lie to you.

As a young reporter, I often played tennis with Lowell Weicker, a three-term Republican senator from Connecticut and later the state's governor. He was an atypical politician – straight-talking, a man of towering integrity with absolutely no use for right wing zealots who were trying to take over the GOP when he was in office. Though nominally still a Republican, he supported Democrat Barack Obama for president. Weicker's bluntness earned him many enemies. He was a dogged competitor: I can't recall ever having beaten him on the tennis court.

Pete McClosky could have been Weicker's twin. As a Marine lieutenant, his heroism in the Korean War earned him Navy Cross and Silver Star as well as two Purple Hearts. Although he was a Republican, he was the first member of Congress to call for President Nixon's impeachment after the Watergate Scandal broke. He later exposed Televangelist Pat Robertson as a liar for claiming combat service in Korea: Robertson's father, a U.S. senator from Virginia, had intervened to keep his son far from the front lines. I knew McClosky well when I covered Congress and greatly admired him. I later lost touch, something I've always regretted.

Yet another maverick completes my "Most Impressive" list – Democrat Bob Casey Sr, who served as governor of my home state of Pennsylvania from 1987 to 1995. Like me, Casey was a graduate of Scranton Prep. Unlike me, he was an outstanding baseball player who turned down a contract offer from the Philadelphia Phillies, choosing to go to college instead. As a leader of the anti-abortion movement, Casey was anathema to many of his fellow Democrats. At age 61, he underwent a lung-heart transplant and lived on for another seven years. We were both honorees at the University of Scranton graduation ceremony in 1995, Casey received a special medal: I was the commencement speaker. At a luncheon following the ceremony, he spoke about my father and mother, both of whom he knew well, and said how proud they would have been of me. It was high praise indeed.

The people mentioned above are, or were at one time, publicly known. Two other unsung individuals – John Kohout and George Candelori – are also among those I regard as inspirational figures. Both are fellow retirees. John is a career Air Force officer who flew B-52 bombers, George, who earned the Silver Star in Vietnam as a helicopter pilot, later flew for United Airlines and worked as a teacher and real estate broker on the side. Nearly every morning we walk several miles together on a riverside trail near our homes. John is conservative, George a liberal. I'm somewhere in the squishy center but lean left when push comes to shove. Every morning we talk politics and almost always find common ground. The key seems to be listening to the other guys' points of view.

Chapter Nine

Sailing, Stateline and Photography

W HAT DOES SAILING have to do with my career as a newsman? Franklin Delano Roosevelt, who was long dead when I joined the White House Press Corps, was the modern president who enjoyed the sport. Because of his polio he couldn't pursue it when he was America's leader. George H.W. Bush was an avid boater but he liked high-powered watercraft, vessels derisively known to sailors as "stinkpots." My involvement with sailing, which spanned more than three decades, supposedly gave me a respite from my high-pressure job but in reality was often just another stressful pastime.

I sailed only once as a child, on a sailing canoe on Lake Wallenpaupack, a man-made lake in Pennsylvania's Pocono Mountains created for hydroelectric and flood control purposes. I was scared to death because I've had a lifelong fear of the water that started when my father insisted I learn how to swim when I was eight or nine years old. He'd drop me off after school at the Catholic Youth Center, our counterpart to the YMCA, and I'd get in the pool with others my age. When it came time to put my head under water, I'd run back to the locker room every time. Getting caught in an ocean riptide at Stone Harbor N.J. briefly when I was 10 or 11 only deepened my hydrophobia.

Nevertheless, in the early 1980s I bought a sailboat, the first of three I owned. It was a 23-foot sloop I named "Connemara" and sailed on the Potomac River. It was the only boat I ever truly enjoyed. I kept it in a small marina a few miles from my home and I could sail it by myself. On a summer evening, Lynn would sometimes come with me. We'd sail out into the river, open a bottle of wine and watch the stars come out. I tried to get my children interested but only Sean, the oldest, ever spent any time on the boat. He was a teenager then and used to sneak it out at night, usually with a girlfriend along.

I've always been driven to play at the highest level at work and at play. Just enjoying myself wasn't enough; I needed a stiff challenge, all the better if it was risky business, the kind of adventure most sensible people would avoid. So soon after I started sailing I jumped at the chance to join some friends sailing a 45-foot ketch from Bermuda to Annapolis. Little did I know then that an east-west ocean passage is likely to be rough because prevailing winds blow from the west, making the voyage upwind. Mother Nature was true to form; we had winds on the nose throughout the eight-day trip, 10 to 20 knots mostly but 30 to 40 during a 48-hour storm, gusting to 52. Seas in and near the Gulf Stream were 12 to 16 feet.

Sailing to windward is always laborious; in this case it was murder. You can't travel in a straight line in a sailboat; you must zig-zag at 45 degree angles from your destination. There were five of us on *Windward*, only two of whom had much offshore experience. The skipper was Russ Ward, then NBC Radio's White House correspondent.

"For me, night sailing in a gentle breeze is one of life's greatest pleasures. But this was challenging, sometimes frightening stuff," I wrote in a *Chesapeake Bay Magazine* article about the experience. "The atmosphere was charged with foreboding as wind, waves and darkness created a Gothic-light setting beyond the red glow of the compass light. 'This is no place for trifling by foolish weekend sailors,' the night seemed to whisper. 'You are treading in the domain of seafarers.'"

I wrote that our 803-mile voyage had taken an eternity by jet age standards, noting that on an Asian trip with President George H.W. Bush we'd left Beijing at breakfast time, flew to Seoul for lunch and thanks to the international dateline got back to Washington in time for dinner.

"Still, the Bermuda-Annapolis passage easily rivalled and in some ways surpassed the drama and excitement of White House travel," I said. "It was a test of character and endurance in an age when such tests are rare, and the rewards were priceless – magnificent oceanscapes even amid the violence of the storm, spectacular sunsets, and, most especially the kind of companionship that probably also exists only in combat."

Notwithstanding my breathless prose, most sensible humans would have been one and done with long distance ocean sailing after that trip which, because of my frequent seasickness, was literally nauseating. Rather than being off-putting however, it whetted my appetite. Soon after the trip, I sold my much-loved Potomac River-based little boat and with a partner purchased a larger one, a 28-foot sloop called *Seanchaithe*, berthed on the Chesapeake. The name is Gaelic for "Story-tellers," a nod to the fact that my partner and I were both writers. We subsequently bought an even larger boat that crushed my finances, ended our friendship and almost brought us to blows. But I'm getting ahead of my story.

The more I got into sailing, the more I wanted. It was selfish and unfair to Lynn, who wasn't at all enamored of what she called my "obsession." It seems clear now my stepped-up involvement in the sport was part of a mid-life crisis that resulted from a career change when I was 56 years old. With little warning, Reuters pulled me out of the White House and stuck me in a desk job editing stories. I probably brought it on myself; I'd gotten pretty full of myself after close to 20 years in what was then considered one of the top jobs in the news business.

I was furious. Heeding the old adage "Don't get mad. Get even," I immediately starting looking for a new job. Soon I found one: managing editor of an Internet startup called Stateline. It aimed to strengthen news coverage of American government at the state level, which was then (and still is) totally inadequate, and it had deep pockets financing, the Pew Foundation.

The work was interesting and I was well paid, considerably better than would have been the case had I stayed with Reuters. The Internet was in its infancy and we learned as we went about cyberspace, creating a valuable new source of information that exists to this day. We gave dozens of journalists their first job. Several went on to highly successful careers; Stateline now counts among its alumni a Pulitzer Prize winner. Moreover, I had a management role, something I'd always wanted. I missed the constant adrenalin rush of covering the White House though and turned to bigtime ocean racing to fill the gap, becoming so consumed I was nearly fired.

The United States Navy was partly to blame. On the basis of my one blue water adventure, which had given me enough hours offshore to qualify, I applied for and was accepted into the U.S. Naval Academy's volunteer sailing coach program. It's a difficult, time consuming commitment; about two dozen volunteers usually are involved. To participate fully, one must demonstrate sailing proficiency and pass a 14-part written exam that tests one's knowledge of a number of seamanship skills, including navigation, weather forecasting, rules of the road, sail trim, diesel engine mechanics, emergency procedures and first aid.

Every Saturday morning for months during the school year, I took classes at the academy to get up to speed on these various skills. When I completed all the requirements, I was awarded a "D-Qual," designating me as a "Senior Skipper Offshore." That meant that in the eyes of the U.S. Navy, I was qualified to command a small boat far out of sight of land. It was a stretch. I would have been in trouble if I'd ever actually been called on to meet that responsibility. Still, it was pretty heady stuff for a weekend sailor.

Two or three afternoons a week in the Fall and Spring I had to leave work early and drive to Annapolis for sailing team practice. I was gone for weeks at a time in early summer doing offshore safety training and actual racing. Ed Fouhy, a former CBS News vice president who was my boss, eventually warned me I was in danger of losing my job. I eased up on my extracurricular activities for a time and succeeded Fouhy as Stateline's executive editor when he retired. I was fortunate: Barbara Rosewicz, a former Wall Street Journal reporter, became my deputy and did such an outstanding job I was able to coast until I hung up my spurs.

While my obsession with sailing didn't reach the level of irresponsibility that it did when I was at Stateline, it was often entwined with my professional life. On visits to California with President Reagan, I got to know the Santa Barbara Yacht Club crowd and frequently sailed with Ian Winspur and Tobe Plough. Winspur, a Scottish hand surgeon with a droll sense of humor practicing in Santa Barbara at the time, owned a 30-foot racing sailboat called *Hazardous Waste.* He and Plough were buddies; in later years we often sailed in the Caribbean together.

One of our most enjoyable excursions involved our wives. In June 1989, Lynn and I joined Ian and his wife Ingrid and Tobe and his wife Sally for nearly a week on Santa Cruz Island, an island the size of Bermuda 25 miles off the California coast. Reachable only by boat or plane, the island covers an 96 square mile area. Just before our visit, it had become the property of The Nature Conservancy and the National Park Service. Previously it was privately owned, the site of a large cattle ranch. We roamed it from one end to the other by four wheel drive pickup truck, reveling in the beauty and privacy. Lynn loved that trip; it was one of the few times she enjoyed my favorite pastime.

When George H.W. Bush was in the White House, I often sailed off Kennebunkport ME on a chartered boat, often taking White House aides along. Bush, as was mentioned previously, was himself was fond of boating; he owned a sleek high-speed Cigarette boat called *"Fidelity"* and could often been seen whizzing along with Secret Service boats chasing behind him, heading a mile or so offshore to go fishing. To my chagrin, my younger children Chad and Becky looked forward to getting a ride on *Fidelity* every August. It was a regular attraction of a daylong picnic the Bushes hosted for the press and their families during their summer vacation. I can't recall if Sean and Jennie ever went along; they might have been too grown up and sophisticated by then.

Illustrating the deterioration of ethical standards that has occurred since, a group of us were out sailing on a chartered boat on a bright and sunny summer Sunday afternoon when someone received a telephone call from Bush's oceanfront estate: White House photographer Susan Biddle needed to report for duty. There was brief discussion of whether a Coast Guard boat could come out and pick her up. That was quickly rejected as an illegitimate use of government property. So we had to return to the dock and drop Susan off, ending what had been a pleasant outing.

When I visited Bush at his Houston office on one occasion after he returned to private life, I gave him a Navy Sailing polo shirt and teased him that wearing it would let him enjoy both worlds: he could continue to operate a power boat but people would think he sailed. Bush told me he did so when he was in Congress, sailing on the Potomac, my training ground. He also told me he'd considered going to the U.S. Naval Academy both before and after World War Two. He didn't explain why he'd changed his mind and attended Yale instead.

The only chief executive I covered who did sail while in office was President Clinton. He and Hillary went out with Sen. Ted Kennedy and Kennedy's wife Vicky on Kennedy's 52-foot schooner Maya during one of their summer vacations on Martha's Vineyard. I was on a power boat following them and kept looking over my shoulder apprehensively at storm clouds building up along the Massachusetts coast.

When we got back into tiny Menemsha Harbor, I spotted a Secret Service agent I knew and expressed surprise that the president and his wife would be out on the water in such threatening weather. The agent assured me that their protective detail was carefully tracking the storms on radar, then suddenly cried out, "Oh, no!" Here was Maya coming into the constricted harbor with Clinton at the helm. At precisely the right moment, the boat swung smartly into the wind and its sails crumbled to the deck. The anchor plunged to the seafloor and all was well.

When Clinton went jogging a day or two later, I was in the press pool and complimented him on his boat-handling skills. I told him few people would dare enter a restricted harbor under full sail. "Oh, I've done that many times," he said. He then apparently remembered I was a sailor and said Kennedy told him what to do. I later learned that someone much more knowledgeable had grabbed the wheel from the president at the last minute and brought the boat to a stop. I've wondered why Clinton claimed a proficiency he clearly lacked and why he thought it important.

My first foray offshore with the Naval Academy ocean racing team ended badly. A tropical storm churned up the East Coast as the 2003 Annapolis to Newport Race began in mid-June, making for a fast ride down the Chesapeake. I was assistant Officer-in-Charge aboard a 43-foot race-boat with a crew of 10 called "Bulldog." It was painted in the U.S. Marine Corps colors of crimson and gold; completing its livery was a fierce-looking bulldog wearing a drill sergeant's hat painted on the sugar-scoop stern. As we sailed out of the bay at dawn on day two of the race, some sloppy steering in the big ocean swells left from the storm caused us to rip our mainsail. We made little headway sailing on jib alone for the next several hours trying to mend the main. When we finally re-hoisted it, it tore again. After that, we dropped out of the race and motored to the Coast Guard station at Cape May NJ. It was an ignominious end to my first ocean race.

I got many more chances at the sport, however, competing in two subsequent Annapolis-Newport Races, two Newport-Bermuda Races, a race from Miami to Montego Bay and four Heineken Regattas off the Caribbean island of St. Maarten.

What I liked about ocean racing was the same thing that thrilled me during my first offshore passage: the magnificent seascapes, beautiful sunsets and, above all, the comradery. I also felt a closeness to nature that sometimes was almost spiritual. In the teeth of a storm at sea, fear quickly gives way to inner peace and acceptance of come-what-may. As a storm begins breaking up, there's quiet elation.

Once, during a rough couple of hours in an Annapolis-Newport Race, a pod of dolphins suddenly appeared beside us on both sides of the boat, leaping and whistling, clearly communicating in some way. It was almost as if they were our guardian angels, assuring us we would come to no harm. It seemed as if there was some sort of spiritual connection between us and the sea creatures. Call it what you may; I thought it was truly a magical experience.

For all my fond memories of sailing, I doubt it was worth it. Looking back over all the days and weeks I spent away from home enjoying the company of strangers, I'm left with a great sense of guilt. Surely Lynn would have liked my company. Surely I could have forged a better bond with my children if I'd spent more time with them than I did. My only excuse is that I liked to sail though my comfort level with it was almost nil. I was deathly afraid of the water. I was fine when I shared the responsibility with others more expert than me. On my own, I was too timid to venture very far from shore.

I owned three different boats in the years I sailed. The last was a 40-foot sailboat – a yacht, really – that I co-owned with a wealthier friend. He sailed "Winsome" most of the time; I paid half the expenses. This was unfair to Lynn. Maintaining a vessel like that is very expensive. My annual cost easily exceeded $10,000. How many missed opportunities did that amount to? How many vacations could we have enjoyed together?

As I neared retirement, I decided I just couldn't afford the boat anymore. Pursuant to our written agreement, I asked my partner to choose one of two options: buy me out or put the boat up for sale. He wished to do neither. Our relationship turned acrimonious. Eventually he agreed to buy me out, but at a steeply discounted price, paid over three years, without interest. I had no alternative – I desperately wanted out. So I accepted the deal. But it wrecked what I regarded as a friendship and left me wishing I'd never met the man.

My last passage with the Navy sailing team was much like the first – problematic. To prepare for the summer ocean races, team members embark on a sail training exercise each spring that consists of circumnavigating the Delmarva Peninsula. During the four day voyage, a half dozen or more Navy sailboats head north on Chesapeake, transit the Chesapeake & Delaware Canal and travel east to the mouth of Delaware Bay. At Cape Henlopen, the fleet heads south along the Atlantic Coast until it reaches Norfolk, where it reenters the Chesapeake and begins a 129-nautical mile homeward leg to Annapolis.

There are all sorts of seamanship tests the way, including crew overboard recovery drills; steering with an emergency rudder; deploying a sea anchor, which is sometimes a storm survival technique; and dealing with flooding – a hole in the boat under the waterline. Midshipmen call the exercise the "Delbarfa" because there's usually at least a bit of seasickness-inducing bad weather.

The 2009 edition, the last in which I took part, is now enshrined in Naval Academy sailing team lore as the "Hellmarva." We expected stormy weather and got more than we bargained for. Making matters worse, the brunt of the storm struck after we reentered Chesapeake Bay, a notoriously shallow body of water where there's little room for maneuver or error. We had a following wind at first and sped along well above hull speed as we surfed down big waves. But the wind backed halfway up the bay, forcing us into a mode of sailing aptly called "beating."

As is often the case, the worst of the worst came after dark. At one point, we saw wind gusts exceeding 60 knots. A deck-sweeping wave tore out the starboard lifelines of the boat I was on, making movement on deck perilous. Though double-reefed (reduced in size), the main blew out. It was too dangerous to try to set storm sails because of the missing lifelines, so we began motor-sailing, making little headway.

Other boats in the fleet had an equally difficult time; one was dismasted. Because I was the Officer in Charge of our 44-foot sloop, I stayed topside most of the night, letting my less-experienced assistant coach remain below in his bunk. That was a mistake. Seasickness and hypothermia eventually forced me to stumble below, where I threw up repeatedly before passing out. I have no idea what happened after that; the midshipman skipper, who later became a Marine Corps fighter pilot, performed magnificently and brought us home safely.

Ironically, I'd reprimanded him earlier for sexually suggestive comments to a female shipmate. I decided after that ordeal I'd gotten too old for the Naval Academy sailing program and resigned as a volunteer coach. My 10-year run was fun while it lasted, mostly. But I'd become more of a liability than an asset.

II

I've always needed a passion to enliven my life. So after sailing I returned to my lifelong love of photography. For my 8th birthday, my parents gave me a Kodak Baby Brownie camera and I've taken pictures ever since. I seem to have a flair for the hobby; one of the first photos I ever took shows a football player in full stride catching a pass at a University of Scranton football practice. The player is in focus, the background blurred. I instinctively used the technique of panning to capture the shot.

When I was in the army I bought a professional caliber Nikon and an array of lenses. I still own that equipment as well as a couple of modern digital Nikons. I usually had a camera with me during my professional travels. In pre-digital days I could always cadge film from news photographers. There was one slight problem: since the film was free, I shot like a pro, making dozens of exposures to capture the right one. But I had to pay for developing, which made my hobby expensive. The digital revolution eased that concern, giving me the best of both worlds.

My love of photography dovetailed with my love of travel. The latter surprised me, because when I retired I swore I'd never get on another airplane. I'd seen the world, traveling First Class all the way. My professional travel was on chartered jetliners or Air Force One. We stayed at five star hotels and ate at the best restaurants, all on expense account. I thought I'd seen it all and didn't think I could bare the comedown if the globetrotting was on my dime. But I found there's a lot of difference between traveling on someone else's schedule and being independent.

I soon learned I'd really seen very little on presidential trips; you see a landmark here, an historic site there and the odd castle or palace along the way. But the overall experience is like watching a Hollywood movie set in some foreign land. Now that I know what I missed, there's nothing I like better than to visit another country and plunge into another culture. Luckily for me, my wife Becky feels the same way.

I instinctively agree with Mark Twain. "Travel is fatal to prejudice, bigotry, and narrow-mindedness, and many of our people need it sorely on these accounts. Broad, wholesome, charitable views of men and things cannot be acquired by vegetating in one little corner of the earth all one's lifetime," he said.

My children and grandchildren don't think twice about traveling near and far. In my lifetime, air travel has gone from being something experienced by a very few to the world's preeminent form of mass transportation. Any destination on Earth is now less than a day away thanks to the range and speed of jet aircraft. It's also relatively inexpensive.

I was in college the first time I flew. It was a night flight between Scranton-Wilkes Barre Airport and Newark aboard an Alleghany Airlines twin engine Convair and took well over an hour. Not until I was in my early 20s did get to travel to another country, becoming the first in my immediate family to do so. I often joke that to make that trip I had to wear a green suit and carry a gun.

While serving as a soldier in South Korea, I went to Japan on R&R twice, visiting Tokyo, the giant Buddha at Kamakura, and the seaside village of Akasaki. I've been back to Japan several times since, and am amazed each time by how modern and densely populated the country is. The same is true of South Korea of course. I've been there several times as well since my tour in the Army. No longer is it the war-ravaged country I once knew. But on a visit with President Reagan in 1983, I saw how dangerous a place it can still be.

Only a month earlier, 21 people had been killed and 46 others wounded in a North Korean attempt to assassinate South Korean President Chun Doo Hwan in Rangoon. Chun narrowly escaped death but among those killed were four senior South Korean officials, including the country's foreign minister. Burmese authorities immediately implicated three officers of the North Korean Army in the attack so the heightened tension was obvious during Reagan's stay in Seoul.

One of the high points of Reagan's visit was a ceremonial dinner at Chun's official residence, a mansion known as The Blue House because of its blue-tiled roof. During the drive there, the press van which I was in got separated from the rest of the presidential motorcade. There we were, racing up and down streets emptied for security reasons when a vehicle pulled in front of us and a half dozen or more heavily armed soldiers climbed out. They surrounded our van and leveled their weapons at us, ignoring our shouts of "White House Press! White House Press!

"ROLL ON THIS! ROLL ON THIS," a television reporter with us yelled to his crew. "Don't ... Do ... That!" I said as calmly as I could. I was afraid that when the bright light affixed to the TV camera lit up the night it would blind the soldiers, who might then instinctively open fire. Unlikely as it seems, the TV people listened to me. Somehow we got the situation defused. I'm convinced to this day it was a very close call.

Notwithstanding such occasional potential nightmares, what I especially love about traveling is how often it lets me connect historical dots. When I was five or six, my father took me to see Japanese Emperor Hirohito's horse. The Japanese emperor's captured white stallion was on display on a street-corner in downtown Scranton, a U.S. Marine Corps horse trailer beside it. Some 40 years later I was in Tokyo for Hirohito's funeral, traveling with President George H.W. Bush. That event graphically illustrated how the world turns. Bush fought Hirohito's forces as a Navy pilot in the Pacific during World War Two and narrowly escaped death when his plane was shot down during a bombing run on the Japanese-held island of Chi Chi Jima.

My first overseas trip as a civilian took me to England and Scotland. I drove from London to Edinburgh, stopping along the way in Oxford, Shakespeare's Stratford-on-Avon and other places I'd read about. I returned to London by train and bus, wending my way through the poet Wordsworth's Lake District and spending a night in industrial Manchester. The night in Manchester was one of the longest of my life because of the bleak oppressiveness of the city, the hotel and my hotel room.

The summer after our marriage in March 1971, Lynn and I visited Ireland, Paris and London on a delayed honeymoon. Ireland was great fun. In a sense, it was a homecoming. We rented a car and traveled west to east, driving on the wrong side of the road (from our standpoint), often picking up hitchhikers to acquire some local knowledge and generally having a ball. Even then I coupled travel with my photography. Some of the pictures I took are favorites still. Lynn was expecting our first child. When we stopped at a crossroads one day so I could capture an interesting landscape, some passing nuns insisted on taking my bride to their nearby convent for a cup of tea. They thought she looked a bit peaked.

I was badly hung over the morning we arrived in Paris. I'd spent much of the previous day drinking in Dublin with some newfound friends who worked for RTE (Radio Television Erin), the state broadcasting system. I quickly recovered though, and day after day for a week or more we walked from one end of the world's most beautiful city to the other. The visit kindled in me a love of Paris that has deepened with each subsequent visit. Nowhere am I as happy as I am walking the narrow streets and broad boulevards of the City of Lights. The first two years after Lynn died, I visited again and again. I spent the week before Christmas there in 2012. Alone with my memories and thoughts, Paris was just what I needed: a place of comfort.

On the Sunday before Christmas, an atavistic impulse drove me to Notre Dame for a Solemn High Mass sung in Gregorian Chant. I arrived early and got to enjoy a service consisting of French Christmas Carols sung by an opera-class tenor and baritone, both of whom were wearing blue cassocks. It wasn't clear if the two were clerics, but it didn't matter; there was a soaring spirituality to the concert. Then the mass began with a long procession of officiants and acolytes led by a cross-bearer and a Friar Tuck lookalike whose outthrust arms held up a book I assumed was the Gospel. The pageantry was awesome.

The best was yet to come. During the Consecration, that moment in time when Roman Catholics believe bread and wine literally become the body and blood of Jesus Christ, the celebrant of the mass raised aloft a snow white wafer the size and shape and of a dinner plate. A half-dozen co-celebrants stood in a circle around him raising their right arms in unison. A step below on the altar meantime, acolytes swung silver pots back and forth, causing clouds of incense to rise toward the vaulted ceiling of the medieval cathedral. It was powerful mojo. One could imagine how dazzling such a ceremony must have seemed to unschooled peasants. It certainly dazzled me.

Afterwards, I treated myself to an old fashioned Sunday dinner at *Le Train Blue*, a magnificent Belle Epoch-style restaurant in the Gare de Lyon railway station. The meal was expensive but worth it. It reminded me of the Sunday dinners of my childhood at home, joyous family occasions rich in food and conversation that is sadly now a thing of the past. I completed the outing by taking the Metro to the Arc de Triumph and joining thousands of other *flanneurs* on a Sunday stroll along the Champs Elysees.

Though immersed in grief, I was cossetted by my abundance, a situation few humans enjoy. As President John F. Kennedy once bluntly explained, "Life is unfair." All my life I've wondered why. Why do a few have so much when most of God's children have so little? How can it be unless the Creator – if there is a creator – is indifferent. Leaving Alexandria, a deeply spiritual memoir by Richard Holloway, a former Episcopal Primate of Scotland, explores such existential questions.

Holloway left his hometown of Alexandria, Scotland at age 14 to enter an Anglican seminary. He grew up poor and the seminary was recruiting young men like him to try to create more diversity in the church's clergy, which drew for the most part from the upper reaches of British society. For much of his priesthood, Holloway ministered to the poor. He found it fulfilling but eventually he began rising in the Anglican hierarchy, an ascent that culminated with his installation as the Primate of Scotland.

Despite his rise he had growing doubts about whether religion played any useful role in human life. He was especially disenchanted by the church's treatment of women and gay people, which eventually caused him to leave the priesthood. His book ends with this coda:

> "I don't expect to meet my maker when I die, but if I do it won't surprise me if he comes smiling toward me over green fields. 'So that's what you made of the hand I dealt you? I know you were strongly tempted by determinism when you were down there, but it is not strictly correct to say the Dealer deserves all the responsibility for the hand. You played it, after all, and some things you could have done differently. But there is no point in feeling shame about any of it now. Want to see what I thought I was doing when I dreamt the whole thing up?'

Holloway didn't expect that to happen *"but if it does I'll accept his invitation because I'm still curious about the mystery of it all."*

There isn't much to add to Holloway's comments. One can argue that evil is a more powerful spirit than goodness. That has seemed to be the case in my lifetime, and indeed the life of the planet. Nine months before I was born, the United States entered World War Two, which destroyed much of Europe and Asia and cost 60 million lives. America has been at war periodically ever since: the list includes Korea, Vietnam and Persian Gulf Wars One and Two as well as skirmishes in Grenada, Panama and the Balkans.

When Lynn and I visited former President and Mrs. Bush in Kennebunkport in 2010 after my semester at Harvard, the conversation at one point turned to books we were reading. I recommended *Matterhorn*, a searing Vietnam War by Karl Marlantes, a Marine veteran of Vietnam who won the Navy Cross. When Bush asked me why I found the book so compelling, I explained that I served in Korea during the early stages of the Vietnam War and felt driven to know what some of those I went through infantry training with faced. "It was a terrible, terrible war. We never should have been there," Bush said, shaking his head sadly.

For all the fighting during my lifetime, there hasn't been another Great Power conflict with its massive destruction and loss of life. Future historians will probably speak of *Pax Americana* in the same way they now speak of the *Pax Romana*, an era in which most of humanity was at peace. For that we need to remember Bush and my Uncle John and all the others who in their lives "fought for life ... and left the vivid air signed with (their) honor. Thanks to them, statesmen were able to cobble together agreements and treaties that have made the world safer for more than three quarters of a century.

As I write however, we're in the midst of one of the darkest periods in U.S. history. Too many Americans seem to celebrate ignorance and accept "alternative facts" instead of truth. This at a time when computer technology enables us to carry mountains of knowledge in our pocket. Though Donald Trump was denied reelection after four years of chaos, his malignant ideology lives on, cheering on those who would betraying our friends and applaud our adversaries, dividing our people and denouncing anyone who dares challenge them.

Nowhere was the lunacy of Trump's presidency more evident than during the Covid 19 Pandemic that paralyzed the country in 2020. More than 250,000 people died of the virus in the first eight months of the crisis, yet under Trump medical guidance that might have saved many lives was totally ignored. Worse, such common sense precautions as wearing face masks were sneered at by the nation's leader and many of the scientific experts faced a torrent of death threats. Despite Joe Biden's indisputable victory in the election, Trump refused to concede defeat and along with many other leading Republicans did his best to make life as difficult for his successor as possible.

Some of my friends thought me alarmist when I warned them during the 2016 election campaign what a disaster for the country a Trump presidency would be. I saw what was coming a long time ago. In a 2003 speech to parents and students at my alma mater Scranton Prep, I said this:

> I am increasingly worried about this country. Maybe that's a perennial worry of old guys like me, but you represent the leadership elite of this country, so I want to share some of my concerns with you.
>
> First and foremost, I am concerned about what I perceive as lack of unity. It used to be, it seems to me, that whatever we were, the most important thing we were was Americans. Yes, there were lots of us – black Americans, Native Americans, many women and others – who didn't fully share the American Dream. But when I was a young man, we were working to fix that. Now I think too many of us identify first as single interest groups: Anti-Abortion, Pro-Choice, Pro-Gun, Gun Control, Conservative, Liberal, Meat eater, vegan. I could go on and on.
>
> Flowing out of all this is my second concern: lack of respect for the other guy's viewpoint. America's genius is that it is a pluralistic society, where the majority rules but minority rights and BELIEFS are respected. Too often these days, it seems to me, instead of trying to find common ground that serves everyone's interests, we tend to align ourselves around the poles and demonize those with whom we disagree. There's only one outcome at the end of that road: civil war.
>
> What concerns me most though is our seeming lack of collective commitment to a just society. In a society as rich as ours, why should any child ever have to suffer a toothache? Why should any old man or woman have to go without prescription drugs (and yes, Virginia, that will continue even with the new Medicare prescription drug benefit program.) Why do stock market swindlers who bilk millions of millions get a slap on the wrist while someone who sticks up a convenience store for a few hundred bucks gets 20 years to life? How many of the most well off in this country actually know ANY of the servicemen and women serving in Iraq or Afghanistan? How many of the most

225

well off (including the decision-makers who deploy our troops)
have a son or daughter in Iraq or Afghanistan? If not, why not?

I pride myself in having served in the military though I served only two years, didn't see combat and rose no further than first lieutenant. To me America's battlefields are sacred ground, particularly the killing fields of Normandy. It was in this pastoral French province that my uncle and thousands like him confronted the greatest evil ever to grip mankind and slowly but surely destroyed it in a blood-soaked struggle still astounding three quarters of a century later. Yet in the twilight of my life, I increasingly fear it all went for naught: the Four Horsemen of the Apocalypse – war, conquest, famine and death – seem back in the saddle again. How else to explain the accelerating collapse of world order.

A great country emulates men like John McCain. As a naval aviator, McCain was shot down during the Vietnam War and spent six years as a prisoner of war in Hanoi, much of it in solitary confinement. McCain was awarded the Silver Star, Bronze Star, the Legion of Merit and the Purple Heart. Yet Trump, who avoided military service during the war because of five questionable draft deferments, scoffed at what McCain endured.

"He's not a war hero. He's a war hero because he was captured. I like people who weren't captured," he said during the 2016 presidential campaign.

Even more infuriating was Trump's boast during an interview with radio shock jock Howard Stern that he felt "like a great and very brave soldier" because he slept with many women while the fighting raged in Vietnam without getting a sexually transmitted disease. "It is my personal Vietnam," he said.

What I can't understand is why millions of Americans who consider themselves patriotic shrugged off these slur. How can anyone not see them as incredibly hurtful, a blood libel of anyone who has ever been a member of U.S. Armed Forces?

Chapter Ten
Waypoints

A LEGEND: MEMBERS OF a White House advance team were in Moscow laying the groundwork for a summit meeting between Richard Nixon and Leonid Brezhnev. After a night of carousing involving much vodka, the group returned to their hotel and went to someone's room for a nightcap. "Surely there's a bug in here somewhere," one of the team members remarked.

A search ensued. When they pulled up the rug in the room, it seemed they'd struck pay-dirt. There was a small cutout in the floor containing a nut, a bolt and a nest of wires. Someone managed to remove the nut and the group heard a very loud noise as the chandelier fell from the ceiling of the ballroom below and crashed to the floor.

The story might be apocryphal but the incidents I experienced or heard about as a working newsman were endlessly interesting and sometimes zany. I traveled constantly during my working life, crisscrossing the country and straddling the globe again and again.

It wasn't unusual to put in 20+ hour days – punch in at 5 AM East Coast Time and end the workday at midnight West Coast Time. There you have it, twenty hours on the clock, although explaining the overtime to my bosses was always easier said than done. For all the miles I traveled – by my conservative estimate, close to a million, perhaps more by the time I retired -- I wound up with zero frequent flier miles. Most of my travel was by chartered plane or Air Force One.

Pan Am usually flew the press charter until the airline folded in 1991. The same pilots and flight attendants worked every trip, so it was one big happy family. "The White House liked the arrangement because it simplified the security vetting, and the Press Corps liked it because the cabin crews were generally all familiar faces, who knew from experience just how everyone liked his steak and what sort of libation to have waiting at the front door after a long day," retired Pan Am Captain John Marshal said.

Writing in Airways Magazine, Marshal recalled that the flying was much different than what he and other pilots were accustomed to. "Captains assigned to White House charters were permitted to choose their own cockpit crews, and their number were normally counted among the ranks of the airline's flight instructors and check flight engineers. During presidential campaigns a single day's flying might entail five or six stops, with legs sometimes as short as twenty minutes. Not exactly the mission its designers had in mind for the (Boeing) 707," he said.

Most of us think of Air Force One as the big blue and white Boeing 747 jumbo jet we see on television. In reality the term is an Air Traffic Control designator, a radio call sign – whatever aircraft the president is aboard is Air Force One. When I started covering the White House, a Boeing 707 was the most commonly used presidential aircraft. The Boeing 747 in use as I write came into service in 1990 during George H.W. Bush's presidency. I was on the inaugural flight on September 6 as a certificate signed by Col. Robert "Danny" Barr, the aircraft commander, attests.

Actually there are two nearly identical Boeing 747s in the presidential fleet: the only distinguishing characteristic is their tail numbers, 28000 and 29000. Both are capable of mid-air refueling and have many other advanced features, including anti-missile systems. The latter goes along on international trips as a backup. There are also several short-range airplanes. In my day, these included McDonnell Douglas DC-9s and several executive jets.

The aforementioned aircraft are only the tip of the iceberg. Presidential trips also involve at least two Air Force cargo planes to haul limousines, helicopters and communications gear. If senior administration officials are along, they often travel on separate planes. So it's not unusual for a presidential air armada to dwarf the size of a small country's air force.

Ronald Reagan had the most relaxed travel schedule of the presidents I covered, making life easier on the rest of us. Perhaps because he was older than any previous chief executive, and with a medical history that included a brush with death when he was shot by John Hinckley and colon cancer surgery, Reagan paced himself. His 1984 visit to China was typical: it began with a week in Santa Barbara, three days in Hawaii, and an overnight on Guam before going on to Beijing.

With Bill Clinton, one of the youngest presidents in U.S. history, whirlwind trips to the U.S. West Coast and Europe were often the norm. In December 1994, he flew to Budapest for a meeting with Russian President Boris Yeltsin and returned to Washington the same day. Almost to the day one year later, he made a whirlwind trip to Paris for a signing ceremony marking the end of a war in Bosnia. During that trip, we flew into the center of Paris by helicopter and went back to the airport the same way. Night had fallen and it was snowing heavily as our Marine helicopter lifted off from a plaza near Place de la Concorde to start the return journey. It was a thrilling experience as the big Sikorsky Sea Stallion lumbered into the sky, making the city below look like it the center of a snow globe. Through the falling snow flakes the Eiffel Tower seemed close enough to reach out and touch.

Clinton's trip to visit U.S. peacekeeping troops in the Balkans a few months later was another unique experience. On a Friday afternoon when most people would have been easing into another weekend, we flew aboard the plane usually reserved for the president from Knoxville TN to an American airbase in Aviano, Italy. There we transferred to a C-17 military transport configured to carry troops and equipment. We were the troops on this occasion, led by the Commander in Chief, so we all settled as comfortably as we could into nylon web seating on both sides and part of the middle of the aircraft.

Our first destination was to have been the northeast Bosnian city of Tuzla where U.S. troops were based, but fog forced a diversion to a military staging area in neighboring Hungary. An armored unit was marshalling there, getting ready to join the peacekeeping forces. I was amazed at how large it was. Dozens of heavy tanks and other lethal-looking machinery stretched as far as the eye could see. It was a far more powerful force than anything I'd seen when I was in the army.

When the weather cleared, we returned to Tuzla and executed an assault landing, a fast, spiraling descent meant to make the plane less of a target for ground fire. A bit dramatic for the low likelihood that we faced any threat, but who knows?

There was more drama when we left Bosnia: an assault takeoff showing the capabilities of the C-17. Once our aircraft turned onto the active runway and was on the centerline, the pilots locked the brakes and spooled up the engines. The plane seemed to quiver like a thoroughbred at the starting gate, then burst its bonds and after a brief takeoff roll literally leaped into the air Three minutes later, we were more than three miles above the earth. A transport with fighter plane characteristics: it was an impressive performance.

I made a subsequent visit to Bosnia with Hillary Clinton, who was accompanied by singer-songwriter Sheryl Crow. We returned to Tuzla (where Mrs. Clinton later foolishly claimed we'd come under sniper fire). Unlike her husband whose visit was confined to the U.S. army base, Mrs. Clinton traveled by helicopter to an outpost where some of our peacekeeping troops were deployed. We flew over several devastated villages with burnt-out roofless dwellings. Serbian militias were to blame. After shooing the Moslem inhabitants away – or worse – they'd climb to the attic of a house and leave a lit candle, then enter the kitchen and open the gas on the stove. A few minutes later, KA-BOOM! Another instance of man's inhumanity.

I thought I'd seen the world when I retired. But I learned I hadn't even scratched the surface. Strange as it seems, traveling with a president is not nearly as glamorous or fulfilling as people think. Yes, you get to go to Buckingham Palace or the Taj Mahal and other landmarks most folks see only in pictures. But it's all work. Hard work. Your focus is on the newsmaker and what *they're* doing. You're also mentally composing a story and otherwise missing the forest for the trees.

This was driven home to me when Becky and I visited Budapest and Prague. It was my third time in each city. But I had no idea how pleasant it is to walk their streets or sit in a café with a glass of beer in hand watching the world go by.

Even a visit to Prague Palace was a different experience. On a trip with Hillary Clinton, our guide was Czech President Vaclav Havel, the writer and onetime dissident who played a key role in freeing his country from communist rule. Here was someone who'd already carved out a niche for himself in history. Yet I found being on a public tour of the palace was better because the pace was slower and I didn't have to worry about missing something. It's much more pleasant to visit museums and monuments when you're there because you want to be, not because you're reporting on someone else's visit.

I started traveling incessantly in retirement after Lynn died. Paris was where I went again and again for the year or two after I became a widower. It remains my destination. Never is the city more magical than Christmastime. As I mentioned previously, I spent the week before Christmas there the first year I was alone. December's grayness matched my mood.

In the Tuileries Garden near the Louvre is a work by the French sculptor Henri Vidal, a statue drawn from the Bible, Cain after killing his brother Abel. It's a powerful expression of grief. The statute became my touchstone: I photographed it over and over until I got the image I wanted. I stayed at a dowdy old hotel on the Left Bank, the Lutitia. James Joyce wrote part of <u>Ulysses </u>there. I didn't know that then. I did know the hotel's notoriety; home to the Abwehr, the German counter-intelligence service, during the World War Two Nazi occupation of the French capital.

It rained much of the time during that stay in Paris. But there were moments of grace, among them discovering a restaurant that remains one of my favorites: 35 Rue Jacob, a few blocks west of the Boulevard Saint Germain. on the Left Bank, a few blocks from the Boulevard Saint Germain. The City of Lights was the right place to be for mourning and starting life again.

I've been on the go much of the time since, solo for the first few years and now with Becky, checking off entries on my bucket list. Lakes in northern Italy, the Swiss Alps, Brittany, Normandy, the Canadian Rockies, Albania and its neighbors, Morocco, New Zealand, Vietnam. India and Nepal. Like the poet Robert Frost, I like to imagine there are miles ahead of me before I sleep.

The latest jetsetter travel wrinkle supposedly is surprise vacation packages. You tell the tour operator what you want to spend and how long you want to be gone. A few days before departure they email a weather forecast and packing list. You don't learn your destination until you get to the airport.

I prefer to make my own arrangements but I also like surprises, and Morocco provided many. In fact, it tops the list of my favorite trips. I'd always envisioned the North African nation as an Arab country noted mainly for the classic movie *Casablanca* and lots of sand. I was wrong. During a two week visit in 2019, Becky and I wandered from the Atlantic coast to the Algerian border and back on a tour conducted by Gate 1 Travel, glimpsing various aspects of Moroccan life. From Marrakech and Casablanca's vibrant atmospheres to the stunning scenery of the Atlas Mountains and the sublime beauty of the Sahara Desert, what we saw was fascinating.

A highlight of Marrakech was the Yves Saint-Laurent Museum, a complex spread over a couple of acres in an upscale residential neighborhood. The complex includes the elegant Majorelle Gardens, named for the French artist Jacques Majorelle. I never knew cactus could be so beautiful. There's also an art gallery and a museum where the French dress designer's most famous creations are on display. To my surprise, I found the latter enchanting even though women's fashion is usually not my cup of tea. I though the museum nearly as interesting as the labyrinth of shops adjacent to Djemma el Fna Square, where acrobats, snake charmers and dancing monkeys compete to amuse hordes of tourists.

Surprise number two was Morocco's geology. Transiting the snow-capped High Atlas Mountains to get from urban coast to the desert isn't for the fainthearted. The road through the 7,410-foot Tizi 'n Tichka pass follows an old caravan route; from November through March it's often shrouded in fog and laden with snow. The weather was sunny and clear for our transit, through several of the steepest stretches of the roadway were unpaved and muddy and a modernization project involving heavy construction equipment made it an obstacle course.

Once in the Sahara, we got to ride camels into the desert to watch the sun set. It's breathtaking; once the sun drops below the horizon there's no twilight, just total darkness. Another desert experience was camel meat. It's like beef but tougher.

Best of all were the nomadic desert people who, it turns out, are not Arab but Berber, a separate ethnic group that comprises about 80 percent of Morocco's population. Everyone we met was friendly. Some were downright intriguing. While a thoroughly modern urban nation, biblical time characterizes the Saharan region, the land of the blue men and one-eyed women.

There's a serenity and a timelessness, which supports a way of life that has gone on for centuries. The Sahara isn't just sand; mile after mile is flat dry scrub-brush, strewn with rocks and boulders. Every so often, a small encampment appears in the middle of nowhere; a rootless family eking out a living. Tourism is a big part of their lives. While clinging to their old ways in terms of *where* they live, many semi-nomads earn a living leading camel rides or driving visitors into the dunes in the equivalent of Jeeps. Dune buggy drivers love to charge up a towering sand hill, wheels spinning and overtaxed engines screaming in protest, then plunge down the other side skidding and sliding. For the passengers, it's an exhilarating experience!

Then there were Morocco's tree-climbing goats. They roam an area in the southwest where Argon trees, an indigenous species, grow wild. The trees need little water and produce a nutty fruit that's ground into an oil used in cosmetics and cooking. Shepherds graze their goats in Argon groves and the animals climb the trees to eat fruit and leaves.

As we traveled through an area thick with Argon trees, there they were, hundreds of tree-climbing goats, some on their hind legs stretching to get to the leaves, others up on the branches and even atop trees. Our bus screeched to a stop and our camera-wielding tour group hastily disembarked, scrambling to record the bizarre scene. This startled the munching four-legged creatures, causing them to leap from their perches three, four and five at a time, making it seem it was raining goats. It was almost biblical, like the plague of locusts or the burning bush.

My personal travel has often given me a new perspective on events I reported on during my working life. So it was with a 2019 visit to Mainz, Germany's wine capital on the Rhine which was once the home of Johannes Gutenberg. I was there with President George H.W. Bush in 1989. The Berlin Wall was still standing. A Cold War between the United States and the Soviet Union still divided East and West. But Bush spoke of a Europe "whole and free."

"As President, I will continue to do all I can to help open the closed societies of the East. We seek self-determination for all of Germany and all of Eastern Europe. And we will not relax, and we must not waver... the world has waited long enough," Bush said. While his speech was largely overlooked at the time, it seems quite visionary rereading it now — this from a president who was often accused of lacking vision. German reunification was not something Britain and France wanted then, let alone Russia.

In 1998, Bush and National Security Advisor Brent Scowcroft published <u>A World Transformed</u>, a book about what they regarded as their foreign policy accomplishments. There was a book party at Washington's prestigious Metropolitan Club; Lynn and I were invited. When we were leaving, I told "41" I looked forward to reading the book. Ever modest, he put his arm on my shoulder and replied, "Gene, it will put you to sleep."

One of my favorite travel writers is an Englishman, Patrick Leigh Fermor. At the age of 18 in 1933, Fermor began walking across Europe, His trek started in Holland and ended in Istanbul, then known as Constantinople. He wrote about his experiences in a trilogy: *A Time of Gifts, Between the Woods and the Water* and *The Broken Road*. It's a work that describes for a reader the look and feel of an historic turning point that rivalled the fall of the Roman Empire.

Hitler was becoming a force in Europe and already there was a deep sense of dread, a sense that the world as then known was coming apart. Becky and I got a whiff of during a 2017 visit to Hungary. Prime Minister Viktor Orban had started to tighten his ultra-nationalist grip on the country. Returning from dinner one night we ran into a series of roadblocks: thousands of university students were in the streets of Budapest near the Parliament building in peaceful protest. Almost as many riot police wearing helmets and body armor and carrying truncheons were formed up in flying squads, ready and perhaps even eager for confrontation.

There was no violence. But the scene that night was disturbing. Orban moved further right as time went on and strains of Nazism began echoing in Poland, Austria other parts of Europe. In the America I knew until Trump came along, advocates of the illiberal policies that stained human history in the 1930s and '40s would get no sympathy. The United States would be second to none in expressing revulsion and its stance would carry weight. That was not the case from 2017 to 2021. I hope Joe Biden will restore the honor and decency of our country but I fear the dark forces that his predecessor mobilized remain and clear and present danger.

The subject of travel came up during a visit with President Bush in Kennebunkport a year before he died. Perhaps thinking about the incessant traveling he once did, he spoke admiringly of our globetrotting. "Gene wants to do the kind of traveling he did with you – flying on Air

Force One, staying at the best hotels and eating at the best restaurants. Well, we can't afford that sort of thing," Becky said.

Bush seemed confused. I sensed he thought she was implying we all lived high on the taxpayer's dollar. I assured him Reuters paid all my expenses back in the day and it was the expense account living that Becky and I couldn't match.

Another misunderstanding occurred closer to home. I was astonished when my son Chad told me he was a nervous wreck as a child whenever I went off on a presidential trip, fearful I wouldn't come back. I thought I was doing a glamorous job, making my family proud. I never imaged I was in any danger, surrounded as I was by immense Secret Service firepower and state-of-the art security measures. Chad's anxiety undoubtedly stemmed from the assassination attempt on President Reagan. He was just shy of age five when it happened and watching a kiddie show on television that was interrupted with news of the shooting. He watched in horror, thinking I was probably in the midst of it all. It's understandable that a child exposed to that kind of experience would be likely to think my job was unsafe.

Chad's fears might not have been groundless. In a book about the Clinton presidency called *The Death of American Virtue*, law professor Ken Gormley writes that the 42d president was the target of an Al Qaeda assassination plot during a visit to the Philippines in 1996. Clinton was in Manila for a set of trade talks with a strange name: Asian Pacific Economic Cooperation, or APEC for short. According to Gormley, the Secret Service learned that Osama bin Laden's terrorist group planned to blow up a bridge as Clinton's motorcade crossed and hastily changed his route. The story has never been confirmed but Ramzi Josef, who attacked New York's World Trade Center with a truck bomb in 1993 and 9/11 mastermind Khalid Sheikh Mohammed were both in the Philippines in the mid-1990s. I was on that Clinton trip and might have been in the motorcade in question.

Looking back, there were also other potential close calls, beyond the incident in Seoul I noted previously. One occurred in 1995 while President Clinton was vacationing in Jackson Hole, WY. The war in Bosnia was raging, and three U.S. diplomats trying to stop the fighting were killed when the armored personnel carrier they were in plunged off a mountain road near Sarajavo. The three were Robert Frasure, Clinton's special envoy to the former Yugoslavia; Joseph Kruzel, deputy assistant

Defense Secretary for European and NATO affairs; and Air Force Colonel Nelson Drew, a member of the National Security Council staff.

Clinton was shaken by the tragedy and arranged to return to Washington for the men's funeral. I was in the press pool. We flew out of Twin Falls ID, the closest airport with a runway long enough to accommodate the president's plane. The press pool was to get there by helicopter but thunderstorms forced us to travel by van instead, traversing a mountain pass between Jackson Hole and Twin Falls.

I was riding in the front passenger seat during the four-hour late night trip when I noticed the driver, a local volunteer, was dozing off. I kept talking to try to keep him awake but when our vehicle drifted off the highway during one of the steepest parts of the trip I insisted on taking over. Someone was watching over us. My initial inclination when the trip began was to grab a back seat and sleep the long ride away.

With all the flying, I guess occasional mechanical problems were to be expected. None seemed life-threatening at the time. Two of my four emergency landings occurred when I was covering President George H. W. Bush. The first was aboard a chartered Boeing 727 press plane during Bush's 1998 campaign. We'd taken off from Chicago's O'Hare Airport bound for Spokane when I noticed a thumping sound as we climbed out over Lake Michigan. Soon the pilot announced he was unable to retract the flaps and would have to return to O'Hare. We circled for 15 or 20 minutes dumping fuel before making an uneventful landing.

Bush was president when a second aviation adventure occurred. We were about an hour out of Los Angeles enroute to Honolulu on a chartered Pan Am Boeing 747 when one of its four engines flamed out. There was no drama: we turned around, returned to Los Angeles and in no time were aboard another plane headed back to Hawaii.

My only other interrupted flights were equally inconsequential: I was the only passenger on a twin engine Beechcraft King Air that lost an engine during takeoff from Springfield IL early in my working life and experienced an unscheduled landing at O'Hare in retirement when the main hydraulic system on an Alaska Airlines flight to Seattle failed.

I'm fatalistic about personal safety. Not that I've ever knowingly taken any unnecessary risks – I'm much too risk averse. But I do believe you're done when your number is up regardless of when and where you are at the time. I'm always excited when a trip begins. As a child, I was fascinated with a supplemental grade school reader that had stories about faraway places and the people who lived there. The Gauchos, Argentine cowboys who galloped across the Pampas, using bolas to round up the cattle. Heavily-laden Chinese peasants, traversing the world's largest country with the Great Wall in the background. One of the greatest joys of my life is that I've actually gotten to see much of that.

Sometimes it's more than just sightseeing. For Becky and me, traveling to Vietnam was an emotional journey, a kind of closure to the young adulthood chapter of our lives. Becky's late husband was in the war as a Navy pilot flying reconnaissance missions. I was lucky I didn't wind up there; I was safely out of the army by the time the fighting was at its height.

As a UPI Audio reporter armed with a microphone and tape recorder, I covered anti-war demonstrations that convulsed Washington and the country starting with the so-called Vietnam Moratorium in 1969. It drew an estimated two million people to the U.S. capital for a largely peaceful protest. Richard Nixon was in the first year of his presidency. During a later demonstration, Nixon made an early morning visit to the Lincoln Memorial and spoke with some demonstrators. Touring Vietnam and meeting some of its people left both of us wondering why the United States ever got involved. President Bush was right. It was a terrible war.

Bill Clinton was the first U.S. president to visit the country after the war. He did so in 2000 but I'd left Reuters by then. Tens of thousands of people greeted Clinton in Hanoi, the first of three cities he visited. "The size and enthusiasm of the crowds was particularly striking because Vietnam's leaders treated the president with polite but distant formality, as if they were still unsure about how far they wanted to take this new opening with a former enemy," the New York Times reported.

Becky and I started our visit in Saigon, now known as Ho Chi Minh City, went from there to Da Nang, a little fishing village named Hoi An, and the ancient capital of Hue before winding up in Hanoi. The people were extraordinarily friendly. They said they hated the Chinese and the French because of a long history of mistreatment by those people. They excused America's involvement in their country as a minor historical misfortune. That's what everyone told us anyway; tourism is an important economic engine in Vietnam and the people we met probably didn't want to offend us. But their sentiment seemed sincere.

Vietnam was seared into America's consciousness because of the war but nothing was as I expected. Take Saigon: the city is still commonly known by that name. Everything is chrome and glass near landmarks familiar from news reports during the war – the Opera House and the Caravelle, Rex and Intercontinental Hotels. It isn't much different from the expensive centers of any of the world's major cities. Within a few blocks is squalor, however.

Though forewarned by travelogues I read before the trip, I was surprised by the endless swarms of motor-scooters jamming the streets. Crossing an intersection was terrifying until you get used to plunging into the stream of traffic. Then it becomes fun. It was amazing how scooter drivers adjusted their bearings and flowed around pedestrians. Walking through the constant commotion makes one feel like Moses crossing the Red Sea.

Da Nang was undergoing massive development, with miles of high-end seaside resorts and condominiums springing up along China Beach, where U.S. troops went for rest and relaxation. In nearby Hoi An, a picturesque fishing village that was once a Viet Cong stronghold, we found hordes of tourists. The village was especially pretty at night illuminated by thousands of colorful paper lanterns.

Some of the war's fiercest fighting took place in Hue, a place we reached after an hours-long bus trip from Da Nang on a serpentine highway through the mountains. The city in Vietnam's central highlands was overrun by North Vietnamese Army regulars during the 1968 Tet Offensive. U.S. Marines eventually got the upper hand but only after more than a month of intense combat.

Today there's little evidence of the blood and thunder of that time. Hue is a bustling city. People crowd the outdoor Central Market, shopping for foodstuffs and other supplies; boats cruise the Perfume River. A massive red and yellow Vietnamese flag flies from a towering flagpole at the Citadel, where the country's emperors once dwelled. Given a slight twist of fate, I could have been among those fighting in Hue. That thought recurred again and again.

I was at the National Press Club in Washington on November 21 1969 when General William Westmoreland, the U.S. commander in Vietnam, famously declared the war was winding up. Though what he said became known as his "light at the end of the tunnel" speech, Westmoreland never actually used those words. "We have reached an important point (in the war) when the end begins to come into view," he said. Ten weeks later the Tet Offensive exploded and savage fighting continued for another eight years.

At a Buddist temple a few miles downriver from Hue, Becky and I saw a pale blue old Austin sedan, a relic of an incident that was a much an inflection point as Tet. In the summer of 1963, the vehicle transported a Buddist monk named Thich Quang Duc to a busy street-corner in Saigon where he burnt himself to death. He was protesting the repression of South Vietnam's Buddhist majority by the country's predominantly Roman Catholic government. The Buddhist uprising that followed was a powerful accelerant to the savage fighting that eventually devoured the U.S.-supported regime.

One Viet Cong stronghold of the war, the Cu Chi tunnels less than 50 miles northwest of Saigon, is now a popular tourist attraction. The area was heavily bombed; U.S. Air Force B-52 bomb craters still mar the landscape. I found the tunnels claustrophobic. I also found them illustrative of something we now realize: the best and brightest in the U.S. government had no idea of what they were up against in Vietnam or how to deal with it. As a result, more than 58,000 Americans died.

The United States dropped three times as much bomb tonnage on the small Asian country than it did throughout Europe and the Pacific during World War Two. But even in North Vietnam, the target of much of the U.S. air assault, there seemed to be no hard feelings. I was amazed by the beauty of Hanoi. Expecting to find a typical communist city full of drab Stalinist architecture and crumbling concrete, what I discovered instead was a sparkling metropolis: it was indeed the embodiment of a description I'd never heard before: the jewel of Asia. Part of Hanoi's allure are the five lakes within its boundaries, including Hoan Kiem Lake in the heart of the city. During our stay, Becky and I went to a water puppet show (an acquired taste); dined at the luxurious Metropole Hotel; and saw the horrors of the Hanoi Hilton.

The latter, formally known as the Hoa Lo Prison, is where John McCain and other American prisoners of war were held. I was in McCain's company several times when he was a U.S. senator. He always brushed off his six years in captivity as a time "when I was in jail." I probably would have voted for McCain when he was the Republican presidential candidate in 2008 had he not chosen Alaska Gov. Sarah

Palin as his running mate. She seemed unfit to be a heartbeat away from the presidency.

When McCain died in the summer of 2018, Becky and I stood in line outside the U.S. Capitol for hours waiting to pay our respects before his flag-draped coffin in the Great Rotunda. So did thousands of others; in honoring McCain, many were obviously showing their support for the high standards he lived by

On the final day of our Vietnam trip, we toured a pair of small villages about an hour north of Hanoi. We first visited a Buddhist temple whose altar was piled high with canned and packaged food, nourishment for the ancestral spirits. At the last stop, an old woman with blackened teeth showed off a coffin that would be her final resting place. It was next to her bed. On the way back to the Vietnamese capitol, we passed a farmers market where dogs were roasting on spits. Showing the power of cultural norms, the sight made me nauseous. It was an image I'd just as soon forget.

In the early 1970s, I toyed with the idea of trading places with Jim Russell, UPI Audio's man in Saigon. He was to come to Washington. I was to fill his job. I was enamored with the idea of becoming a war correspondent. It was a crazy idea and never went beyond the talking stage.

One of the things I've learned in life is the truth of William Faulkner's observation: "The past is never dead. It isn't even past." This was vividly underscored during a trip Becky and I made to Albania, Montenegro and Slovenia. In this mountainous region of southeastern Europe, tribal grievances and ethnic differences dating back to the 10th century still drive the culture.

Not too long before we visited, Albania was the North Korea of Europe -- desperately poor, isolated, paranoid and ruled by a madman, Enver Hoxha. During Hoxha's reign, tens of thousands of military bunkers were erected throughout the country because he feared invasion. It was still poor when we were there and "blood feuds," revenge killings pitting one clan against another, were still prevalent in the northern part of the country. Roads were primitive and the driving was perilous -- until recently few Albanians owned a car. In the capital of Tirana, one of the landmarks is Skanderbeg Square, which honors an Albanian nobleman who led a rebellion against the Ottoman Turks in the 15th century. The square covers several blocks. Seen from our hotel, people walking across it looked like swarms of ants.

Fourteen miles away, in the tiny village of Fushe Kruje, is a nine-foot tall statue of George W. Bush. "43," as he likes to be called, is in shirtsleeves, waving his left hand in greeting. The statue commemorates Bush's visit to the village in 2007 when someone might have stolen his wristwatch. According to our guide, as Bush shook hands among a cheering crowd his watch was filched. The White House denied it, insisting that Bush removed the Timex timepiece and handed it to a Secret Service agent. But a video of the incident certainly makes it look like a quick-fingered crowd member came away with a presidential souvenir.

I've long been fascinated with the Balkans. Because of the mix of religions – Roman Catholicism, Orthodox Christianity and Islam -- it's where the tectonic plates of Western Civilization meet, resulting historically in near-constant political upheaval.

The spark that set off World War One was the assassination of Austro-Hungarian Archduke Franz Ferdinand in what's now Bosnia. More recently, Orthodox Christian Serbian aggression in predominantly Moslem Bosnia was the scene of the most massive European bloodletting since World War Two. Trying to end that genocidal war was what cost Robert Frasure, Joseph Kruzel and Nelson Drew their lives.

Montenegro, a nation the size of Connecticut with a population of 680,000, sided with Serbia in the war. More than 20 years later, we discovered bitter feelings lingered. There was a long wait for clearance at the border crossing between Montenegro and Croatia and our guide told some of our traveling companions who'd picked up souvenir Montenegro baseball caps to put them away until we left the country.

The best part of seeing the world is the education it offers. How the simplest things mean so much for so many. When Hillary Clinton visited Nepal, she brought along birthing kits that cost U.S. taxpayers less than 15 cents apiece. The kits consisted of a small plastic sheet, a safety razor and a shoelace. Sepsis, a potentially deadly bodily response to infection, was a widespread problem for poor Nepali women and infants after childbirth. The plastic sheet would provide better sanitary conditions for the mother during birthing; the razor blade was to sever and tie off infants' umbilical cords. Simple, cheap and supposedly effective enough to save the lives of thousands of women and their babies. What could be a better investment for the American people?

Together with Becky, I returned to Nepal 25 years later. I found it as fascinating as the first time I was there. Kathmandu was heavily damaged by a 2015 earthquake and the cleanup was still going on. But the mix of colorfully painted dwellings and elaborately decorated Hindu and Buddhist temples give the city and its surrounding area an exotic "Toto, we're not in Kansas anymore" feel.

During our visit we observed ritual cremations on the banks of the Batgami River, which bisects Kathmandu. Some might find the ceremonies macabre but I thought them moving. There were about a dozen pliths along the riverback. At the start of each cremation, timbers were piled on the one to be used. Then the corpse, wrapped in a sheet and draped with garlands of flowers was placed atop them.

While the pyre was prepared, a Hindu holy man shaved the head of the person officiating, normally the oldest son of the deceased. Bare-chested and wearing an ankle-length white sarong, this person would piled straw on the pyre and set it ablaze. The cremation took about four hours. A guide told us that when it was completed the ashes would be pushed into the river, adding nitrogen to the water. Downstream the river would irrigate farm fields, enriching the crops. It was a cycle of life I found intriguing.

We also visited India on the trip. As mentioned previously, I'd seen the Taj Mahal with Hillary Clinton. On that occasion, the grounds were cleared – we had the monument all to ourselves. So I thought it would be anticlimactic to see it with throngs of tourists. On the contrary, it was even more magnificent. The crowds added to the excitement.

Something I hadn't seen on my previous visit was the sickening squalor and seemingly endless human misery that surrounds what is arguably the most beautiful monument in the world. Our guide told us to ignore the women and children who surrounded us with outstretched hands and pleading looks at every stop because they were part of a begging industry run by unsavory bosses. But it was okay to give to the grotesquely crippled people we saw because they obviously couldn't work and had no social safety net to fall back on. The visit to India was a constant reminder of just how lucky we are.

The Gospel according to Luke, 12:48, teaches that "to whom much is given much is required." Americans enjoy riches beyond measure, yet we're among the world's stingiest nations when it comes to sharing wealth with others. For as long as I covered U.S. politics, foreign aid was a highly contentious issue. Only about one percent of the federal budget – about $34 billion a year – goes to helping others. The biggest U.S. aid recipients are Israel and Egypt, hardly poor countries. Surprisingly, the Peoples Republic of China is the world's most generous country according to researchers at Virginia's College of William & Mary. They estimate that the bulk of PRC aid goes to infrastructure: energy generation and supply, transportation, storage and communication.

In Montenegro China is doing is building a superhighway through the mountains that give the country its name. I'm no expert on road construction but given the topographical challenges we saw, the project clearly involved spectacular engineering. I'd previously seen another Chinese project in the Caribbean: a huge sports stadium in Grenada. While we begrudge others a helping hand China arguably is winning hearts and minds and expanding its global influence.

Reagan's visit to China in 1984 included a banquet at the Great Hall of the People in Beijing's Tiananmen Square. Everyone in his entourage was invited. The dinner was my first and only exposure to shark's fin soup, which was delicious. Chinese opera singers provided the entertainment. One song was so hauntingly beautiful I've tried to find it for years to no avail.

The trip also included a visit to the Great Wall of China near Beijing. We also traveled to Xian and Shanghai.

A day or before our departure, I was among a small group of reporters at a Los Angeles Dodgers baseball game. We visited the Dodgers' clubhouse afterwards and when Manager Tommy Lasorda heard we were bound for China he insisted we take along a bagful of major league baseballs to hand out to children there. I gave mine to several little girls who greeted us at stop in Shanghai, then watched incredulously as they were confiscated by women I assume worked for the Public Security Bureau, the Chinese secret police.

I got to Australia twice during my career. Once with President Bush. Once with President Clinton. On the Bush trip, we were in Sydney on New Year's Eve and saw one of the most spectacular fireworks displays I've ever witnessed. Hundreds of brilliantly colored skyrockets and pinwheels dazzlingly danced in the night sky high above the Sydney Harbor Bridge, welcoming in the year 1991.

We also went to Canberra and Melbourne on that trip. I was a guest at a state dinner honoring Bush in Australia's capitol. A host of other notables including tennis great John Newcomb were also on the invitation list. There was a change in the dress code just before the glittery event; instead of tuxes and gowns, everyone was told to wear business clothes. I bought a new tie to go with my suit – a cravat in Australia's green and gold speckled with dozens of little kangaroos. "Where'd you get that tie, mate? No-one in Oz would be caught dead wearing that tie," one of the leaders of the Australian Parliament teased.

I had another of those close calls that are quickly forgotten while covering Clinton's trip. Like Bush he visited Sydney and Canberra, then flew to Port Douglas in the north of Australia to see the Great Barrier Reef. Clinton's visit to that maritime wonder must have been private; I have no memory of it. But I do vividly recall swimming for hours with colleagues in a kind of Water World rich with coral and sea twenty miles off the Australian coast.

There was a floating restaurant and large deck for sunbathing. Just beyond was a vast saltwater playground hundreds of square yards in size. Although I've never been a strong swimmer, I was lulled into a false sense of security as I snorkeled along, mesmerized by schools of colorful fish. Suddenly and without warning the wind came up and I was in trouble, trying to swim in increasingly choppy seas. I rolled onto my back and concentrated on staying afloat. But I was far from safety and afraid no one saw me. I was fighting panic when a rescue boat came along and pulled me out of the water. I then had to pretend I'd been okay all along.

When Lynn and I were young parents we were befriended by New Zealand Embassy diplomats and I always wanted to visit their country. But it was far away and seemingly out of reach; its denial of its waters and ports to U.S. Navy warships that were nuclear powered or carrying nuclear weapons strained relations with Washington and kept American presidents from visiting for decades. My daughter Becky visited when she was in medical school and came back raving about the country. When I finally got there with my wife Becky it was all that I'd imagined.

Our visit was bittersweet because it became a reminder that nowhere in the world is safe anymore. I'd always regarded New Zealand as a kind of earthly paradise with great natural beauty and civic tranquility. But six days after our arrival, a right wing terrorist shot and killed more than 50 Moslem worshippers at two mosques in Christchurch.

The Kiwi response was a model of national unity. Prime Minister Jacinda Ardern donned a *hajib* to show solidarity with her country's Moslem citizens. Many New Zealand women followed her example. She also announced that her government would seek to ban assault rifles, a move that won almost unanimous parliamentary approval a few weeks later. Even before the ban was approved, many New Zealanders voluntarily surrendered rapid-fire weapons. "Black, white or brown, Muslim, Christian or Hindu, Asian Islander or Maori: This is New Zealand. We are one," said a makeshift memorial on a beach in Queenstown.

As an American, it was embarrassing to learn that the accused assailant, an Australian white supremacist, was inspired by Donald Trump. In a 74-page manifesto, he praised the president as "a symbol of renewed white identification and common purpose." Equally dismaying was the Trump administration's refusal to support an international drive to outlaw live-streaming of terrorist acts by the social media (as was briefly the case with the New Zealand attack). Its excuse: the proposed violated the First Amendment to the U.S. Constitution.

My favorite part of the New Zealand trip was a helicopter sightseeing tour of the Southern Alps, a mountain range that stretches along most of the country's South Island. During the flight we touched down on Franz Josef Glacier and I got to wander around it.

The trip had other memorable moments as well: Seeing a Maori *Haka*, an ancient war dance of New Zealand's indigenous people at a cultural center in Rotorua. Marveling at cute, gawky little blue penguins as they returned after a day in the ocean to their Oamaru coastal habitat. A scenic cruise on Milford Sound. An informative wine tasting session on Waihake Island near Auckland and a drive through the Central Otago region, which looked like Montana. All in all, New Zealand was what I imagined America to be during my childhood: a land of great splendor, blessed with bountiful resources and friendly people. Vaguely menaced, however.

Interesting events and constant movement: the story of my life. In closing, let me reecho, what now is surely a familiar refrain: history's lessons must be respected. The world has come full circle since I was born. In 1942, fear enveloped the globe: the United States and its allies – Great Britain, Canada and the Soviet Union – were in the throes of a horrifically bloody world war with Nazi Germany and Japan. While there were glimmers of hope – German offensives blunted in Russia and Africa and a much-needed U.S. victory in the Battle of Midway in the Pacific, the outcome was anything but assured. The values and standards of Western civilization, equality, freedom and justice, hung in the balance.

I was too young to know any of this while it was happening. But I was soon all too familiar with one of the saddest chapters of human history. From overhearing adult conversation, reading beyond my age level and looking at picture books. (A Life Magazine history of World War Two owned by my Uncle John was a favorite) and because of the looming threat of nuclear war, I was gripped by a sense of foreboding when I was young. I knew that unless we collectively were very careful we'd be very sorry. What eight-year old kid is driven to write to the president to bitch about his having fired a general?

More than three quarters of a century later – a lifetime that surpasses my expectations – I worry that the shadows are reasserting themselves. Not only in the United States, clinging by a thread to the values and standards we profess to cherish. But also in Britain, a once-powerful kingdom unable to adjust to its loss of empire and assimilate with its neighbors. And also in France, Italy, Austria, Poland and Hungary where the ugliness of Fascism rises again. China and Russia on the march. The Middle East poised for a cataclysmic explosion. It's a deeply disturbing state of affairs.

I wish I could be as inspirational as William Faulkner, who was awarded the Nobel Prize for Literature in 1950. Speaking at the height of America's "Red Scare" when demagogic politicians fanned groundless public fears of a communist takeover of the U.S. government and a widespread dread that the world would end in a mushroom cloud, Faulkner famously declared: "I believe that man will not merely endure: he will prevail.

"He is immortal, not because he alone among creatures has an inexhaustible voice, but because he has a soul, a spirit capable of compassion and sacrifice and endurance," he said.

In the twilight of my life, I worry about the future. There've been at least eight major historic events during my time on earth: World War Two; Korean War; Cuban Missile Crisis; Vietnam War; the assassinations of John F. Kennedy, Martin Luther King and Robert Kennedy; Watergate; a resurgence of authoritarianism marked by the rise of Donald Trump and the Covid 19 Pandemic. We're in the throes of the latter as I write: in the first 10 months of a health crisis that turned the world upside down, the American death toll approached 300,000. Much of this was the result of the Trump administration's utter incompetence.

Joe Biden's defeat of Trump in the 2020 election was a ray of sunshine but I believe America remains in a bad place, still at risk of a resurgence of Trumpism because of the division and hatred that continues to plague the country. There's not much I can do about it now. That's for the next generations. What I plan to do is to love and cherish my wife and children, proudly watch my grandkids grow up and try to help other whenever I can. I'll also walk on a riverside path near my home as much as I can and travel to places I haven't been. Patagonia, Machu Picchu, Antarctica...

Acknowledgements

M Y WIFE BECKY and Marlin Fitzwater deserve much of the credit for this book. Becky insisted I write it and kept after me until I did. Marlin, the only individual to serve as White House Press Secretary to two presidents, Ronald Reagan and George H.W. Bush, read the book and suggested changes and corrections. He then encouraged me to publish it and helped me in the endeavor. To both of them I'm eternally grateful. Jim Carrier, author of <u>The Ship and the Storm</u>, cast an eagle eye on my manuscript and offered helpful suggestions. Bob Cotter did an extraordinarily swift and thorough copy editing job, making this a much better, cleaner read. Graphic Artist extraordinaire Eric Grover designed the book cover and Carol Powers, a White House photographer during George H.W. Bush's presidency, made the image (in Istanbul) that Eric used as cover art. Thanks to both of them.

I'm also grateful to my family, without whom my adventures would have been impossible. To my late wife Lynn, who did much more than her share of looking out for our family. She didn't live to enjoy the fruits of her labor, something I'll always regret. To our children, Sean, Jennie, Chad and Becky, who supported my career in many ways they'll never know even though they probably would have preferred to see more of their dad growing up. Each of you make me very proud.

My seven grandchildren were also an inspiration for this book: Charlie, Eli and Hobbes, Zoe and Lily, Libbie and Nell. I hope they'll read it one day, know that they are loved more than words can tell and get to know their grandparents better.

The contributions of my brothers Charlie and Joe, with whom I share a love of putting words together, were immense. They've driven me to far surpass what I expect of myself since the days we were children. I've known many impressive people in my life. None more so than them.

When it comes to others who deserve acknowledgement, William Butler Yeats put it best: "Think where man's glory most begins and ends, and say my glory was I had such friends." John Kohout and George Candelori, beloved walking companions whose wise counsel has guided me well; Jerry Seib and Barbara Rosewicz, while not related the same as family; Susan Biddle and Lou Mazzatenta, world class professional photographers from whom I've learned so much about the craft, and life in general.

I also owe a tip of the hat to my Cotter cousins, Tom, Mary, Michael, Susan, Trudy Ellen and the aforementioned Bob. Although we don't see each other as much as we should anymore, they'll always be more like siblings than extended family. They're always in my thoughts.